MARXISM IN INDIA

★ FROM DECLINE TO DEBACLE ★

OTHER LOTUS TITLES

Ajit Bhattacharjea	*Sheikh Mohammad Abdullah: Tragic Hero of Kashmir*
Amarinder Singh	*The Last Sunset: The Rise and Fall of the Lahore Durbar*
Anil Dharker	*Icons: Men & Women Who Shaped Today's India*
Aitzaz Ahsan	*The Indus Saga: The Making of Pakistan*
Alam Srinivas & TR Vivek	*IPL: The Inside Story*
Amir Mir	*The True Face of Jehadis: Inside Pakistan's Terror Networks*
Ashok Mitra	*The Starkness of It*
Dr Humanyun Khan & G. Parthasarthy	*Diplomatic Divide*
Gyanendra Pandey & Yunus Samad	*Faultlines of Nationhood*
H.L.O. Garrett	*The Trial of Bahadur Shah Zafar*
Hindustan Times Leadership Summit	*Vision 2020: Challenges for the Next Decade*
M.J. Akbar	*India: The Siege Within*
M.J. Akbar	*The Shade of Swords*
M.J. Akbar	*Byline*
M.J. Akbar	*Blood Brothers: A Family Saga*
Maj. Gen. Ian Cardozo	*Param Vir: Our Heroes in Battle*
Maj. Gen. Ian Cardozo	*The Sinking of INS Khukri: What Happened in 1971*
Madhu Trehan	*Tehelka as Metaphor*
Mushirul Hasan	*India Partitioned. 2 Vols*
Mushirul Hasan	*John Company to the Republic*
Mushirul Hasan	*Knowledge, Power and Politics*
Nayantara Sahgal (ed.)	*Before Freedom: Nehru's Letters to His Sister*
Nilima Lambah	*A Life Across Three Continents*
Robert Hutchison	*The Raja of Harsil: The Legend of Frederick 'Pahari' Wilson*
Sharmishta Gooptu and Boria Majumdar (eds)	*Revisiting 1857: Myth, Memory, History*
Shrabani Basu	*Spy Princess: The Life of Noor Inayat Khan*
Shashi Joshi	*The Last Durbar*
Shashi Tharoor & Shaharyar M. Khan	*Shadows across the Playing Field*
Shyam Bhatia	*Goodbye Shahzadi: A Political Biography*
Thomas Weber	*Gandhi, Gandhism and the Gandhians*
Thomas Weber	*Going Native: Gandhi's Relationship with Western Women*

FORTHCOMING TITLES

Indian Express	*The Prize Stories*
Mohammed Hyder	*October Coup: Memoir of the Struggle for Hyderabad*

MARXISM IN INDIA

★ FROM DECLINE TO DEBACLE ★

KIRAN MAITRA

Lotus Collection 2012

The Lotus Collection
An imprint of Roli Books Pvt. Ltd.
M-75, Greater Kailash II Market, New Delhi 110 048
Phone: ++91 (011) 4068 2000. Fax: ++91 (011) 2921 7185
E-mail: info@rolibooks.com; Website: www.rolibooks.com
Also at Bangalore, Chennai, & Mumbai

Cover Design: Devan Das
Layout: Sanjeev Mathpal
Production: Shaji Sahadevan

ISBN: 978-81-7436-847-8

Typeset in Garamond by Roli Books Pvt Ltd
and printed at IBH Printers, Noida

Contents

To my granddaughter, Anushka

Preface

The socialist revolution in Russia was a phenomenon of worldwide importance. It was hailed across the colonial world, much to the discomfort of the imperialists, as it promised to eradicate the poverty of the common masses, and held aloft the ideal of the equality of men, irrespective of nationality and religion.

India was fighting her own battle for freedom. The leaders of the Indian struggle for independence were, however, elated at the success of the socialist revolution, but did not take up socialism themselves. Only a few young men with little or no political experience took to the study of socialism and adopted the socialist mode of struggle to fight the colonial ruler. Since a significant part of the freedom movement in India had chosen to be non-violent, the prospect of armed revolution of the Soviet kind was reduced.

Further, when the Communist Party was formed in India, it found the Communist Party of Great Britain as its natural guardian for advice and support from the Comintern. The marxists did not, rather could not, grow their roots in India.

Marxism had begun as an intellectual movement. The common people who were drawn by its unduly emphasized populist image were soon disillusioned and sought an escape route. This was also the case in the Soviet Union and the East European countries. The people of China, Cuba, North Korea and Vietnam are also waiting to avail the first opportunity to throw off marxism.

In India, too, marxism has failed to make a dent in the political landscape. Marxist leaders have been clearly unequal to the task of guiding such a gigantic intellectual movement, in terms of their honesty, integrity and political vision. The party's presence is now confined to a few pockets of the country.

Marxism in India, divided into nine chapters, traces the course of the communist movement in India, from its inception to proletarian revolution to the turn to constitutional benefaction .

I am grateful to my wife, Renuka, for having borne with the many inconveniences that I might have thrust upon her in the course of preparation of the manuscript. My daughters Manjari, Indrani and Pallavi have helped me by taking the responsibility of typing the manuscripts and checking the copies, as well as in numerous other ways.

I am grateful to my friend Shri A.K. Nanda who has been kind enough to go though the text with a toothcomb, making changes and suggesting improvements that I value most.

Kiran Maitra

I

India and the Socialist Revolution

The socialist revolution in Russia came at a time when half the world was under imperialist occupation. India too was under the rule of Great Britain, the greatest imperial power of the day. People who were striving to end British rule in India were elated with the success of the socialist revolution, but were not prepared to accept socialism or the socialist mode of struggle themselves. Under the leadership of Gandhi, India accepted non-violence as the weapon to end British rule in India and was not prepared to change to any other form of struggle – although after the First World War, the emotional and intellectual climate of the country was receptive to the ideas of socialism. Its appeal was universal as it promised to eradicate poverty of the common masses and bring about equality of men, irrespective of religion or nationality. But no political leader worth the name came forward to make use of the situation. Only a few young men with no political patronage or financial assistance, inspired by a vague idea of socialism, stepped forward to end British rule in India, following the method adopted by socialists in Russia. The success of the socialist revolution had a tremendous impact on these youths.

Disillusioned and disheartened by the mode of struggle adopted by Gandhi, these youths thought of treading a new path. In Bombay (now Mumbai), Sripad Amrit Dange; in Bengal, Muzaffar Ahmed; in Punjab, Ghulam Hasan; in Madras (now Chennai), Singaravelu Chettiar; and in the United Province (now Uttar Pradesh), Satya Bhakt and Shaukat Usmani formed small, insignificant groups to study marxism, and if possible, to build a communist party in India. These were individual efforts and not the outcome of any decision taken jointly. In fact, these men did not even know each other.

Dange, who was earlier a follower of Gandhi and took part in the non-cooperation movement, soon became disillusioned and took to the study of marxism. After gaining some rudimentary knowledge of marxism, he wrote a book, rather a booklet, *Gandhi vs Lenin* – an amateurish exposition of Gandhi by a young and enthusiastic marxist. The booklet attracted the notice of a disgruntled gandhiite, R.B. Lotvala, a small industrialist in Bombay. Lotvala liked not only the booklet, but also its author. He called Dange to his residence and advised him to read more of marxism before taking to writing. He also enquired about his means of livelihood, and after getting to know about his financial difficulties, he fixed a monthly allowance for his upkeep.[1] Thereafter, Dange became a regular visitor to Lotvala's private library to enrich his knowledge of marxism.

After studying marxism for some time, Dange gained confidence and brought out a newspaper financed by Lotvala. In August 1922, *The Socialist*, an English weekly edited by Dange saw the light of day. The weekly made Dange known to people and helped him draw around him a number of young radicals, such as S.V. Ghate, R.S. Nimbkar, K.N. Joglekar, and a few others.

Like Dange in Bombay, Muzaffar Ahmed became the pivot of marxism in Bengal. But unlike Dange, Ahmed had no experience in politics before he became a marxist. Even in the hey-days of the *khilafat* non-cooperation movement, he kept himself aloof from politics, though he claims that he decided to make politics rather than literature the pursuit of his life, at the beginning of 1920.[2] In July 1920, along with Qazi Nazrul Islam, Quttbuddin Ahmed and a few others, Ahmed started an evening daily in Bengali, *Navayug,* financed by Fazlul Haq, leader of the Krishak Praja Party.[3]

While editing *Navayug,* Ahmed became interested in the problems facing workers and purchased a few books of Marx and Lenin to gain some knowledge of the working class movement. It was his first exposure to marxist literature and Ahmed did not conceal his initial inability to understand Marx. With humility he confessed, 'I did not know what I was going to do with them (books). I had not read any marxist literature previously'.[4] However, Ahmed soon acquired some knowledge of marxism and formed a marxist group around him.

The lead in Madras was taken by Singaravelu Chettiar, a lawyer by profession and, initially, a believer in the ideology of the Congress; in Punjab, Ghulam Hasan, a teacher of economics in the Islamia College, Peshawar; and in the United Province, Shaukat Usmani and Satya Bhakt.

These amorphous marxist groups were neither strong nor influential. They existed more on paper than in reality. Yet, there existence was no mean achievement: at least they provided a foothold to marxism in India.

The situation abroad was a little different. Indians who were working in Europe to end the British rule in India came in contact with French socialists, long before the socialist revolution in Russia. Madam Cama and S.R. Rana attended the International Socialist Conference held in Stuttgart in 1909 as self-appointed representatives of India and spoke for India's independence. And Lala Hardyal, one of the founders of the Ghadar Party in America, penned down a short biographical sketch of Marx as far back as 1912. Hardyal found in Marx a great lover of humanity and a friend of the downtrodden, though he never subscribed to his views.[5]

However, with the success of the socialist revolution in Russia, quite a few Indians working abroad for India's independence made friends with Russian socialists. The most notable among them were V.N. Chattopadhyaya, V.V.S. Ayer, Tirimul Acharya, Abdur Rab Nister and Mohammad Safiq. They met Lenin and made all kinds of efforts to urge him to help India in its struggle for independence, but achieved little. Lenin expressed his sympathy, while asking them to learn more about socialism. Their knowledge of socialism was naïve as it was submerged in nationalism.

The most dynamic and fascinating among the Indians who took to marxism was Narendranath Bhattacharjee alias Naren. Naren was a revolutionary before he became a marxist. He came under the spell of the revolutionaries at a very early age and acquired a lopsided view of revolution. He firmly believed that the basic requirements for a revolution were arms and money. If these two things were available, revolution would be child's play. The prospect of getting arms brightened with the outbreak of the First World War, when Germany promised arms to Indian revolutionaries. These arms never reached India. Disillusioned and disheartened, Naren disguised himself as C.A. Martin and left India in search of arms. After dashing through Batavia, Shanghai and Tokyo, he landed in San Francisco and from there left for a nearby town, Palo Alto, hoping to reach Berlin to contact the German Foreign Office for arms and money. At Palo Alto, he became a guest of Dhanagopal Mukherjee, the younger brother of his comrade in India, Jadugopal Mukherjee. Mukherjee knew Naren, but did not expect to see him at Palo Alto. After the initial shock was over, Mukherjee advised Naren to wipe off his past and start a new life. Naren liked the idea. The same evening, M.N. Roy was born in the campus of Stanford University.[6] Soon thereafter, Roy left for New York to fulfil his mission.

In the campus of Stanford University, Roy met Evelyn, with whom he fell in love and eventually married. Roy's marriage with Evelyn supplied fodder to scandalmongers. It became the hottest gossip among Indian revolutionaries in New York. Lala Lajpat Rai took pity on the young couple and offered them shelter, along with some money to pull on with.[7]

Lajpat Rai's company was conducive to Roy in more ways than one. Through Rai, Roy came in contact with American socialists. Both Rai and Roy were nationalists and had no belief in the doctrine of social revolution. They were opposed to marxian materialism.

Yet, both became friendly towards socialists because of their sympathy towards the cause of India's independence. However, to refute the arguments of socialists, Roy took to the study of socalist classics.

While Roy was busy with the study of socialism, a momentous event took place that revolutionized his entire thinking. Lajpat Rai was invited to speak at a meeting of socialists. His vivid description of the poverty of the Indian masses under British rule moved the audience. All those present were avowed enemies of all forms of exploitation of man by man, and thus appreciated Lajpat Rai. However, one person from the audience got up and posed an embarrassing question, 'How did the nationalists propose to end the poverty of the Indian masses?' Lajpat Rai's evasive reply failed to satisfy the interrogator. There followed a heated exchange of words. The interrogator proved his point further by asking provocatively, 'What difference would it make to the Indian masses if they were exploited by native capitalists instead of foreign capitalists?' Lajpat Rai flew into a terrible rage and retorted, 'It does make a great difference whether one is kicked by his brother or a foreign robber.'[8] Initially, Roy shared Lajpat Rai's indignation, but soon he realized that something was lacking in his argument. Roy left the hall alone, quite confused and vaguely visualizing a different picture of freedom. Keeping away from friends, he delved deep into the study of Karl Marx's works for an answer.

His immediate concern, however, was to go to Berlin for arms to bring about a revolution. While Roy was waiting in futility for this trip, America declared war on Germany in support of the allied powers and put under arrest Indian revolutionaries in America on the charge of violating the neutrality of America through a worldwide conspiracy to embarrass its ally, Great Britain. Roy and Evelyn were taken into custody, but were let off after interrogation. Roy was put under arrest again for violating immigration laws and sent to the lock-up for one night, after which he was released on bail. Shrewdly enough, Roy jumped the bail and fled to Mexico in the company of Evelyn, with a letter of introduction to General Alvarado, the

Governor of the State of Yucatan, from David Starr Jordon, the President of Stanford University.[9]

Roy landed in Mexico as a stranger and put up at *Hotel de Geneva.* He did not know a single person there, nor had he established any contacts before. His only hope was the letter of introduction addressed to General Alvarado.

On enquiry, Roy came to know that the State of Yucatan was far away from the city of Mexico. To reach the state, one had to travel on land a distance of about a thousand miles through the wilderness of the states of Tabasco and Chiapas. There was no railway connection between the city of Mexico and the State of Yucatan. The usual route was across the Gulf of Mexico. But the ships were all American, and as a rule, after leaving the Mexican port of Veracruz, they called at some American port. Roy, much against his wishes, thought of keeping himself away from the hazardous journey.[10]

Roy's disappointment was over quite soon though. He managed an interview with the minister of defence, who happened to be the son-in-law of General Don Venustiano Carranza, the President of the Republic of Mexico. The minister welcomed Roy and asked for the letter to Alvarado. The content of the letter is not known, but after going through it, as Roy states in his *Memoirs*, the minister was satisfied and assured him of his safety in his country. The minister further informed Roy that the general was expected at the capital any day and promised to inform him about his arrival in the city.

The letter of introduction to Alvarado and the interview with the minister of defence enhanced Roy's prestige. It gave the people the impression that Roy had friends in high circles. The next day, he received a letter from the editor of *El Pueblo*,[11] one of the leading dailies of the city, inviting him to his office. Roy met the editor at the appointed hour. After the exchange of niceties, free from the usual Mexican extravagance, the editor informed Roy that the hotel in which he was putting up was not a safe place and that he should move out of it at the earliest opportunity. However, the editor of *El Pueblo* did not know that Roy's fortune lay buried in that hotel.

Before Roy moved out, he came to know by a freak of chance about the presence of a few Germans in the hotel. They had escaped either from the Far East or from America to evade arrest. However, the presence of so many Germans in the hotel aroused Roy's curiosity. Quite unexpectedly, one morning, a German dropped in his room to deliver the happy news that two Germans whom Roy had met earlier at Batavia were staying in the hotel and would be pleased to meet him. Roy, whose zeal for armed revolution had been dampened by now, welcomed the news and decided to meet them.

The reunion was extremely fruitful for Roy, though not for armed revolution in India. After exchanging notes about their respective adventures, Roy settled down to talk business. He put forward his *China plan,* still hovering over his mind.[12] The Germans not only appreciated the plan, but to the surprise of Roy, offered necessary financial assistance to implement it. Roy welcomed the windfall. The little money that he had brought from America was practically exhausted and Roy did not even have resources to pay for his next meal. But now, to his surprise, he found himself a rich man – adventurism had started paying its dividends. As promised, the Germans gave Roy 10,000 gold pesos[13] to begin with, before he moved out of the hotel.

No sooner had Roy moved into a house in a respectable quarter of the city called *Colonia Roma* with 10,000 pesos in his pocket, than he received an invitation for dinner from the Germans, for which he was not prepared. The question that haunted his mind was, were the Germans really serious about the plan? Roy accepted the money as his share of the loot, to meet his own expenses. After years of struggle and instability, he was now looking for a settled life – the logical end of a petty bourgeois. He was no more a desperado. He was married and not very keen to plunge into the unknown again. Besides, he had already begun to realize that a shipload of arms would not bring about revolution in India. And even if it did, it would not end the exploitation of the toiling masses. It would simply transfer the instrument of exploitation from the hands of the imperialist to that of the Indian bourgeoisie. Yet, opportunism won at the end.

He accepted the dinner invitation from his German *friends* at the appointed hour, prepared to dupe them again.

The dinner was not a general get-together. It was a business meeting under the cover of a social function. As soon as it was over, the Germans asked Roy about the progress of his plan. Roy not only put forward a rosy picture of his sincere attempt to resume contact with the revolutionaries to fulfil the *China plan*, but gave the impression that, if necessary, he would himself make a trip to China. The Germans were satisfied. Within a week, Roy's coffers swelled to 50,000 gold pesos,[14] soon to be followed by another $50,000.[15]

The news that Roy had dipped his hands into the gold sack of Kaiser made the Indian revolutionaries in America conscious of their *duty*. They proceeded post-haste towards Mexico to have a share of the loot, which, they perhaps quite rightly thought, belonged to them. But Roy was not to be outwitted so easily. Except in a few cases, he placated most of them with meagre sums. However, to save himself from the hands of the *patriots* and to assure the Germans about his sincerity, Roy left the city of Mexico on the pretext of going to China in quest of arms.

Armed with a semi-diplomatic passport, Roy left the city of Mexico quite reluctantly. 'The heart was not in the adventure,' writes Roy, 'it was undertaken under the force of habit, but the conviction was lacking.'[16] However, after a hazardous journey through Guedaljara and Manzanillo, Roy reached Salina Cruz, a small port town on the Pacific coast, only to learn that the expected ship was not calling at the port. The next ship was due only after a month. The news, though disappointing, was a great relief to Roy. He had undertaken the hazardous journey to dupe the Germans to convince them of his sincerity to the cause. With the latest news, this adventure was over and Roy's return journey began. Mexico beckoned him again. Roy reached Mexico via Veracruz, happy and gay, appreciating on the way the country's landscape and Tehuanan beauties.[17]

The failure of the mission affected Roy in the least. His contacts with the high-ups in Mexico gave him social prestige and the German gold, the required affluence. 'My mode of living,' confessed Roy, 'was not exactly proletarian,' and it was true. He took up his residence 'in the plutocratic *Colonia Roma*, furnished with green satin-covered Louis XV furniture'.[18] To match the standards, he engaged a Spanish tutor, learnt the game of chess, started visiting fashionable cafés with friends and made inroads into the high-level snobbish quarters of the capital's cosmopolitan societies. Further, to fit the standards of an aristocrat, Roy took to riding every morning, accompanied by a pair of Alsatians, exploring the neighbourhood and making friends among the country folk.

After he was done with hobnobbing with the Germans, Roy set his sight on socialism – an ideology that promised both revolution and reconstruction of the society to bring in a new era. He resolved to exploit the new field of adventure with no regret for the failure of the past. Roy was fortunate. He reached Mexico when it had no political party in the true sense of the term. Numerous groups that were based around individual adventurers in the name of revolution were struggling to attain power. Their common aim was the distribution of land to land-hungry peasants and employment to agricultural labourers. It was a sheer bird's call to rally the poverty-stricken rural masses under the banner of revolution.

Away from this anomalous situation, the bulk of the middle class was looking for a political party that would restore order and peace to the country. The people were conscious of the fact that ninety per cent of the population lived on land and a programme of radical agrarian reform could end perpetual poverty. But there was no political party, because people had little faith in parliamentary reform. The leftists who could bring order to this chaos were scattered and formed a hopeless minority. Roy assessed the situation and thought of organizing the left.

On enquiring, he came to know about the existence of a socialist party, rather a group, under the leadership of an elderly lawyer, Ignazio Santibanez. Roy decided to meet him.

Before meeting Santibanez, Roy, at the request of the editor of *El Pueblo*, published a series of articles on British rule in India. This was his second experiment with writing,[19] and was quite successful.

For at the very first meeting, Santibanez told Roy that he and other members of his party had read his articles in *El Pueblo*. The members were so impressed that they wanted to contact the author and 'invite him to speak at a party meeting'.[20] Roy's meetings with the socialists took place in the backdrop of a conflict in Mexico, between President Carranza and General Obregon – the chief architect of Carranza's military victory.

The cry of the adventurists during the struggle for political power in Mexico was *tiere liberated*. And the Mexican peasants rallied around whosoever came forward with the requisite programme. Carranza was essentially a landed gentleman, yet he came forward with this popular slogan and quite successfully rallied a band of followers behind him to fight against Villa and Zapata, who were landed gentry and equally adventurist. They wanted to grab power with the same slogan as that of Carranza. In this struggle for power, Carranza found in Obregon a popular and capable military commander, while Obregon found in Carranza a person providing better opportunity to realize his ambition than Villa or Zapata. However, by October 1915, Carranza, supported by Obregon, made his position quite secure and controlled a major part of the country by throwing away Villa and Zapata into the native woods, as well as boosted his position further by gaining recognition from the USA.

However, Carranza failed to come up to the expectations of the people. Being conservative, he preferred the status quo and did little to change things. Worse, perhaps, he permitted his regime to sink into corruption. Aware of the weakness of his policies, Carranza was on the lookout for an opportunity to conceal the internal struggle.

Shortly before the situation became desperate, General Alvarado, an aspirant for the presidentship of the republic, brought out a paper to garner support for himself in the next presidential election. The tone of the paper, according to him, was to be socialistic, based on his experiment at Yucatan. But because of the distinct American influence on Mexican political life, Alvarado was anxious to enlist America's support in his favour. This was an impossible task: preaching socialism through the eyes of imperialism. However, the radicals headed by Roy came forward to take responsibility and *El Heraldo de Mexico* was launched. Roy undertook to write for the paper a series of articles on the Monroe Doctrine, aimed more at his advantage than Alvarado's. 'The work gave me,' writes Roy, 'the occasion for a fairly comprehensive study of the history of the new world, practically since the American war of independence. It was a very useful knowledge to acquire, which greatly helped in the development of many political ideas and understanding of the contemporary world.'[21]

When Roy decided to write for the *El Heraldo de Mexico,* he was not a member of the Socialist Party of Mexico, though he had come in contact with the socialists and succeeded in moulding the opinion of the radicals in accordance with his views. The success encouraged him to think about joining the Socialist Party of Mexico to cast it in his mould. Roy called on Santibanez, whom he called the Karl Marx of Mexico, and expressed his desire to become a full-fledged member of the party. Santibanez was almost ecstatic. For want of money, the activities of the party were limited to the publication of a four-page paper titled *De Lucha de los classes.* It was a small ineffective group of half a dozen people confined to the capital. Roy's enrolment in the party would at least solve the financial problem. The *Indian Prince,* known for his wealth, might come forward to help the party. And this was no unjustified expectation. After all, the *Karl Marx of Mexico* did not waste his time in futile exercise. With the help of Roy, the party purchased a press and converted the four-page *class struggle* into a regular weekly of eight pages.[22]

While Roy was hobnobbing with the socialists, the situation in Mexico was fast deteriorating to the disadvantage of Carranza. Confronted both from within and outside, Carranza started looking for popular support. Roy's association with the socialists and his articles on the Monroe Doctrine with an anti-American stance attracted the notice of Carranza. He found in Roy both a friend and a scapegoat. As a friend, Roy could be asked to rally the socialists behind the regime and intensify the anti-American propaganda. If the situation worsened, however, he could be disowned as an obscure foreigner. With this end in view, Carranza sent an invitation to Roy for dinner.

However, long before Carranza thought of Roy or about winning the support of socialists, Roy was quite active in moulding the opinion of socialists in favour of the corrupt Carranza regime. Having found asylum in Mexico, Roy was always on the lookout for an opportunity to be useful to Carranza. Thus, when on the appointed day Roy was ushered into the magnificent reception hall of the Chepultaken Castle, accompanied by Dom Manuel, head of the legislative branch of the state, his mind was already set.

Before Carranza came out with his plan, Roy informed him that his articles on the Monroe Doctrine were aimed at raising the bogey of Mexican nationalism against foreign intervention to remind the socialists of their duty towards their motherland. This was exactly what Carranza wanted Roy to do. Over a glass of wine, Carranza congratulated Roy. Roy felt flattered and promised to do everything in his power to save his adopted country, and in effect, Carranza.[23]

The unqualified support to Carranza was, however, based on personal gratitude rather than on any ideology. It was motivated by opportunism. Carranza was the elected head of a so-called democratic state, but he was a feudal lord by both birth and action. Roy knew that to support Carranza would mean to support a corrupt bourgeois regime. If the present regime was allowed to continue, it would add to the misery of the people. But Roy defied the norms of a revolutionary and justified his action on the ground that 'preparatory to capturing power, the proletariat must organise itself as a decisive factor in the political life of the particular country, and that it was a very opportune moment to do so'.[24]

The socialists were on the horns of a dilemma. They objected to Roy's 'theory of opportunism', but were not prepared to lose the *Indian Prince* from their ranks. The *Indian Prince* may not be sincere to the cause, but had sufficient dollars in his coffers to give the Socialist Party of Mexico a sound financial footing. Thus, after much hesitation and prolonged discussion, the socialists put their seal on Roy's *theory of opportunism* as a sure step towards a social revolution.

Having got the mandate from the party and the blessings of Carranza, Roy arranged the first conference of the Socialist Party of Mexico to rally the working class and the socialist intellectuals in support of the Carranza regime.

The conference proved to be a great success. The Socialist Party of Mexico ceased to be a small intellectual group and emerged as a national organization. It changed its name from the Socialist Party of Mexico to *El Partido Socialista Regional Mexico*; elected an executive committee and office-bearers; and Roy, a non-Mexican, became the general secretary of the party.

The success of the socialist conference seemed to have given a fresh boost to Roy's prestige in Mexico. He started meeting 'the president quite frequently, the formalities of interview were dispensed with'.[25] Roy claims that thenceforth he became a friend and unofficial adviser to President Carranza – a claim difficult to corroborate, yet impossible to refute.[26]

No sooner was the conference over than there appeared a mysterious visitor in Mexico. No one at that time knew who he was, but all took it for granted that he was a Russian bolshevik, though his manners were more akin to a bourgeois than to a friend of the proletariat. The curiosity around the gentleman heightened when he knocked at the doors of the *El Heraldo* office and enquired for Roy, the general secretary of the Socialist Party of Mexico. Roy was not in office, and on being asked about his identity, the man introduced himself as Mr Brantwein. He left the office as suddenly as he had come, with a request to inform Roy about his presence. After he left, speculation was rife for quite a few days, until it became clear that the gentleman was no stranger, but Michael Borodin alias F. Gruzenburg.

Borodin had come to Mexico under peculiar circumstances. After the failure of the 1905 revolution in Russia, he emigrated to the United States and stayed there till tsardom was overthrown. With the news of the success of the socialist revolution, Borodin reappeared in Russia and wasted no time in encashing on his friendship with

Lenin. Lenin selected him for a risky job – to smuggle a large quantity of crown jewels to the United States out of sheer necessity.

In 1918, the Soviet Union sent a trade delegation to Washington. The Government of United States granted *de facto* recognition to the delegation, but refused to allow international banking facilities and the services of diplomatic couriers. This put the delegation into immense financial difficulties, and eventually, it was stranded in a hostile and expensive capital. Borodin was entrusted with the job of relieving the delegation out of the sale proceeds of the crown jewels.[27] On the way, however, he lost track of the precious cargo and landed in New York empty-handed. In New York, he was soon spotted as a dangerous alien and had to escape to Mexico, practically penniless, to evade deportation.

In Mexico, Borodin came across the name of M.N. Roy in Gale's magazine,[28] as the general secretary of the Socialist Party of Mexico. He immediately decided to meet Roy and called at the office of *El Heraldo*, with the hope of getting some help.

At the very first meeting, Borodin took Roy into confidence and made no secret of his financial difficulties. Over a glass of *hock,* Borodin narrated the story of his woes and aspirations. Roy understood the problem and came forward to his rescue. He invited Borodin to stay with him to relieve him from paying the hotel bill and promised to meet his financial ends.[29] Borodin felt obliged and soon the two became close friends.

The contact with Borodin was useful to Roy in more ways than one. It was through Borodin's influence that Roy shed his ignorance. A few years ago, when he had left India in quest of arms, Roy's idea of revolution and international relations was rather naive. During his short stay in the USA, he had studied contemporary political and economic issues in detail, and started realizing the contradiction between social idealism and cultural nationalism upon which the Indian revolutionaries based their movements. Nationalism, whether revolutionary or constitutional, cultural or social, political or economic, rests primarily on emotional appeal to the heart rather than to the head because of its lack of rationale. Roy understood it, but found it difficult to forsake his old ideas. His reading added to his knowledge, but failed to make any fundamental change to either his outlook on life or his national chauvinism. A few months before meeting Borodin, Roy wrote, 'History teaches us that the Indian people under the Hindu monarchs were universally literate and educated. Daily reading of selections of the Holy Scripture was a welcome obligation for the Hindus. So illiteracy was an almost unknown phenomenon among the Indian people during the period. Institution was always free in India.'[30] But there came a change in his attitude when he came in contact with Borodin. Borodin taught Roy the history of European culture and the intricacies of hegelian philosophy to prepare the ground for the study of marxism. 'My faith in the special genius of India faded,'[31] writes Roy in his *Memoirs*.

The news that Borodin had shifted from the hotel to the residence of Roy trickled down to the members of the Socialist Party. The members thereupon promptly demanded 'an extraordinary conference of the party to define its attitude towards the socialist revolution and make a declaration about its international affiliation'.[32]

This was Roy's opportunity. He introduced Borodin to the party executive and put forward a suggestion to convert the Socialist Party of Mexico into the Communist Party of Mexico. This was accepted with alacrity. The party resolved to convene a broad-based conference of all the parties sympathetic to the socialist revolution.[33]

The extraordinary conference met from 25 August 1919 to 4 September 1919. Roy and Evelyn chaired most of the meetings.[34] However, there arose a dispute between the right and the left at the very start of the conference on the question of the sitting of Luis Morones. The left wing led by Linn Gale accused Luis Morones of being the agent of Samuel Gompers.[35] But Roy favoured Morones and Gale lost the day. However, soon after the conference was over, Gale along with his supporters held a rump session and declared his faction as the *Communist Party* of Mexico.[36]

Gale's opposition hampered the conference, but with Borodin's support, Roy managed the show. The Socialist Party of Mexico converted itself into the Communist Party of Mexico and declared its affiliation to the Communist International.[37] A small faction of the old Socialist Party of Mexico remained aloof; it neither agreed with Roy nor with Gale.

Borodin was happy with the proceedings. He came to Mexico as a stranger, but now, to his surprise, he found himself sitting among the prominent men of the city's political circle. He thought of conveying the news of his achievement and Roy's exploits to Lenin, which, under the circumstances, was a difficult task. With tsardom overthrown, all the European countries snapped their diplomatic relations with the new regime in Russia. Russia virtually lost all postal connections with the world. The only way to establish communication with Moscow was through Scandinavian countries, which had *de facto* diplomatic relations with Russia and *de jure* with Mexico. Communication with Russia could only be established with the help of the Mexican government. Borodin turned to Roy again.

The task before Roy was much easier than expected. With the collapse of Germany, Carranza lost his only ally in his fight against the USA. Given an opportunity, he might have reconciled his relations with the powerful neighbour. But by the time he realized his mistake, it was too late to think of reconciliation. Besides, news trickled in that Obregon had managed to get the support of the Yankees and was preparing for a showdown. The news made Carranza nervous. He started looking frantically for an ally. Roy sought to exploit the situation. He invited Carranza to his place for dinner and introduced him to Borodin.[38] Carranza gained nothing from this meeting. It all went to the advantage of Roy and Borodin. The manoeuvre shot up Roy's prestige in the eyes of Borodin. And Borodin exploited the friendly gesture of Carranza to get in touch with Moscow under the cover of semi-diplomatic privilege.[39]

When the channel of communication cleared, Borodin conveyed to Lenin his diplomatic victory and Roy's successful adventure. What Borodin wrote to Lenin about Roy is not known, but one can imagine it to be unusual praise, since it made even Lenin a bit prejudiced against the critics of Roy.

Within a few days, Borodin received a message from Lenin, inviting Roy to visit Moscow. Borodin suppressed the news until the newly formed Communist Party of Mexico received an invitation to send a delegation to the second congress of the Third Communist International.

The choice of delegates posed no problem. Roy, Mrs Roy and Charles Philips, a friend of Roy, and the editor of El Heraldo formed the delegation to represent the Communist Party of Mexico at the world congress.[40]

As the day of departure drew near, Roy called on Carranza to bid him farewell. Since both Roy and Carranza were inherently fond of adventure, they had developed a soft corner for each other. Roy stayed in Mexico for only two years and a half, but within this short period he had made his existence felt and carved out for himself a place in Mexican politics. This was no mean achievement for a stranger without any academic distinction or political background of any substance. Yet it became possible because of his cool and calculated moves and the indulgent attitude of the Mexican government, i.e., Carranza. Carranza found in Roy a friend in need and, perhaps, wanted him to stay in Mexico as his friend till the end. Thus, when Roy begged for leave, Carranza, with a heavy heart, gave him his last piece of advice: 'Don't gamble with fate.' Carranza did not know that gambling is a part and parcel of politics. All politicians gamble with fate in the most crucial hour of their destiny. Whether it was Caesar or the Tsar, Napoleon or Lenin, all gambled with fate at one time or another to make a mark in politics. Roy was no exception. The advice fell on deaf ears. The lure of adventure was too much to resist. Roy got ready to leave for Moscow.

Notes

1 Muzaffar Ahmed, *Myself and the Communist Party*, India, 1920-1929, Calcutta, 1970, pp 134-35

2 ibid

3 ibid

4 ibid

5 Lala Hardyal, 'Karl Marx, a Modern Rishi', *Modern Review*, Calcutta, March 1912. Following Hardyal's portrait, another biographical sketch, almost similar to that by Hardyal, was published in Malayalam by one Rama Krishna Pillai.

6 M.N. Roy, *Memoirs*, Calcutta, 1964, p.22

7 Lajpat Rai, *Recollections of his life and work while living in the United States and Japan 1914-1917*, (MSS, National Archives of India, New Delhi), pp 40-41

8 *Memoirs*, p.28

9 ibid. p.48

10 Roy was keen to go to Yucatan not only to have a friend in General Alvarado but also to see for himself the socialist experiment initiated by the general. He was eager to have a firsthand knowledge of the practice of economic theories of socialism which had just begun to capture his imagination. The socialist experiment of Yucatan was in practice a sort of state capitalism. The state monopolised the export of aloe sisal fibre which was under the control of the American capitalists.

11 *El Pueblo* 'The People' was the non-official mouthpiece of the Government of Mexico

12 At Tokyo, Naren met Sun Yat-Sen and proposed an alliance between the peoples of China and India in their common struggle for freedom, and as a token of alliance asked for Chinese arms that were lying with the Yunan and Szechnan rebels, to help the underground revolutionaries in India. Sun Yat-Sen liked the idea but asked for five million dollars which only the Germans could pay.

13 *Memoirs*, p.71. Gold Peso, Mexican currency, worth 50 per cent of the American dollar at that time.

14 *Memoirs*, p.91.

15 Gene D. Overstreet and Marshall Windmiller, *Communism in India*, Bombay, 1960, p.23.

16 *Memoirs*, p.98.

17 ibid., p.103.

18 ibid., p.148.

19 While in America, Roy had prepared a thesis on war and colonialism stating that 'colonialism being the cause of war, liberation of the subject

people, particularly of India, was the condition for durable peace'. The essay was published with the title *The Way of Durable Peace*, shortly after he left for Mexico.

20 *Memoirs*, p.76. At Santibanez's place Roy met a few American slakers viz., Charles Francis Phillips alias Frank Seamen, Michale Gold alias Irwin Grannich, Carlton Beals, Henry Glintenkamp, Maurice Baker, etc., who had escaped to Mexico to evade the draft introduced in America soon after she joined the war.

21 *Memoirs*, p.124

22 ibid., p.131

23 ibid., p.139. Roy could not come up to his promise. Nearly two years after he had left Mexico, Carranza lost the game and was butchered by his rivals. Many years later when Roy sat to write his *Memoirs* he remembered Carranza and his tragic end. With a drop of tears he writes: 'had I remained in Mexico, I would have stood by him – until the bitter end'. *Memoirs*, p.158.

24 ibid., p.120.

25 ibid., p.151.

26 ibid., p.191.

27 For the story of Tsarist jewels see *Memoirs*, pp.196-203.

28 Gale was one of those Americans who crossed over to Mexico to evade conscription, Roy in his *Memoirs* (pp.184-6) has given a disparaging account of Gale and his activities. In August 1919, Roy wrote an article in Gale's magazine 'Hunger and Revolution in India' (Gale's -III, pp. 5-25; Gene D. Overstreet and Marshall Windmiller, op. cit., p.124). This shows that before they fell out they were not on bad terms. Nowhere in his *Memoirs* Roy has mentioned this article.

29 *Memoirs*, pp 198-99. Roy, true to his words, in spite of feeble protest from Borodin, sent $ 500 to Mrs Gruzenburg and $ 10,000 to Washington to relieve the trade delegation. Borodin married in America. After the revolution when he left America for Russia his wife and two grown-up children continued to stay in Chicago. Since he left America he did not know how the family was pulling on without any means of subsistence.

30 M.N. Roy, *La India: Su Pasado, Su Presenta Y Su Porvenir* (Mexico: 1918) Quoted: Gene D. Overstreet and Marshall Windmiller, op. cit., p.24.

31 *Memoirs*, p.195.

32 ibid., p.204.

33 ibid., pp.204-5.

34 Roy has conspicuously ignored Evelyn, who it is said, played an important role in Roy's life until their separation in 1925. Nowhere in his *Memoirs* has Roy mentioned the name of Evelyn.

35 Gene D. Overstreet and Marshall Windmiller, op. cit., p.24. Gompers and Morones were Americans who had shifted to Mexico during the First World War to evade conscription.

36 ibid., pp.24-5.

37 On the basis of Cerleton Beals account, Overstreet and Marshall Windmillar states that Roy's attempt to get the Socialist Party of Mexico changed into Communist Party of Mexico failed and he was then obliged to secede from the Socialist Party and formed a second Communist Party, Gale's being the first. The account of Beals is biased. Beals was jealous both of Roy and Borodin. While analysing the reason of close friendship between Roy and Borodin, Beals writes: 'Borodin, I later discovered, had told Roy that if he would found a communist party in Mexico, then get himself named delegate to the second international congress in Moscow, he, Borodin, would assist him to promote Hindu independence, a bigger opportunity for Roy than remaining marooned in Mexico, far from the theater of activities'. Carleton Beals, Glass Houses, Philadelphia, 1938, p. 50. Quoted: Overstreet and Windmiller, op. cit., pp.25-6.

38 *Memoirs*, p.205

39 ibid, p.206

40 It is said that Gale's faction had also decided to send a delegation to the Communist International but the idea had to be dropped because of financial difficulties. Gale's group then gave credentials to a young Japanese, Keikichi Ishimoto. Ishimoto had visited Mexico a year before and was known to Gale. On the eve of the second congress he had written to Gale from New York expressing his desire to go to Moscow to attend the congress. In the absence of any other plan Gale sent him a detailed report of the communist movement in Mexico. Gale hoped that its delivery at the congress would discredit Roy. Ishimoto, however, could not attend the congress for unknown reason.

2

Scramble for Comintern Support

Towards the close of November 1919 – armed with semi-diplomatic passports from the Mexican government, issued in the fake names of Mr and Mrs Robert Alleny Viela Gracia – Mr and Mrs Roy boarded the Spanish trans-Atlantic liner *Alfanso XIII* at Veracruz. The immediate destination was Madrid, and from there, Moscow, via Genoa, Zurich and Berlin. Roy selected the route in consultation with the Mexican government to avoid the risk of being arrested or kidnapped by the British police. His conspiratorial nature made him more cautious than necessary. He justified his action on the ground that his name had figured in the sedition committee report in connection with the Indo-German conspiracy, though the war was over and the conspiracy in which he had been implicated had ended in a fiasco.

Roy reached Berlin in December 1919. It was his first visit to the city, which was no longer a dreamland. His idea of revolution and opinion about the Indian revolutionaries had changed considerably. 'I no longer believed in political freedom without the content of economic liberation and social justice,' writes Roy in his *Memoirs.*[1]

The statement seems doubtful. It was perhaps an afterthought, or at best, an emotional outburst in conformity with his newly acquired socialist idea of revolution. He was still a nationalist to the core and believed that a truckload of arms and ammunitions could bring about enough revolution in India to drive the British out of the country. Thus, the change, if any, was merely peripheral to suit his convenience and that of other Indian revolutionaries of his time. There was no secret about it. The debacle of Germany and the subsequent liquidation of the Berlin Committee disillusioned the Indian revolutionaries abroad. They all got scattered and were on the lookout for new avenues of adventure. The only difference between Roy and other Indian revolutionaries was that while others were roaming in wilderness to acquire a berth, Roy had already got it and improved his position considerably. Borodin's company gave him a footing in marxist circles and the German gold relieved him of his financial difficulties, with which most Indian revolutionaries were then struggling. Roy was aware of his enviable position, which led him to believe that his affluence and position in marxist circles would certainly prove to be an eyesore to his one-time comrades. He, therefore, decided to treat the members of the erstwhile Berlin committee with considerable indifference. However, in the course of his short stay in Berlin, Roy decided to meet Bhupendranath Dutta, the only member of the erstwhile Berlin committee present in the city.

As expected, Dutta demanded from Roy a full report of his activities ever since he left India, and also an account of the large sums of money he had received from Germans on behalf of Indian revolutionaries.[2] Roy refused to comply with the demand. He contended that he had received the money from Germans in his personal capacity and he was only accountable to the Germans and no one else. To his advantage, none of those Germans were around to question him regarding the money. Roy abruptly closed the chapter much to the annoyance of Dutta.

While in Berlin, Roy also came in contact with several leading German communists, notably Thalheimer, with whom he became friendly. Roy claims that he attended a few secret meetings of communist leaders in Berlin and discussed the problems facing the revolution. 'Thalheimer took great pains to give me the English rendering of the discussions and asked for my opinion.'[3] The claim seems to be exaggerated. Roy's knowledge of the communist movement at that time was limited to what he had gathered from a few books, and supplemented with heavy doses of imagination and ambition. Thus, it is quite unlikely for Thalheimer to ask Roy for opinion. However, the stopover in Berlin was helpful to Roy. Apart from being acquainted with German communist leaders, he witnessed the debacle of the proletarian revolution in Germany. This had a significant impact on him, which lasted until he was asked to quit the Comintern. Roy visualized that 'the proletariats in the metropolitan countries would not succeed in their heroic endeavour to capture power unless imperialism was weakened by the revolt of the colonial people'.[4] This was a new thesis and a new approach to proletarian revolution in an immature mind.

The causes that led to the failure of the revolution in Germany were far different from what Roy had imagined. The revolution in Germany was carried out following proletarian means and methods at the call of the spartakists, but it did not proceed beyond the bounds of a bourgeois democratic revolution. It did away with the monarchy, but did not destroy the power of the bourgeoisie. The new government formed in the name of a socialist republic was a government of the right social democrats and the centrists. It utilized its power in the interests of the bourgeoisie, backed by the more gullible section of the masses. The revolutionaries believed, however mistakenly, that with the overthrow of monarchy and the setting up of a republic, the 'soviets' had brought power into the hands of the proletariat and would now proceed towards the building of socialism. But the right social democrat leaders successfully split the movement and this kept it within the bourgeois democratic limits, because the working class was not adequately organized for the occasion. Leaders of the right social democrats, in collaboration with reactionary forces, dealt a heavy blow that led to the debacle of the proletarian revolution in Germany. But Roy viewed it otherwise. Following his new thesis from Berlin, he issued a *manifesto,*[5] calling upon workers from all countries, especially Great Britain, to help India achieve a revolution.

In this curious *manifesto*, Roy applied his newly acquired socialist idea of proletarian struggle to the national democratic liberation struggle in India, ignoring the very basis of a colonized country's struggle for freedom. Instead of wanting to make the freedom struggle broad based, he propagated a sectarian outlook by contraposing the two tendencies in the national liberation movement. This becomes clear when he states in the *manifesto*, 'Today there are two tendencies in the Indian movement distinct in principles and aims. The nationalists advocate an autonomous India and incite the masses to overthrow the foreign exploiter upon a vague democratic programme or no programme at all. The real revolutionary movement stands for the economic emancipation of the workers and rests on the growing strength of a class-conscious industrial proletariat and landless peasantry. This later movement is too big for the bourgeois leaders and can only be carried out with the social revolution. This manifesto is issued for those who fill the ranks of the second movement ... we declare our aim is to prevent the establishment of a bourgeois nationalist government which would be another bulwark of capitalism. We wish to organise the growing rebelliousness of the Indian masses on the principle of class struggle, so that when the revolution comes it will be social revolution. The idea of the proletarian revolution distinct from nationalism has come to India and is showing itself in unprecedented strikes. It is primitive and not clearly class-conscious so that sometimes it becomes the victim of nationalist ideas. But those in the van see the goal and the struggle and reject the idea of uniting the whole country under nationalism for the sole purpose of expelling the foreigner, because they realise that the native princes, landlords, factory-owners, moneylenders, who would control the government, would not be less oppressive than the foreigner ... we call upon the workers of all countries especially Great Britain to help us to realise our programme.'[6] Yet, it would be wrong to suppose that Roy did not understand the two distinct stages of the socialist revolution in their totality. He was quite aware of them, when in the same *manifesto* he states, 'The first step towards the social revolution must be to create a situation favourable for organising the masses for the final struggle. Such a situation can be created only by the overthrow or at least the weakening of the foreign imperialism which maintains itself by military power.'[7]

Here again, Roy committed the same mistake. While accepting the two distinct stages of the socialist revolution, he ignored the class implication of the first stage, i.e., the stage when the proletariat has to play the role of the builder of a united anti-imperialist and anti-feudal front, along with the national bourgeoisie. The forces of the movement for national independence and the struggle of the workers and peasants for ultimate liberation – the two stages of a socialist revolution – were mixed up in a way that could only lead to a sectarian approach to the detriment of the formation of a united national front necessary to achieve the first stage of the socialist revolution.

By about the end of March or the beginning of April 1920, Roy left Berlin and proceeded towards Moscow on board *The Soviet*. *The Soviet* sailed from Stettin, and travelled as far as Reval, the capital of the Estonia Republic. Then, from Reval, Roy travelled by rail to Moscow via Leningrad.

In 1920, Moscow – the dreamland of revolutionaries all over the world – was gasping. The civil war had just ended and law and order had taken a firm grip over the city. Distinctions between the rich and the poor had vanished by a single stroke. Everything – bread, shelter, transport – in fact, all the necessities of life, though scarce, were regulated by the principle of social justice. But Roy did not have to feel the scarcity. He got down from the train and headed straightaway for the 'Gutchkov Mansion' in a large limousine, escorted by Schlipkin.[8] He was a state guest and lived with reasonable comfort in the midst of scarcity.

Long before Roy, quite a few Indians had come in contact with bolshevik leaders and landed in Soviet Union. They risked their lives to identify an effective method to fight British rule in India. In fact, Indian revolutionaries were not attracted so much to communist ideals as to their applicability as a means to drive out the British. Both within the country and outside, Indian revolutionaries were attracted towards the Soviet Union 'by the fact that it had proclaimed the right of nations to self-determination and had liberated the colonial peoples of the Russian Empire from the yoke of Tsardom, thereby showing to the other eastern peoples the way to national independence'.[9] Yet, it would be wrong to suppose that Indian revolutionaries were ignorant of the impact of the socialist revolution on people. They were quite conscious of the social aspect of the revolution. 'The ideas of social equality, social justice, even of an agrarian anti-feudal revolution, were by no means alien to some of the revolutionaries. What is more, quite a few of them were deeply influenced by these ideas, but they understood them in a utopian, petty bourgeois revolutionary nationalistic manner.'[10] This is no aspersion on the Indian revolutionaries. The Indian revolutionaries had lived and grown in a social and economic atmosphere that taught them to brood on past glories rather than look forward. This prevented them, for quite some time, from comprehending the marxist-leninist theory in its totality. Indians who had come to Soviet Union, and finally to communism, came via the anti-imperialist movement, carrying with them many old ideas, wholly alien to the new ideology. It is for this reason that 'most of the Indian revolutionaries, even after they had proclaimed themselves communists, did not become so in a real sense for quite some time'.[11] Only Roy studied and understood a bit of marxism in its true form, which was why he among all the Indian revolutionaries, could impress bolshevik leaders.

Roy had twin advantages. A clever and intelligent manipulator, he had Borodin's unqualified support. He was accepted as the sole spokesman for India after he reached Moscow. Others who had come before him lacked both intellect and patronage, and they had no one to introduce them to the top brass or shield them from difficulties, as Borodin protected Roy. There was much grumbling among Indian revolutionaries in Berlin against Roy's supremacy in the bolshevik circle, but hardly any challenge. The little challenge that came from the Indian revolutionaries stationed at Berlin was quite belated – long after the second congress of the Third International – when Roy had become powerful enough to counter all challenges quite successfully. Soon after Roy reached Moscow, Borodin introduced him to the higher echelons of the bolshevik leadership, which Roy exploited to his advantage against his critics.

For the people of the East, the second congress of the Third Communist International or the Comintern had special significance. It examined threadbare a wide range of problems concerning the East at a time when it was groaning under the heel of imperialist oppression. From an altogether different plane, it examined the socioeconomic structure of a colonial society and the nature of its freedom struggle, the role of the national bourgeoisie and the peasantry in this struggle, as well as the role that the Comintern was going to play to help the colonized people free themselves from imperialist oppression. The congress met from 22 July 1920 to 7 August 1920. The sessions for the first four days were held in Petrograd, and thereafter, in Moscow. The congress was attended by 217 delegates from 67 organizations of 37 countries.[12]

At this important international congress, several Indians, including Roy, were present. Roy attended the conference in the assumed name of Robert Allen-Roy, as a delegate from the Communist Party of Mexico, but, in fact, represented India. He was the only Indian with a right to vote. All others, Abani Mukherjee, M.P.T. Acharya, and Roy's wife, Evelyn, had a voice but no vote; and Mohammad Shafiq was only an observer.[13]

Before the opening of the Congress, Lenin had circulated a preliminary draft of his thesis on the national and colonial question for discussion among the delegates acquainted with the problems of the East. Roy, in Moscow at that time, received a copy of the draft for 'criticism and suggestion'.[14] Thereafter, Roy met Lenin a number of times. He is known to have discussed the problems of liberation and social emancipation of the colonial countries of the East, particularly of India. During the course of discussions,

Roy seemed to have disagreed with Lenin on a number of points, but, with a great deal of tolerance and understanding, Lenin gave him a patient hearing. Roy flattered himself on this. 'By quoting Plekhanov's authority, I shook his theoretical position… I had the rare privilege of being treated as an equal by a great man…,' writes Roy in his *Memoirs*.[15] How far Roy shook Lenin's theoretical position or was treated by Lenin as an equal, the less said the better. But one thing was certain: the 'naivety of a novice' must have amused Lenin. However, Lenin asked Roy to draft a supplementary thesis on the national and colonial question for discussion.

Lenin had a clear vision about the nature and course of liberation movements in colonial and backward countries. While advancing his idea, he 'proceeded from the fact that feudal or patriarchal-tribal relations were prevalent in the colonial and dependent Asian countries. The feudal landlords, the tribal chiefs, as a rule, supported foreign imperialist domination, whereas the growing national bourgeoisie came out against imperialism'.[16] Lenin's opinion was based on the real state of affairs. After World War I, a powerful liberation movement headed by the national bourgeoisie emerged in all the eastern countries, especially in India. Lenin, therefore, found it quite necessary on the part of communists to support the liberation movements, in alliance with the anti-imperialist bourgeoisie, for a determined struggle to establish independent nation states.

The support that Lenin was prepared to extend was, however, conditional. He was aware of the bourgeois democratic content of the national liberation movements led by the bourgeoisie in backward and colonial countries. Thus, he laid down certain specific conditions while defining the role and task of the rising communists and the Comintern vis-à-vis the national liberation movements. In his thesis on the national and colonial question, he clearly stated: 'The Communist International should support bourgeois democratic movements in colonial and backward countries only on conditions that in these countries the elements of future proletarian parties, which will be communist not only in name, shall be brought together and educated to understand their special tasks, viz., to fight the bourgeois movements within their own nations. The Communist International must enter into a temporary alliance with bourgeois democracy in the colonial and backward countries, but should not merge with it, and should under all circumstances uphold the independence of the proletarian movement even if it is in its most embryonic form.'[17]

It is clear from the above that Lenin's thesis on the national and colonial question was primarily aimed at two things: that the communists in oppressed countries must become an independent force and they must join hands with bourgeois democratic forces to form an anti-imperialist united front in the struggle for national liberation. This new principle was opposed by Roy.

Roy disagreed with Lenin on the necessity for the communists to support the liberation struggle headed by the national bourgeoisie. He refused to accept a historically revolutionary role for the national bourgeoisie in the liberation struggle. According to Roy, 'bourgeoisie even in the most advanced colonial countries, like India, as a class, was not economically and culturally differentiated from the feudal social order: therefore, the nationalist movement was ideologically reactionary in the sense that its triumph would not necessarily mean a bourgeois democratic revolution'.[18]

Roy based his arguments on the assumption that India was already a capitalist country with its subordination to the power of British imperialist capital, in which the national bourgeoisie had become an ally and close collaborator of British imperialism. The struggle of the Indian people, therefore, 'did not have, in the main, a national content, but was rapidly acquiring the nature of a struggle for economic and social emancipation and for the abolition of all class domination'.[19] He contended that in the colonies, especially in India, the liberation struggle was essentially an economic struggle. The bourgeois democratic nationalist movements are limited to the small middle class that does not reflect the aspirations of the masses. It strives for the establishment of a free nation state to perpetuate exploitation. The Comintern, therefore, must not find in bourgeois democrats the means through which the liberation movement in colonies should be helped. 'The mass movements in the colonies are growing independently of the nationalist movements. The masses distrust the political leaders who always lead them astray and prevent them from revolutionary action.'[20] Therefore, support to bourgeois democratic movements in the colonies would amount to fuelling the growth of a national spirit to the detriment of the awakening of class consciousness among the masses. It would be worthwhile to encourage and support revolutionary mass action through the medium of a communist party of the proletariat to bring 'the real revolutionary forces to action which will not only overthrow foreign imperialism, but also lead progressively to the development of soviet power, thus preventing the rise of a native capitalism in place of the vanquished foreign capitalism, to further oppress and exploit the people'.[21]

Lenin and Roy differed fundamentally on the role of the national bourgeoisie. Lenin believed that the national bourgeoisie was playing a historically revolutionary role in the liberation struggle in colonies and backward countries, and the communists should support it in the struggle against imperialism. Roy, on the other hand, believed that it was anti-imperialist but not revolutionary. Ideologically, it was reactionary and not worthy of support. Roy further asserted that 'in most of the colonies there already exist organised socialist or communist parties, in close relation to the mass movement. The relation of the Communist International with the revolutionary movement in the colonies should be through vanguard of the working class in their respective countries'.[22] As against this, Lenin believed that there were no proletarian organisations of any consequence at the time; so the idea of helping the revolutionary movement through proletarian parties was out of question.

The theses of both Lenin and Roy were placed before the commission for discussion. Roy tried to defend his thesis, but his 'voluntaristic, left-sectarian' views were considered unscientific and harmful. 'You will have to base yourselves on the bourgeois nationalism', said Lenin, 'which is awakening, and must awaken, among those people and which has its historical justification.'[23]

However, though Roy's thesis was rejected, he succeeded in getting Lenin's wordings slightly modified. Lenin in the preliminary draft of his thesis had stated:

> In respect of the more backward countries and nations with prevailing feudal or patriarchal and patriarchal-peasant relations, it is necessary to bear in mind especially:
>
> The necessity of all communist parties to render assistance to the bourgeois democratic liberation movement in such countries; especially does this duty fall upon the workers of such countries upon which the backward nations are colonially or financially dependent.[24]

The final amended version reads:

> In regard to the more backward States and nations, primarily feudal or patriarchal or patriarchal-peasant in character, the following considerations must be kept specially in mind:
>
> All communist parties must support by action the revolutionary liberation movements in these countries. The form which this support shall take should be discussed with the communist party of the country in question, if there is one. This obligation refers in the first place to the active support of the workers in that country on which the backward nation is financially or as a colony, dependent.[25]

After this change was made, Lenin's thesis – along with Roy's supplementary thesis on the national and colonial question, with Lenin's amendment – was placed before the commission and accepted unanimously.[26]

In his report to the plenary session, Lenin put forward an explanation for this change: 'The significance of this change is, that we, as communist should and will support bourgeois liberation movements in the colonies only when they are genuinely revolutionary, and when their exponents do not hinder our work of educating and organising in a revolutionary spirit the peasantry and the masses of the exploited. If these conditions do not exist, the communists in these countries must combat the reformist bourgeoisie …'[27] Lenin therefore did not make any concession to Roy, as far as the general strategy of the struggle for liberation is concerned. He still maintained that the proletarian party in colonial and backward countries must unite with the national bourgeoisie without loss of identity and play an independent role in the fight against imperialism and its local bastion, viz., the pre-capitalist social structure. However, what Lenin conceded was in the tactics of the application of the general theoretical position – that in the fight for national liberation, the tactics should be decided through consultation between the Comintern, the proletarian party (if there is any) of the country concerned, and the working class of the metropolitan countries. Therefore, Roy's claim to have shaken Lenin's theoretical position by quoting Plekhanov is open to doubt.

Roy suppressed the truth and distorted what had actually happened at the congress, because, in spite of Lenin's repeated 'warning against sectarianism', he could not give up his left-sectarian views. It is hard to believe that Roy did not understand the danger of 'leftism' in the growing communist movement – which turns the party of the working class into a sect. Before attending the second congress of the Comintern, Roy had gone through Lenin's latest brochure on the dangers of sectarianism.[28] Lenin prepared this brochure on the eve of the Comintern's second congress to share his experience of proletarian revolution with other comrades for their benefit. In the brochure, Lenin stated in clear terms that 'to reject compromise on "principle", to reject the permissibility of compromise in general, no matter of what kind, is childishness, which it is difficult even to consider seriously. A political leader who desires to be useful to the revolutionary proletariat must be able to distinguish *concrete* cases of compromises that are inexcusable and are expressions of opportunism and *treachery*; he must direct all the forces of criticism, the full intensity of merciless exposure and relentless war, against *those concrete* compromises, and not allow the past masters of "practical" socialism and parliamentary Jesuits to dodge and wriggle out of responsibility by means of disquisitions on "compromises in general"…. There are different kinds of compromises. One must be able to analyse the situation and the concrete conditions of each compromise, or of each variety of compromise'.[29] Lenin further proceeded and laid down several brief fundamental rules for analysis of concrete compromises to avoid any misrepresentation. The brochure, as Roy said, 'was a piece of communist literature of historical significance. It must be read and understood by all the faithful'.[30] Roy read the brochure and claimed that the title of the brochure, *Leftwing Communism, an Infantile Disorder,* was his suggestion, which Lenin had accepted.[31]

Even if Roy suggested the title of the brochure, he did not follow its content. He continued to hold his left-sectarian views. But these views turned out to be suicidal for the communists in India. Indian communists, in those days, knew only Roy, and following his footsteps, they too also developed a sectarian attitude towards the bourgeois-liberation movement in India and isolated themselves from the main currents of the liberation struggle. This strengthened the rightist elements among the national bourgeoisie and made the leftists rather wary of the communists. Following the tactics suggested in Roy's got-up version of the thesis on the national and colonial question, not only did the national movement suffer at the hands of the communists in India, but it also distorted their image.

The second congress of the Comintern was a momentous event in Roy's life. It enhanced his prestige among the communists manifold. The delegates who attended the congress were both amused and amazed at the cheek of a young man, barely in his twenties, who could dare challenge Lenin. Actually, Roy had neither the capacity nor the mind to challenge Lenin. He was quite conscious of his limitation. Yet, he came forward for a simple reason – should the Comintern decide to support the bourgeois democratic leaders in the colonies to direct the anti-imperialist movement in their respective countries on behalf of the Comintern, then Virendranath Chattopadhyaya would certainly be in a better position to direct the movement in India than

Roy. The fear was not totally unfounded. While in Berlin, Roy had an inkling that Chattopadhyaya would attempt to exploit the Comintern for political and financial support to the struggle against imperialism in India. And as suspected, Chattopadhyaya did try to influence the Comintern, but being slow, unwittingly allowed Roy sufficient time to establish his position.

Soon after the second congress, the executive committee of the Comintern met in a formal session and set up a 'small bureau' of five persons as the supreme policy-making body of the Comintern. The main task before the 'small bureau' was to plan the strategy of revolution to liberate the oppressed people of Asia. This was thought to be easy after a temporary setback in Europe. To gear up the movement, the 'small bureau' passed two resolutions: to hold the first congress of the oppressed people of the East at Baku, and to set up a Central Asiatic bureau of the Comintern at Tashkent.

The people behind the Baku congress and the setting up of a Central Asiatic bureau of the Comintern were Zinoviev, Bela Kun and Radek, supported by Lenin. Roy opposed the idea initially, but agreed when Lenin asked him to do so. 'After days of discussion,' writes Roy, 'Lenin advised me to suspend judgement until the benefit of Stalin's authoritative opinion was available.'[32] However, in spite of Lenin's advice, Roy declined to attend the congress at Baku and suggested the name of Abani Mukherjee instead. Roy considered the Baku congress 'a wanton waste of time, energy and material resources in frivolous agitation', and went to the extent of calling it 'Zinoviev's Circus'![33]

Roy's opposition to the plan was purely sentimental. Despite his prominence at the Comintern's congress, he was not given a place in the executive committee of the Comintern. The only Asian included as a member of the executive was Sen Katayama. Roy's claim of having declined to accept the membership on the body cannot be true. Roy became a candidate-member of the executive committee of the Communist International at its fourth congress in 1922 and a full voting member only in 1924. Roy felt sore about this negligence and let out his anger through opposition. Lenin understood it, but in the absence of any other alternative, he thought it fit to keep Roy in good humour. Roy was not slow to understand this and changed his position from opposition to one of cooperation by accepting a membership in the Central Asiatic bureau.

The Central Asiatic bureau was composed of three persons. Besides Roy, there were Sokolnikov and Georgi Safarov, commandant of the 'propaganda train'.[34] Both Sokolnikov and Safarov left Moscow for Central Asia soon after the second congress, but Roy stayed back. He was not in a hurry to leave Moscow. Though now a professed communist, his idea of the struggle to liberate India from the clutches of British imperialism remained unchanged. The only difference between him and his terrorist colleagues was that while his terrorist colleagues were enjoying their blissful slumber, he came out of it to exploit the new situation arising from the socialist revolution by painting his nationalism red. He was still an adventurist and wanted to gain everything through adventure. 'I had no intention of leaving Moscow,' writes Roy, 'without being amply provided with the sinews of war material to make a revolution in India. I had failed in a similar attempt in the Far East. Then the Germans duped us. This time I wanted to succeed, the Russian bolsheviks were reliable allies.'[35]

While Roy was busy making plans of new adventures, the congress of the oppressed people of the East met at Baku on 1 September 1920 under the presidentship of Zinoviev. However, it failed to achieve anything tangible. It was a 'conglomeration of motley people'. The congress was attended by 1,891 representatives of thirty-two nationalities, mostly from the Caucasus and Central Asian territories of the Soviet Union. It included quite a few Turks and Persians and seven Indians.[36] The Indian delegates, excepting one, sat through the proceedings as mute spectators. The one who spoke appealed in flamboyant terms for the unity of the people of the East to get rid of world capitalism.[37] To further its programme, the congress established a council of forty-seven people representing twenty nationalities and brought out a periodical for propaganda.

But within a year, both the council and the periodical had to be wound up because of inactivity.[38]

When the Baku congress was planning the future of the liberation struggle in the oppressed countries of the East, news trickled in from Central Asia to Moscow about the presence of *muhajirs* – a group of pan-Islamists who had left India in search of *Dar-ul-Islam* and, if possible, to take part in a *holy war* against the British in defence of Turkey and its Caliph. But not all of them were anti-British or *holy-war* maniacs. Quite a few of them had joined the melee to try their fortune in a new land. It was a peculiar religious immigration movement of Indian Muslims. It commenced in the middle of 1920, when batches of Indian Muslims, mostly shopkeepers, peasants and a few young, educated people sold all their possessions and left India, initially, for Afghanistan.[39]

The failure of the Baku congress and the presence of *muhajirs* in Central Asia went to the advantage of Roy. He drew a psychological satisfaction from the failure of the congress, and in the *muhajirs*, saw possible recruits for an army of liberation to free India from the hands of British imperialists. By exploiting the anti-British sentiment of these ignorant and unfortunate religious fanatics, Roy thought of raising and equipping an army of liberation. Using the frontier territory as the base of operations, and with necessary support from the tribesmen, he expected the liberation army to march into India and occupy some territory and establish a civil government. On the face of it, the plan looked brilliant, and for Roy, it was foolproof.[40]

Ever since Roy joined the freedom struggle, he had two things uppermost in his mind – arms and money. Being a terrorist at heart, he firmly believed that if these two things were freely available, there was nothing in this world that could not be achieved. He never thought for a moment that no revolution could take place without being propped up by the masses inspired by a revolutionary ideology. The masses must be educated gradually towards a definite goal. Until this is achieved, no amount of arms or money would help bring about a revolution. It could, at best, create chaos to the advantage of anti-social elements in society and mar the prospects of revolution. However, Roy was not alone in thinking thus. Terrorists all over the world suffer from such lopsided thinking. What puzzles us is how the leaders of the Comintern, and especially Lenin, could agree to such a wild scheme. Writing in *Left-Wing Communism: an Infantile Disorder*, Lenin stated in clear terms that 'victory cannot be won with a vanguard alone. To throw only the vanguards into the decisive battle, before the entire class, the broad masses have taken up a position either by direct support for the vanguard, or at least of sympathetic neutrality towards it and of precluded support for the enemy, would be not merely foolish but criminal. Propaganda and agitation alone are not enough for an entire class, the broad masses of the working people, those oppressed by capital, to take up such a stand. For that, the masses must have their own political experience. Such is the fundamental law of all great revolutions ...'[41] Yet, Lenin gave a fillip to Roy's petty bourgeois adventurism.

It is possible that Lenin's knowledge of India at that time was rather poor.[42] He miscalculated the intensity of the freedom movement in India under the leadership of Gandhi. The Khilafat non-cooperation movement with its apparent mass character was half a mass and never a revolutionary movement. According to Morarji Desai's estimate, in a population of 40 crore, not more than 2 lakh, i.e., 0.05 per cent fought the British.[43] By no stretch of imagination could this be called a mass movement. Besides, Gandhi did not take pains to educate people about the idea of a mass struggle towards a definite goal. There was deplorable lack of clarity in his thought and in the campaign that he had formulated for the ensuing struggle.[44] He simply exploited the emotion and anti-British sentiment of the petty bourgeoisie. The role of workers and peasants was minimal and momentary. Everything was in a melee. Chaos was the logical outcome and it did come with Chauri Chaura. Chauri Chaura was the first indicator of chaos. The violence was an unplanned and isolated action of a group of people charged with emotion and anti-British sentiment. There was nothing revolutionary in it. Gandhi knew it. He knew that chaos would never lead to anything positive; rather, if allowed to flourish, it would jeopardize the leadership. No leader would like to put the last nail in his coffin. So, to his satisfaction, Gandhi passed the Bardoli resolution after Chauri Chaura. Long after the Khilafat non-cooperation movement, Gandhi whispered the truth to Shaukat Ali at the Belgaum congress.[45] Yet, in all fairness, it must be accepted that Gandhi was the only leader in our struggle for freedom who understood the people, shared their woes and aspirations, and became one with them. Other leaders, great or small, failed to identify themselves with the people as Gandhi did. They were conscious of this fact and that was why, though they considered the withdrawal of Khilafat a betrayal of the cause, they did not dare to revolt. They accepted Gandhi's decision with a murmur and looked to him again for new answers.

Personality plays an auxiliary role in the evolution of leadership in politics. People choose their leaders in consonance with the prevailing socio-political conditions and the circumstances emanating out of them. It is because of this reason that different ages produce different types of political leaders, and no two leaders are alike, as neither the socio-political condition nor the circumstances ever remain static. Gandhi was a product of the then-prevailing socio-political conditions and circumstances. His semi-medieval obscurantist ideas suited the Indian mind. People found in him the traits of a leader who could meet their needs, and set aside the claims of those who were far more intelligent and rational than him. Thus, in their own interest, the people thrust greatness upon Gandhi and made him pre-eminent in Indian politics. Gandhi was not slow to take advantage of the situation. Like all great personalities in history, he too exploited people's trust in him and exerted his will, while turning a deaf ear to the opinions of others. Gandhi was more of a prophet than a politician. He always acted according to his inner conscience, without caring for its political implications.

Lenin did not know this inherent weakness of our freedom movement. He had no direct contact with the Indian leaders. He was too preoccupied with the problems of his own country to have any time to look exclusively at India to understand the true character of its freedom movement and its leaders. Under the circumstances, he believed Roy and gave his consent to his adventurous plan.[46] Great men are often susceptible to great follies.

With the sanction of the council of people's commissars and Klansky, the deputy chairman of the Revolutionary Military Council, Roy, towards the close of October, set on his journey to liberate India with large quantities of arms, ammunitions and plenty of money.[47] The immediate destination was Tashkent, and from there India, with his would-be liberation army.

Roy was under the impression that he would be the first Indian to reach Central Asia to organize the Indians there. He did not know that two other Indian revolutionaries, Abdur Rab and Trimul Acharya, were already in Central Asia and working among the Indians. Both Rab and Acharya were as good adventurists as Roy, but less fortunate. Rab and Acharya stepped into the Soviet Union and came in contact with Comintern leaders before Roy. They met Lenin at the beginning of 1919 as members of a delegation led by Mahendra Pratap, president of the provisional government of India in Kabul.[48] Since that time, they were active in Soviet Turkistan, building contacts with Indian traders and deserters from the British Indian army. Together they organized an association of Indian revolutionaries in Tashkent, with branches at Samarkand and Baku.[49] Rab and Acharya's achievement was, however, limited. Yet, Roy considered this limited achievement as an obstacle to his success – an encroachment on his authority. Thus, instead of taking Rab and Acharya into confidence, he ignored them altogether, as he did in the case of the Berlin Indian revolutionaries. 'Elevated to the key position in the Comintern apparatus and placed in charge with ample resources and arms and material to try out a plan of organising an India's liberation force, Roy went about the task individualistically, ignoring Rab and Acharya and the work they had done among the Indians in Soviet Turkistan before his arrival.'[50] He dismissed 'Rab as an imposter and Acharya as an anarchist'.[51] This scurrilous attitude of Roy brought him in conflict with Rab and Acharya and led to groupism.[52]

While Roy was brooding over the future course of action, news reached him that a group of *muhajirs* who were proceeding towards Turkey had been taken prisoners and were being mistreated by the Turkoman rebels. The news was shocking, yet it warmed up Roy's dampened zeal. He found in the *muhajirs* possible recruits for his army of liberation and managed to send a detachment of the Red Army to rescue those unfortunate men from the jaws of death. The detachment was sent just in time. A few days' delay would have caused the loss of about fifty heads. These *muhajirs*, as Roy puts it, were mostly 'urban riff-raff in rags and tatters', hardly able to move because of the long period of starvation and inhuman treatment. They undertook the hazardous journey to an unknown land with the fond expectation of going to heaven by laying down their lives in *jihad*. Religious fanaticism so overwhelmed their minds that even savage treatment at the hands of their coreligionists failed to shake off their belief in Caliph or *jihad*. Thus, no sooner did they recoup, than they insisted on being sent to Turkey. No amount of argument would work. They refused to be trained politically. They were all anti-British; so there was nothing for them to learn.[53]

Roy was in a fix. The whole plan of utilizing the *muhajirs* for the liberation of India was about to fizzle out. Thus, persuasion continued till at last a solution was found to the satisfaction of both the parties. Quite a few of the *muhajirs* agreed to receive military training on condition that when the training was over, they would be sent back to India with 'plenty of arms and money to fight the British'.[54] Roy heaved a sigh of relief. He could now boast of forming the nucleus of a liberation army to drive the British out of India. Yet, the main question remained unsolved: for which ideal they would fight the British? They were all religious fanatics and were sure to misuse the arms, unless they were politically educated. They must know what revolution means and learn to work for a democratic setup. Unless this minimum was achieved, it would be potentially dangerous to supply arms to these people. Roy understood this and continued his efforts to make them amenable to political education. At long last, the educated young men among the *muhajirs* agreed to be politically educated. Accordingly, in pursuance of the plan, a military school was set up at Tashkent in October 1920.[55]

However, it was soon clear that its high-pitched aims were not going to be realized. Several problems cropped up, making the situation increasingly difficult by the day. The earlier expectation that a sufficient number of *muhajirs* would be available to form a suitable army of liberation proved illusory. The number of persons available for military training was only 26 out of a total of nearly 200, who had crossed over to the Soviet Union in two *khafilas,* each consisting of about 100 persons.[56] Further, the Afghan government refused permission to transport arms to India across its territory.

Roy's repeated and insistent appeals to the Afghan consulate in Tashkent were of no avail.[57] This was totally unexpected. Russia had helped King Amanullah of Afghanistan to throw off British influence during the war and was quite hopeful that, henceforth, Amanullah would depend more on Russia than on Britain. But events proved otherwise. Amanullah patched up his differences with the British, hampering Russian interest. Lenin had anticipated this. He knew that the British would never abandon their strategic position in Afghanistan without making a last bid to regain it. He is said to have remarked that the British would be willing to bombard Amanullah's citadel with silver and gold bullets, if necessary, in a bid to regain control over Afghanistan.[58]

And, in reality, the British did support Amanullah financially, against the Russians. Besides, Amanullah was afraid of socialism more than anything else in this world, as it stood for the abolition of the feudal and capitalist social order. To a power-hungry despot, nothing could be more serious than the institution of democracy and socialism. Amanullah, therefore, did not like to jeopardize his existence by supporting Indian revolutionaries through the Soviet Union, against the British in India. Further, to add to the trouble, Rab and Acharya, whom Roy had castigated earlier as 'imposter' and 'anarchist', respectively, sprung up at the forefront with a new challenge. They declared themselves communists and proceeded to set up, much to Roy's discomfort, a communist party at Tashkent with the approval of the Turk-bureau of the Communist International.

The debacle of the lofty plan of the formation of a liberation army and a successful revolution in India, along with the news of the attempt to form a communist party at Tashkent, upset Roy. But he was not the person to be disheartened easily. To vindicate his honour before the leaders of the Comintern, or to be more precise, before Lenin, Roy patched up his differences with Rab and Acharya. Much against his wishes, he agreed to the setting up of an emigree communist party at Tashkent, hoping to liberate India at a future date.

The emigree Communist Party of India was founded in a modest way at Tashkent on 17 October 1920. It consisted of seven persons, with a small executive committee of three persons – Roy, Acharya, and Shafiq.[59] The party was founded in accordance with the principles of the Comintern to work out a programme suitable to the conditions in India. It was expected to work 'under the political guidance of the Turkistan bureau of the Comintern'.[60]

The party founded at Tashkent could hardly be called the Communist Party of India. Of the seven members, Evelyn and Rosa were Indians only by marriage. They had never been to India during their life-time. The party had neither any link with India, nor any programme for it. In a sense, it was worse than a government in exile. Neither Roy nor Acharya was serious about the party and its programme. It was the brainwave of Acharya, who wanted to hoodwink Roy. And for Roy it was simply a face-saving device.[61] Later, when Roy sat down to write his memoirs, he recalled the incident and confessed that the party had no 'right to speak on behalf of the workers of India, not to mention the Indian people as a whole'.[62]

The news of the formation of the emigree Communist Party of India was a rude shock to the members of the erstwhile Berlin committee. They considered it a personal achievement for Roy and a defeat for themselves. Under the spell of an illusion caused by Roy's modest achievement, they imagined a monster who would soon emerge as the sole leader of the liberation movement in India on behalf of the Comintern. Instead of proceeding in a cool and calculated manner, they moved hurriedly to throw a challenge to Roy. This was a wrong move, simply because none of the members of the Berlin committee knew Roy intimately. They did not know that Roy's weakness was his own ego – the common fault of an adventurist and a gambler of fate. He was sure to expose himself in due course, as he actually did a few years later. However, headed by Virendranath Chattopadhyaya, the Berlin group confronted Roy with the hope to oust him.

Virendranath Chattopadhyaya was a known figure among Indian revolutionaries, both at home and abroad. It is an indisputable fact that Chattopadhyaya was the main spirit behind the activities of the Berlin committee from the day of its inception.[63] He had a good social standing, which in a bourgeois social order is reckoned as an asset. In comparison, Roy, so long as he was in India, was never regarded as a leader; at best, he was a good subordinate with hardly any social standing. Therefore, in the eyes of the Berlin revolutionaries, Roy was an upstart who had come to position by a freak of chance. Roy was conscious of this fact and was always keen to make his presence felt by disregarding the opinion of others.

Around 1917, when it became clear that Germany was going to suffer defeat in the war, Chattopadhyaya sensed the danger and shifted to Stockholm to set up a branch of the Indian Independence Committee. At Stockholm, he came in contact with Troyanovsky and Madam Balavanova.[64] In 1918, he received an invitation from Comrade Wronski, asking him to proceed to Petrograd, but due to certain difficulties he could not avail of this opportunity.[65] Had Chattopadhyaya succeeded in meeting Lenin before Roy, he would probably have been in a better position to deal with Roy.

In November 1920, while Roy was in Tashkent, Chattopadhyaya reached Moscow to explore the possibility of gaining the support of the Comintern. Quite hopeful of his mission, he contacted Comintern leaders to apprise them of the political situation in India and, perhaps also, to claim leadership. What actually transpired between Chattopadhyaya and the Comintern leaders is not known. It is said that the Comintern leaders advised Chattopadhyaya to return to Berlin and organize the Indian revolutionaries there.[66] Accordingly, Chattopadhyaya came back to Berlin and established a committee of the Indian revolutionaries as a preliminary step to follow up his mission.[67]

The news of Chattopadhyaya's mission to Moscow, his contact with the Comintern leaders, and the subsequent establishment of the Indian Revolutionary Committee in Berlin reached Roy in due course. On the pretext of attending the third congress of the Comintern, he hurried back to Moscow to counter the movement of the Berlin group, leaving behind in Tashkent a bundle of chaos and confusion – a group of 'troublesome lot', as Roy himself puts it, to be managed by Abani Mukherjee, a person whom Roy disliked from the very beginning and was always suspicious of.[68] Roy reached Moscow around March 1921, a few days before the leaders of the delegation of the Indian revolutionaries. He started his work in right earnest and set the stage for a drama to be enacted by the Indian revolutionaries, beginning with the epilogue.

Financed by the Comintern, the delegation of the Indian revolutionary committee of Berlin reached Moscow around April 1921.[69] It comprised fourteen members, Chattopadhyaya being the leader of the group.[70] The main drawback of the delegation was that it was not properly organized and included persons of all kinds of ideas. They had come to Moscow with two specific aims – to establish their claim to the leadership of the communist movement in India and to wage 'a determined struggle against the Roy clique'.[71] Roy was not slow to apprehend the danger. Thus, to soften the opposition, he tried to become friendly with the members of the delegation. The response to his gesture, as Roy puts it, was cool, rather hostile.[72] However, in spite of the differences, the revolutionaries sat in a joint meeting with Roy to iron out their problems. But in the course of the discussion, new squabbles cropped up and the meeting, as expected, ended in mudslinging.[73]

The Comintern appointed a commission to discuss the problems of Indian revolutionaries and their views on the communist movement in India. It was headed by Rutgers and included Borodin, Quelch and all the Indian revolutionaries.[74] But no sooner did the commission get to work, than Chattopadhyaya raised a question on the procedure of writing to be followed. Instead of accepting Chattopadhyaya as the leader of the group and discussing problems with him, Rutgers preferred calling upon individual members and asking them to express their views.[75] Chattopadhyaya objected to the proceedings and staged a walkout, followed by other members of his group. A deadlock ensued and the commission was dissolved.[76] Rutgers reported to the leaders of the Comintern that 'the Indians were not prepared to cooperate with the commission'.[77] Three months later, a new commission was set up to resume the work. The Berlin group gained time, but wasted it in internal bickering instead of patching up the differences. The new commission was headed by James Bell, with Borodin, Troyanosky, Thalheimer and Rakosi on behalf of the Comintern, and the different groups of Indian revolutionaries as its members.[78] Before the commission sat to work, Chattopadhyaya objected to Borodin's presence and threatened to boycott the commission again. And on being told that Borodin was a member of the commission on behalf of the Comintern, Chattopadhyaya staged a walkout.[79] This time he was all alone, no one followed him. He was no longer the leader of the group. This was a defeat for Chattopadhyaya and a triumph for Roy.

Three main theses were put before the commission for discussion. One was by Roy. His amended thesis on the national and colonial question was accepted by the second congress of the Comintern. Of the other two theses, one was by Chattopadhyaya, Luhani and Kankhoje; while the other was by Bhupendranath Dutta and his group.[80] Roy's being an established thesis, the discussion was mainly on the other two. The main point in Chattopadhyaya's thesis was that the destruction of British imperialism should be considered a priority as far as India was concerned. With a view to achieve this, the Third International should establish a 'revolutionary board' and extend all help to Indian revolutionaries through this board. Chattopadhyaya's 'thesis stressed the national, anti-imperialist aspect of the Indian revolutionaries but underestimated or ignored the social aspect of the same'.[81]

The thesis submitted by Dutta and his group had an altogether different tone. It was more in line with Roy's thesis. Its basic point was that as long as the country was under foreign domination, the various classes should work together to organize a political revolution. In this connection, to substantiate his arguments, Dutta quoted profusely from Marx's *Civil War in France* and added that the communist party must be organized from the very start to achieve a social revolution immediately after the political revolution to establish socialism in the country.[82]

The commission sat for two days. The theses of both Chattopadhyaya and Dutta were rejected outright for different reasons. Chattopadhyaya's thesis was purely nationalistic in character. It was politically wrong as it was impregnated with sectarianism. Dutta's thesis had hardly anything new in it. It was more in line with Roy's thesis, except for the jugglery of words. The verdict of the commission, therefore, went in favour of Roy. The Berlin revolutionaries further wanted to meet Lenin but that did not materialize. Chattopadhyaya held the view that 'his opponents had sabotaged this'.[83] This seems to be a conjecture. The opponents might have tried to prevent Lenin from meeting the Berlin revolutionaries, but was Lenin so credulous?

The failure of the mission was a foregone conclusion. Roy enjoyed the confidence of the then-leading comrades of the Comintern. He had the support of Trotsky, Zinoviev, Borodin and Radak.[84] He was known for his supplementary thesis on the national and colonial question, however drastically it might have been reformulated by Lenin. As against this, the Berlin revolutionaries had practically no support from the high-ups. Their theses were weak on several vital points. Instead of trying to gain support through lobbying and improving upon their theses, in conformity with the accepted views of the Comintern, they roamed in wilderness with the vain hope to establish what they considered their just claim. They ignored the rudimentary principles of power politics, in which right or wrong hardly has any meaning. Justification is the first and last word in power politics. The Berlin revolutionaries failed rather miserably to justify their stand on all counts.

Victory over the Berlin group of Indian revolutionaries was a morale boost to Roy. Barring a few, most members of the Berlin group were apolitical. They called themselves revolutionaries, but had no idea of revolution, and even if they had any, it was woefully inadequate. Most of them landed in Europe to either study or learn a vocation. It was out of sheer youthful longing for adventure that they had joined hands with Chattopadhyaya and come to Moscow to oust Roy. Their approach was devoid of sincerity. Their understanding of marxism or international politics was naive. Roy proved beyond doubt that his understanding of international politics, and particularly of marxism, was far more superior to that of his adversaries. The Berlin group realized this truth rather late. The only member of the Berlin group for whom Roy had some regard was Chattopadhyaya. Roy did not anticipate Chattopadhyaya would oppose him. Thus, his hostile attitude hurt him. Yet, he did not accuse Chattopadhyaya, rather, exonerated him and put the blame on Agnes Smedlay, a socialist and admirer of Chattopadhyaya, whom he later married. 'I was very glad when he (Chattopadhyaya) came to Moscow. He was known to be a very intelligent and energetic man, having lived a rather stormy life for years in Europe. I expected to find in him a valuable colleague in the revolutionary work .... His attitude in Moscow was largely the result of the influence of Agnes Smedlay.'[85]

With the failure of the mission, the members of the Berlin group, excepting Gulam Ambia Khan Luhani and Nalini Gupta, left Moscow for Berlin 'without being able to convince the comrades about the real character of Roy and his people'.[86] Luhani and Nalini stayed back for reasons of their own. They had come to Moscow with the Berlin group in search of a livelihood. Thus, after the third congress of the Comintern, when the Berlin group left Moscow, Luhani patched up with Roy, and through his help got an assignment in the international department of the Comintern.[87] Nalini was a destitute. The Berlin group brought him to Moscow to leave him there to his fate to earn a livelihood.[88] Nalini knew it and planned his future accordingly. Having no ideological conviction, he found it convenient to align with Roy for his own survival, in preference to the Berlin group. From the day he reached Moscow, he became an agent of Roy. It was through Nalini that Roy obtained information about the movement of the Berlin group in Moscow.[89] This was a great help to Roy and he utilized the information to outwit his adversaries.

The struggle between Roy and the Berlin revolutionaries was basically for power and position, leadership and hegemony – a struggle for careerism in the backdrop of marxism. As the Berlin revolutionaries got ready to leave Moscow, Dutta called on Roy to bid him goodbye. Roy was in a jubilant mood. He consoled Dutta with a flush of sarcasm, 'Don't feel sorry for my victory, you be here and take charge of the work.' Dutta retorted, 'Neither you have won nor I have lost. You make your career here I make my career elsewhere.'[90] Dutta's cynically frank retort had the tinge of optimism that he could make his career elsewhere. It is a truth that the world is broad enough to accommodate everybody, and yet may not be so munificent as to provide equal opportunities to all. Dutta came back to India in 1925 and, thereafter, slowly sank into oblivion. In spite of his optimism, he could not make his career in politics.

Notes

1 *Memoirs*, p.219.

2 Bhupendranath Dutta, *Aprakasita Rajnaitik Itihash* (Bengali), Calcutta, 1953, p.249.

3 *Memoirs*, p.277.

4 *Memoirs*, p.306.

5 The 'manifesto' was written by Roy sometime in February or March 1920 and was signed by Abani Mukherjee, Santi Devi (Roy's wife) and Roy himself. It was published in the *Glasgow Socialist* in July 1920. The manifesto in its shorter form is preserved in the National Archives of India (Home Political Department, File No. 110, August 1920.)

6 G. Adhikari (Ed.), *Documents of the History of the Communist Party of India*, New Delhi, 1971, Vol. I, pp.152-4.

7 ibid., p.155.

8 *Memoirs*, p.315. The 'Gutchkov Mansion' originally belonged to Count Gutchkov, a noble man and an industrialist in Tsarist Russia. In Tsarist Russia he was known as the 'sugar king' for his large share in sugar business. The revolution abolished private property, so the mansion was taken over by the state. The ground floor was converted into a residential accommodation for Karakan, Vice-Commissar of foreign affairs and the upper storey was kept reserved for distinguished state guests.

9 M. Persits, 'Transition of Indian National Revolutionaries to Marxism-Leninism', *Soviet Review*, No. 23, 16 May 1974, p.25.

10 ibid., p.26

11 ibid., p.31.

12 Bernard Isaac, *Outline History of the Communist International*, (Translated from Russian), Moscow, 1971, p.76.

13 M. Persits, 'Colonial Question and Second Congress of Comintern', *Soviet Review*, No. 26, 3 June 1974, p.35.

14 *Memoirs*, p.340.

15 ibid., p.380.

16 M. Persits, 'Colonial Question and Second Congress of Comintern', *Soviet Review*, No. 26, 3 June 1974, p.36.

17 Draft thesis on national and colonial question prepared by Lenin, Documents, Vol. I, p.159.

18 *Memoirs*, p.379

19 M. Persist, 'Colonial Question and Second Congress of Comintern', *Soviet Review*, No. 26, June 1974, p.38.

20 Draft thesis on national and colonial question (supplementary) prepared by M.N. Roy, *Documents*, Vol. I, p.184.

21 ibid., p.188
22 ibid., pp.184 and 186.
23 V.I. Lenin, *Collected Works*, Vol, 30, p.162.
24 The Second Congress of the Communist International Proceedings, p.478. Quoted: G.D. Overstreet and M. Windmiller, op. cit., p.28.
25 Thesis on national and colonial question adopted by the congress, Documents, Vol. I, p.203.
26 Bernard Isaac, op. cit., p.85.
27 V.I. Lenin, *Collected Works*, Vol. 31, p.242
28 On the eve of the Comintern's second congress, Lenin wrote a book *Leftwing Communism, an Infantile Disorder*, to pool his experiences with those of other communists. In the book Lenin condemned 'leftism' as a dangerous weakness of the growing communist movement as it would lead the communists to isolation from the masses and turn the party of the working class into a sect.
29 V.I. Lenin, *Collected Works*, Vol. 31, pp.37-8.
30 *Memoirs.*, p.318
31 ibid
32 *Memoirs*, p.390.
33 ibid
34 During the years of civil war the Soviet Government filled a train with all sorts of propaganda material to carry the message of liberation to the farthest accessible corner of the country, it had a tremendous impact on the people as it helped them to visualise the actual happenings and the future of their country.
35 *Memoirs*, p.395.
36 *Documents*, Vol. I, pp.47-8.
37 ibid., p.47.
38 William. Z. Foster, *History of the Three Internationals*, Delhi, 1956, Vol. II, pp.30-31.
39 The mass exodus of the Muslims was known as the hijrat movement. Among the Muslims there was a lone Hindu, an M.A. from the Banaras Hindu University, Banaras. The actual number of emigrants that left India in the wake of the hijrat movement has been estimated variously. According to Pattabhi Sitaramayya, 18,000 (*History of the Indian National Congress, 1885-1935*, Vol. I, p.129); A. Toynbee, 18,000 (*Summary of International Affairs*, Vol. I, 1925, p.555); M.N. Roy, 50,000 to 1,00,000; (*Memoirs*, p.455); Shaukat Usmani, 36,000 (*Historic Trips of a Revolutionary Sojourn in the Soviet Union*, p.4.)
40 *Memoirs*, p.420. The amateurish plan had nothing new in it. During the course of the first world war, Indian revolutionaries had hatched out a

similar plan. They tried to form an army of liberation from among the prisoners of war in Turkey and Germany. Attempts were also made to contact the frontier tribes but nothing came out of it.

41 V.I. Lenin, *Collected Works*, Vol. 31, pp.92-3

42 In January 1921 or early February, Roy came to Moscow from Tashkent. He met Lenin on 9 February, and apprised him of the political condition in India and Central Asia. What Roy actually said to Lenin is not known to us. But soon after, on 14 February, Abdur Rab met Lenin and gave a picture different from Roy's in his discussion about the Indian political situation. Lenin, thereupon, asked Rab for a list of books on India with a view to gaining knowledge about the political condition of India for himself, instead of relying on others. For the list of books, see Chinmay Snehanabish, *Rush Biplob O Prabasi Bharatiya Biplobi* (Bengali), Calcutta, 1983, pp.199-201.

43 Rani Dhavan Sankardass, *The First Congress Raj – Provincial Autonomy in Bombay*, New Delhi, 1982, p.15.

44 Subhas Chandra Bose, *Collected Works*, Calcutta, 1981, Vol. II, pp.58-9.

45 At the Belgaum congress, sitting in a tent surrounded by leaders, Shaukat Ali asked Gandhi the reason for withdrawing the khilafat non-cooperation movement. Gandhi replied, 'If I had not called off the movement for which people blame me, you and I would not have been here today'. Harindranath Chattopadhyaya, *Life and Myself*, Bombay, 1948, Vol. I, p.191

46 *Memoirs*, p.417

47 ibid., p.421

48 *Documents*, vol. I, p.220.

49 ibid., p.54

50 ibid., p.59

51 *Memoirs*, p.464

52 Three groups were formed – one led by Roy helped by Abani Mukherjee and Mohammad Ali; another led by Abdur Rab supported by Acharya and Khalil Bay; and the third led by Shaukat Usmani, having leanings towards the Roy group.

53 *Memoirs*, p.57

54 ibid., p.461.

55 The military school offered three courses: one for airforce pilots and officers, another for infantry officers and the third for infantry soldiers. The educated cadres were selected for the first two courses and the uneducated for the third course. General political education was given to all, but the better educated were given an impressive political education course.

56 *Documents*, Vol. I, p.51.

57 ibid., p.242.

58 *Memoirs*, p.493

59 M.N. Roy, Evelyn Trent Roy, Abani Mukherjee, Rosa Fitingof, Mohammad AH (Ahmed Hasan), Mohammad Shafiq, and Trimul Acharya. Minutes of the meeting held on 17 October 1920, *Documents*, Vol. I, p.23.

60 Letter from M.N. Roy, secretary in-charge, Turkistan bureau to the central committee of the Communist Party of Turkistan, Tashkent, 20 December 1920.

61 The conflict between Roy and Acharya did not end with the formation of the emigree Communist Party of India. It continued unabated on the question of jurisdiction and methods of work among the Indian emigrees outside the USSR. Roy wanted to work within the USSR through the Turk bureau of the Comintern. Acharya did not agree. He wanted Roy to take charge of the propaganda and literary work on 'behalf of the party. Roy disagreed.

For details see: Minutes No. 30, meeting of the Turk bureau 6, cc, RCP, and Bureau cc, CPI dated 31 December 1920. *Documents*, Vol. I, pp.231-3.

62 *Memoirs*, p.479.

63 Abinash Chandra Bhattacharjee, *Europe' Bharatiya Biplober Sadana* (Bengali), Calcutta, 1968, pp 132-8.

64 Bhupendranath Dutta, op. cit., pp.240-41.

65 It is said that the German Government did not appreciate the idea of the Indian revolutionaries coming in direct contact with the Soviet leaders. This opposition of the German Government prevented Chattopadhyaya from proceeding to the USSR. He could reach Moscow in November 1920.

66 Bhupendranath Dutta, op. cit, p.263.

67 ibid., p.270.

68 *Memoirs*, p.476. Roy in his *Memoirs* has devoted one full chapter (pp.295-301) on Abani Mukherjee. The title of the chapter is 'An Embarrassing Associate'. The chapter leaves no doubt about Roy's attitude towards Abani Mukherjee.

69 Cecil Kaye, *Communism in India* (Reprint) Calcutta, 1971, pp.2-3.

70 *Documents*, Vol. I, p.254.

(1) Virendranath Chattopadhyaya
(2) Bhupendranath Dutta
(3) P.S. Khankhoje
(4) Birendranath Dasgupta
(8) Herambalal Gupta
(9) Nalini Gupta
(10) Barkatulla Khan
(11) Abdur Rab Peshawari

(5) G.A.K. Luhani
(6) Md. Hasan Mansoor
(7) Dr. Hafiz
(12) M.P.T. Acharya
(13) Abdul Wahad
(14) Pramattanath Dutta

71 *Documents*, Vol. I, p.86.
72 *Memoirs*, p.478.
73 Bhupendranath Dutta, op. cit, pp.283-4.
74 ibid., p.285.
75 ibid.
76 ibid.
77 ibid.
78 ibid., p.291
79 ibid., p.289.
80 ibid, pp.283-4.
81 *Documents*, Vol. I., pp.81 and 255. Chattopadhyaya sent a copy of his thesis to Lenin for comments. Lenin after going through the thesis wrote back to Chattopadhyaya: 'I have read your thesis. I agree with you. British imperialism must be destroyed. When I can meet you will be communicated to you by my secretary'. Bhupendranath Dutta, op. cit, p.290.
82 *Documents*, Vol. I, p.255. Following Chattopadhyaya, Dutta also sent a copy of his thesis to Lenin for comments. Commenting on the thesis Lenin wrote to Dutta, 'I have read your thesis, we should discuss about the social classes. I think we should abide by my thesis on colonial question. Gather statistical facts about Peasants' League, if there is any'. Bhupendranath Dutta, op. cit., pp.290-91.
83 *Documents*, Vol. I, p.87.
84 ibid., p.86
85 *Memoirs*, p.487.
86 *Documents*, Vol. I, p.86.
87 *Memoirs*, p.491.
88 Bhupendranath Dutta, op. cit., p.278
89 *Memoirs*, p.481
90 Bhupendranath Dutta, op. cit, p.298

3

Marxism Comes to India

The Moscow visit of the Berlin group of Indian revolutionaries, as Roy puts it, 'was an important interlude'. To a large extent, it destroyed his illusion about the famous revolutionaries and interfered with his active participation in the third congress of the Comintern.[1]

The third congress opened in Moscow on 22 June 1921. After assessing the political conditions prevailing in the world, the congress came to the conclusion that the post-war revolutionary ferment was over. It brought to the fore the necessity of winning over the masses with the slogan of a united front. It renounced immediate armed uprising and acknowledged the need for a longer period of preparation. The congress was attended by 605 delegates from 103 organizations of 52 countries.[2] India was represented by four delegates, but only Roy's name was mentioned in the proceedings.[3] The congress discussed several issues of international importance, but the national and colonial question, with which the oppressed people of the colonial world were concerned, did not figure in the agenda. In fact, it was taken up for discussion only after Roy made a protest against its non-inclusion. Roy, the sole representative of the Comintern to propagate marxism in India, was given only five minutes to speak on the issue, on the closing day of the congress.[4]

After the congress, the Turkistan bureau was abolished and an eastern section of the Comintern was opened in Moscow to promote and guide revolutionary movements in the colonial world. The military school that was opened with much fanfare and high hopes to train the *muhajirs* for a revolution in India was closed down *sine die*.[5] The experience had proved the futility of continuing the work. Moreover, it had become detrimental to Soviet interest. The British, with whom the Soviet Union was trying to improve its relations, objected to the Comintern plan of imparting military training to *muhajirs*.[6]

The closure of the Indian military school and the India House, the home temporarily set up for the *muhajirs*, posed no problems, however. In course of time, the fanatical enthusiasm of the *muhajirs* to proceed to Turkey and fight in defence of *khilafat* cooled down. The majority of the *muhajirs* expressed their willingness to settle in Tashkent and earn a livelihood, or if possible, go to Afghanistan and try their luck. Only a few volunteered to return to India and fight British imperialism. Accordingly, a fair amount of money was distributed to the *muhajirs* to help them go along their chosen way.[7] Only twenty-two opted to go to Moscow to study at the University of the Toilers of the East, and the three who preferred to join the Red Army were allowed to do so.[8]

The University of the Toilers of the East was set up in Moscow in April 1921. It was a university with a special objective: to train revolutionary cadres, as opposed to turning out, year after year, young men with academic brilliance ready for the rat race. It had no entrance qualifications. The courses of study included political economy, programme and tactics of the Comintern, and some rudiments of natural sciences.[9] The students were either from the republics of the Soviet East or from colonial and dependent countries of the East, who were striving hard to achieve national independence. In fact, there were two distinct groups of students

– one from the Republics of the Soviet East and the other from colonial and dependent countries of the East. Each group had a different role to play in its respective geography.

The socialist revolution of Russia liberated the republics of the Soviet East from imperialist oppression. This was only the first stage of the revolution. In the second stage, they were to be developed and brought on a par with the Soviet West to facilitate the work of establishing socialism.[10] Students belonging to the Soviet East had joined the university to acquire knowledge that would be helpful for achieving this aim. But the students who had come from colonial and dependent countries of the East had an altogether different task. They joined the university to learn the theory and practice of leninism to become real revolutionaries, 'capable of carrying out the immediate tasks of the liberation movement in the colonial and dependent countries with all their heart and soul'.[11] The *muhajirs* joined the University of the Toilers of the East to achieve this aim.

The closing of the military school at Tashkent affected the Roys in the least. Soon after the third congress of the Comintern, Evelyn wrote to a correspondent in Paris, 'All work is to be carried out by the Communist Party which already exists here: here will be established the bureau of our work and the training school for such of our people as wish to avail themselves of it … the International cannot aid nationalists' causes except through a Communist Party as intermediary. Every effort will be bent upon building a strong Communist Party within the country, using those elements which we have outside who are really communists, as preliminary workers. Head-quarters will be here, and a journal issued.'[12]

The experience at Tashkent, though unfortunate, was useful to Roy. His contact with a cross-section of Indian masses dispelled his illusion and made him realistic about a revolution in India. 'I was convinced,' writes Roy, 'that the Indian revolution was still a long way off, and an uphill path lay ahead. Arms and money would not make the revolution. The army of revolution should be first trained politically.'[13] This is a confession without regret. Roy accepted his failure with grace and closed an exciting chapter of his life to look forward to other ways to usher in a revolution in India.

In spite of the failure at Tashkent, Roy had carved out for himself by now a place in the galaxy of marxists. He became the accepted representative of the Comintern to propagate marxism in India. 'My work in future,' wrote Roy to B.K. Sarkar, 'will be to clarify the ideology of the Indian movement and to assist it in emerging from the narrow limits of bourgeois nationalism and to launch it into the arena of the class struggle.'[14] It was not a hard job for Roy to clarify the ideology of the Indian national movement from the marxist point of view. He had acquired sufficient knowledge of applied marxism. But it was a stupendous task for him to carry the movement from the narrow limits of bourgeois nationalism and launch it into the arena of class struggle, till then unheard of in India.

The challenge before Roy was to renew his contact with his one-time comrade-in-arms, the contact having been lost due to his long absence from India. Further, because of the lost contact, his knowledge about the political happenings in India was limited to scrappy news that reached Moscow through the British press. Yet, to keep up his image on the basis of those scrappy reports, Roy wrote – rather manufactured – a few articles for the Soviet press. The common people in the Soviet Union read those concocted stories of the freedom struggle in India and regarded them as authentic and authoritative reports. 'None more than myself,' writes Roy, 'deplored inadequacy of reliable information and my ignorance of what was actually happening in India.'[15]

This 'deplorable situation' did not continue for long, though. To Roy's delight, Borodin, on his way back home from the conference of the International Postal Union at Madrid, brought a huge stock of Indian newspapers. This gave Roy an opportunity to update himself about what was happening in India. On the basis of these newspaper reports, Roy assessed the political situation in India from the point of view of his newly acquired philosophy and came very near the unpleasant truth that the Khilafat non-cooperation movement was politically immature and had no viable economic programmes. The middle class, which was at the back of the movement, was drawn into the struggle by patriotic sentiments and the personality of Gandhi. With this assessment of the movement, Roy came to the conclusion that popular enthusiasm would not sustain for long. Hunger would soon compel the middle class to repent the rashness of giving up jobs and it would then be eager to re-enter the lost paradise.[16] Roy thought of making the best use of the situation.

The next annual session of the Indian National Congress was to be held at Ahmedabad under the presidentship of C.R. Das, a philanthropist known for his sympathy for the poverty-stricken masses. In the light of the newspaper reports, Roy could assess that Das did not fully share Gandhi's ideas, but erroneously believed that he might favour an 'alternative method of mass revolutionary struggle, if a programme of developing it was submitted for his consideration'.[17] The idea was enthusiastically welcomed by all. Roy, in collaboration with Abani Mukherjee, prepared an appeal and got it approved by Lenin.[18]

In the appeal, after analysing the social background and the weaknesses of the national movement, Roy made some concrete suggestions to make the Indian National Congress a true people's organization. 'In order to deserve the name and to be able to execute the difficult task before it, the National Congress must not permit itself to be carried away by the sentiment and idealism of a handful of individuals, however great and patriotic they may be, it must take into consideration the cold material facts, it must survey with keenness the everyday life of the people – their wants and sufferings.... Several thousand noisy irresponsible students and a number of middle-class intellectuals followed by an ignorant mob momentarily incited by fanaticism cannot be the social basis of the political organ of a nation. The toiling masses in the cities, the dumb millions in the villages must be brought into the ranks of the movement if it is to be [of] potential.... Let the Congress reflect the needs of the nation and not the ambition of a small class.'[19] The appeal was printed in Moscow and signed by Roy and Abani Mukherjee.

As the appeal was ready, the question of sending it to India came up and posed a problem, but it was solved before long. Nalini Gupta, Roy's confidante, volunteered to go to India with the appeal. He claimed to have acquaintance with C.R. Das, to whom he would deliver the appeal on his arrival in India.[20] True to his word, Nalini left Moscow in August 1921 with a bundle of the appeal for distribution to the delegates of the Ahmedabad congress. Roy heaved a sigh of relief.

Nalini Gupta alias Jharu Das reached Colombo in November 1921 and spent around six weeks before reaching Calcutta on 23 December.[21] In Calcutta, Nalini did not have to take the trouble of meeting C.R. Das, who was already in jail. He did not attend the Ahmedabad congress either to distribute the appeal. Yet, the appeal, which was taken as the manifesto of the 'Communist Party' of India, reached the Congress delegates through certain other sources and created ripples in the ranks of the non-violent *non-cooperators*.[22] Inspired by the appeal, the republican Muslim leader Maulana Hasrat Mohani, supported by Swami Kumarananda, moved a resolution defining *swaraj* as complete independence, freedom from all foreign control. This was done much against the will of Gandhi and Hakim Ajmal Khan, the acting president of the Congress. Gandhi struck hard in opposition because, in his opinion, the resolution lacked responsibility, and he secured its rejection.[23]

The distribution of the appeal was only a fraction of the job assigned to Gupta. His actual task was to meet underground revolutionaries in Bengal and help Roy re-establish contact with his erstwhile comrades and if possible, recruit a few young men for training in marxism to assist Roy in his work. Gupta knew a few underground revolutionaries, but was never a member of any secret society. He had no knowledge of the movement either. The absurd statement he made before the police against Amrit Lai Hazra, alias Sashanka, the main accused in the Raja Bazar Bomb case, gives an inkling of his ignorance about the activities of the underground revolutionaries in Bengal.[24] However, after making the statement, he disappeared from Bengal and nobody bothered to remember him. Thus, in 1921, when he reappeared in Bengal and stayed for about two and a half months, he achieved very little. To the underground revolutionaries, he was a renegade and, therefore, according to a rule of the secret societies, a *persona-non-grata.* No underground revolutionary was prepared to discuss politics with him. After persistent efforts, he could only come in contact with one or two underground revolutionaries and a few marxists, viz. Muzaffar Ahmed and Qazi Nazrul Islam. Muzaffar and Nazrul reposed high hopes on Gupta, because of their eagerness to know about the organization of the Comintern and the communist party, but were disappointed. On being asked to explain these things, Gupta delivered a lecture on bombs and explosives, making it clear that he knew something about bombs and explosives, but nothing about communism and the communist party.[25] That was practically the end of Gupta's hobnobbing with the marxists. Although he maintained contact with Muzaffar, he was never taken seriously. With the underground revolutionaries, he fared no better. Under the circumstances, Gupta could lure only one 'worthless and non-political' young man, Jatindranath Mitra, to come to Berlin to help Roy in his work and study marxism. Gupta left Calcutta in March 1922 and, soon thereafter, Mitra reached Berlin to help Roy, but instead, became a burden. Roy considered Mitra 'a downright ass'.[26]

While Nalini was trying to establish contact with the underground revolutionaries in Bengal, Roy, sitting in Moscow, was brooding over his plan of action for India. While drafting the appeal for the Ahmedabad congress, Roy visualized that 'the predominating social factor in contemporary India was not feudalism. Therefore, it was not correct to regard the national bourgeoisie as a revolutionary force.'[27] This was contrary to the prevailing notions of the then bolshevik leaders about India. The thesis of Roy attracted the notice of Chicherin, the foreign minister of the Soviet Union, who asked him to prepare a report on the basis of his findings.

In the report, Roy 'emphasised the fact, that although colonial economy tended to galvanise feudal relations, it could not altogether prevent the growth of native capitalism and the consequent rise of bourgeoisie as an ambitious class. The established order, to some extent, thwarted their ambition. But at the same time, they had stakes in the status quo and, therefore, could not lead a revolution for its subversion'.[28] After carefully going through the report, Lenin expressed the view that it could be elaborated in the form of a book to portray a realistic picture of contemporary Indian society and open up the perspective of the Indian revolution.[29] Roy liked the idea. In collaboration with Abani Mukherjee, he prepared the manuscript and titled it *India in Transition*, because, according to Roy, 'the basic feature of the contemporary Indian society' was 'gradual decay of feudal economy and slow but steady rise of capitalism'.[30]

India in Transition was the first book attempted by an Indian marxist to enquire into the past, investigate the present and visualize the future of India, from the point of view of historical materialism. The objective of the book, as Roy puts it, was 'first, to point out the material forces that are pushing the various classes of the Indian people in the present struggle; second, to point out the deep-rooted social character of the present unrest; third, to analyse the social tendencies embodied by the two principal schools of nationalism; and fourth, to indicate the revolutionary trend of the growing mass movement and impress upon the concerned the necessity of confirming this programme and tactics ...'[31] The book underestimated the political potential of Gandhi and gave an exaggerated account of the rise of capitalism in India on the basis of manufactured data. Yet, it was a stimulating piece of literature and drew the attention of the intellectual world.

Along with *India in Transition,* Roy wrote another book, rather a booklet, *What Do We Want*. In this booklet, Roy made no secret of his objectives, by calling upon the people to overthrow British rule from India for the benefit of the common populace. 'Our goal is not to secure political power and economic aggrandisement for the native landlords, financiers, merchants and manufacturers, but to put an end to the economic slavery of the masses of the population'.[32] As the books were published and a few copies reached India, their entry into the country was banned under the sea customs law.

Gupta, on his return from India, met Roy around April 1922. Although he did not travel within thousand miles of Ahmedabad, he concocted a story of the impact of the appeal on the delegates at the Ahmedabad congress. He presented before Roy a dazzling account of his exploits, along with a list of persons with whom contact could be established for the furtherance of the work in India.[33] Roy believed Gupta and, advised by him, shifted to Berlin 'to establish standing connection with India through correspondence and publication of propaganda literature'.[34]

Before leaving for Berlin, Roy thought it prudent to send back the *muhajirs* who were under training at the University of the Toilers of the East to India. Apparently, this was a step to prepare the ground in India to accept marxism but, in fact, it was a measure of caution. The *muhajirs*, with no stake in the quarrel between Roy and the Berlin group, were disappointed with the news of the breakdown of the talks, because they considered it the closing of 'the doors to the setting up of an unified Indian revolutionary command abroad'.[35] Shaukat Usmani, who always stood by Roy, accused him for the breakdown of the negotiations with the Berlin group and, in sheer disgust, expressed his desire to part company with Roy and return to India to take active part in the freedom struggle.[36] Not only Usmani, but the entire group of *muhajirs* held the same view and quarrelled with Roy.[37] Wisely enough, Roy did not like to leave behind in Moscow a group of disgruntled followers, who could create trouble in his absence.

No sooner did Roy reach Berlin, than he came into confrontation with the Berlin group once again. The rebuff at Moscow disheartened the Berlin group only temporarily. By no means did they give up the desire to gain the support of the Comintern or to counter Roy's influence in the marxist circle. On return to Berlin, Chattopadhyaya, helped by Bhupendranath Dutta, opened an Indian 'news and information centre' for the benefit of Indian students who came to Germany after the war. Later, they established the Hindustan Association of Central Europe and a sham communist party.[38] To strengthen his position further,

Chattopadhyaya sent letters to a number of Indian revolutionaries living abroad to come to Berlin and join him.[39] Chattopadhyaya wanted to organize all the Indian revolutionaries abroad under one central organization and put up a unified opposition to Roy. But, as it happened, the Indian revolutionaries failed to come together. S.N. Kar, who had come from America to work with Roy, soon joined hands with Abani Mukherjee, who in the meantime had deserted Roy and shifted his loyalty to Chattopadhyaya. In turn, Bhupendranath Dutta deserted Chattopadhyaya and joined hands with Barkatullah, who by now had arrived in Berlin and organized the Indian Independence Party to achieve complete and absolute independence for India by all possible means. Barkatullah preferred to extend cooperation, in or outside India, to all organizations with a socioeconomic revolutionary programme. Chicherin, who was friendly to Barkatullah, seemed to have approved the plan and asked the Comintern to provide funds.[40]

These formations of parties, groupings and regroupings, were done with the singular aim to come closer to the Comintern and assume leadership of the Indian independence movement by ousting Roy. In this situation, while others were passing away their time in futile exercises, Roy and his wife, Evelyn alias Santi Devi, took some positive steps in isolation to propagate marxism in India.

The accepted policy of the Comintern with reference to India was to work in cooperation with the national bourgeois revolutionary parties, i.e., the Indian National Congress, as against the small underground revolutionary groups to which Roy belonged. In the dictum of the Comintern, Gandhi was a revolutionary so far as he was fighting against British imperialism in India. But Roy thought of Gandhi differently. Politically, Gandhi might put up an imposing appearance of a revolutionary, but being a religious and cultural revivalist, he was bound to be reactionary.[41] His religious ideology and the 'doctrine of trusteeship' suited the medieval mentality of the landlords and big capitalists who supported the Congress financially.[42] Roy asked Lenin 'whether an anti-imperialist movement inspired by reactionary social ideas and burdened with religious belief could be politically revolutionary?'[43] Lenin only said, 'experience would enable us to make a correct judgement.'[44] Roy was not prepared to wait for experience to gain correct judgement. He was convinced about the role of Gandhi and the Indian National Congress. He was on the lookout, from the very outset, for an opportunity to discredit Gandhi and the Congress in the eyes of the bolshevik leaders, hoping that the Comintern would realize its mistake and revise its stance vis-à-vis Gandhi and the Congress at a not too distant date. Yet, much against his will, Roy accepted the verdict of the Comintern. For him, it was 'Hobson's choice'.

The Indian National Congress was an assembly of a heterogeneous group of people with widely different ideas but a common aim to fight British imperialism in India. Roy thought of exploiting the situation. Thus, instead of working in cooperation with the Congress, as directed by the Comintern, he planned to tackle the Congress differently: first, by forming an opposition bloc within the Congress with the people who had already accepted marxism as their political ideology; and second, by drawing congressmen with liberal social views, but not actually marxists, into the marxist fold. In a letter to Dange dated 2 November 1922, Roy revealed the inner structure of his plan of action. 'The opposition will embrace all truly revolutionary elements with a non-offensive name that would not raise the communist bogey, but its political direction should be in the hands of communists and socialists who alone can be the custodians of the interest of the toiling masses. However, side by side, an illegal communist party should also continue to exist.'[45] To accomplish this task, Roy brought out a journal, *The Vanguard of Indian Independence*, later on named *The Advance Guard*, and thereafter, *The Masses of India*, to shape the Indian mind into the marxian mould.

The Indian students at the University of the Toilers of the East were sent back home in batches of at least two. The decision was taken in a hurry and without proper planning. No precaution was deemed necessary for their safe passage to India. They were left to their own wit. As a result, most of the *muhajirs*, were intercepted by the Indian intelligence on the borders and taken into custody with ease.

The *muhajirs* who were supplied with arms and money on the disbandment of the military school at Tashkent were settled in either Central Asia or Afghanistan. The few who were still gung ho about a holy war proceeded towards Turkey to take part in a *jihad*, but when the Turkish government refused entry, they took the road to India as the last resort. The first batch of these 'holy warriors' reached Peshawar in June 1921 and was intercepted by the Indian intelligence. It was from these people that the Government of India came to know the details of the *muhajirs* who had gone to Moscow to join the University of the Toilers of the East.[46] Thus, the plan for arresting Roy's vanguard was on the cards. It was only a question of time. The *muhajirs* thus entrapped were indicted in the Peshawar Conspiracy cases.

Between 1922 and 1927, there were altogether five Peshawar Conspiracy cases implicating seventeen persons. Two among the accused were acquitted, and another two, Ghulam Ahmed and Fida Ali, who turned approver, were pardoned, while the rest were sentenced to varying terms of imprisonment.[47]

The Peshawar Conspiracy cases were a sham affair. Actually, there could not be any case of conspiracy against the *muhajirs*, except that they had been to Moscow and studied in the University of the Toilers of the East. Yet, the trial was of great importance to the British and the *muhajirs* needed to be punished to show how Soviet Union was persistently trying to infuse bolshevism into India. Roy, in his usual flamboyant style, castigated Curzon, the brain behind the sinister move and raised a few pertinent questions never to be answered. 'If to have been in Russia is a crime,' wrote Roy, 'then why Mr George Landsbury is a member of the British Parliament and Shaukat Usmani is a prisoner? Why is Mrs Showden a respectable British subject and an Indian youth is considered to be an enemy of the Empire? There is more than one communist in Great Britain; why is it such a dreadful thing for an Indian to be a communist? Communist literature is legally published in England, why are a few leaflets exhorting the Indian workers and peasants to organise in the defence of their interest enough to convict a number of individuals as rebel against the King? … We put these questions to the British Labour Party ….'[48]

However, Roy's plan to utilize the *muhajirs* for the propagation of marxism in India was a dismal failure. Very few could elude the Indian intelligence. Among the few, only Shaukat Usmani did some work to the best of his ability. The rest, on reaching India, melted away in the multitude, bothering the least about marxism. But Roy was not disheartened. He continued his pursuit with unbounded zeal to disseminate marxism through his pen, preparing the ground for its acceptance by exposing the leaders of the freedom struggle to create a cleavage in the ranks of the bourgeois leadership.

The failure of the Moscow-trained *muhajirs* was only a temporary setback to Roy. He had no illusion about the capacity of his boys. Soon after the *muhajirs* left Moscow for India, Roy wrote to Dange, 'A number of boys who had received training in Moscow have been sent to India. They are all members of our party. Originally, they were not very suitable material, being khilafat pilgrims on their way to Angora, but we got hold of them and could make some of them come over. Their intellectual calibre, however, is not to the mark, nor are they proletarian. But they are good boys and have received a fairly good marxian training. They will develop in practice. Four of them are already in India and seven more are on the way. One of them, Shaukat Usmani, writes me about you …. He is a good earnest chap, but rather erratic in his ways. He needs strong control. I have instructed him to work under your direction and get all our boys in touch with you. We must centralise our activities. Please get hold of these boys and their work.'[49]

Roy's advice to these neo-marxist groups was that their final aim to establish a classless society should be connected to the question of national liberation. They must adopt programmes that rally the working class in the struggle against foreign domination.[50] However, there were a few in these small groups who refused to go by Roy's advice. They advocated that the question of national liberation was of no concern to a working class party in India, as any such action would bring the wrath of the government on the party and jeopardize the nascent movement. They wanted to limit the objective of the working class party so as to bring economic relief only to the working class.[51] In fact, these neo-marxists, from the very start, failed to develop a cohesive view on the strategy and tactics to be adopted in India with regard to the national liberation movement. This lopsided view was suicidal for the marxists in India. In a subservient country, no movement can flourish if it keeps itself aloof from the mainstream liberation struggle against foreign domination. The neo-marxists failed to realize this basic truth, perhaps due to the lack of proper understanding of marxian strategy and tactics. They were yet to study Marx and understand Lenin in the true perspective of working class movements. Roy was, however, consistent in his plan of action. To begin with, he sought to influence congressmen C.R. Das and Subhas Chandra Bose in Bengal and Sampurnanand in the United Province.

C.R. Das, a Bar-at-Law by profession, came closer to politics at the time of the Alipur Conspiracy case. While defending Aurobindo, the main accused in the case, he became sympathetic to the underground revolutionaries. Like many others in Bengal at that time, he was moved by the boldness and lofty ideals of these young men. Later, though he joined constitutional politics as a co-worker of Gandhi, his early impression about the underground revolutionaries remained unchanged. His conscience did not allow any compromise with Gandhi's anti-revolutionary stand. Roy, as an underground revolutionary, had the opportunity of coming in contact with Das and of knowing his leanings. After the lapse of more than a decade, Roy thought of exploiting his earlier contact by making Das not a diehard marxist, but a co-traveller. There is evidence of Roy's effort to establish direct contact with Das through correspondence, but whether Das reciprocated is anybody's guess. Yet, for quite some time, British authorities suspected that the two were in direct communication. The basis of this suspicion was Das's occasional outburst showing sympathy for the poverty-stricken masses and the use of marxian terminology.

Besides Das, Roy tried to influence Subhas and Sampurnanand. In the case of Subhas, it was a dismal failure. Subhas refused to accept communication from Roy and the matter ended there[52] Sampurnanand came somewhat close at the initial stage, but subsequently retracted. According to Shaukat Usmani, Sampurnanand promised to circulate literature and books (marxist) among his trustworthy friends.[53]

Apart from making futile attempts to establish direct contact with bourgeois Congress leaders, Roy, through the pages of *The Vanguard of Indian Independence* and *The Advance Guard,* opened a new front and attacked the programmes of the Congress and its leadership. In the garb of a manifesto, he put forward a programme for the toiling masses of India. 'The Congress,' wrote Roy, 'should at once launch a programme advocating the fight for higher wages for the workers, an eight-hour-a-day, better housing, recognition of unions, right to strike, equal pay for equal work, abolition of landlordism, reduction of rents and taxes, strong measure for the abolition of usury and such other means as will correspond to the immediate necessities of the masses.... Hoist the banner of *swaraj* and rally the people under it with the slogan of living wages to the workers and land to the toilers ...'[54] Not content with the programme alone, Roy openly advocated the use of force to overthrow British rule in India. 'The government maintained by violence and brute force,' wrote Roy, 'cannot be overthrown without violence and brute force ... we will no longer exhort the hungry people to suffer for some visionary *swaraj* to be attained by 'soul force' purified in the fire of poverty. Although it will be stupid to talk of premature violence, we, nevertheless, are of the opinion that non-violent revolution is an impossibility ...'[55]

The attack on the Congress and the bourgeois leadership through the pages of *The Vanguard* and *The Advance Guard* continued unabated with the sole purpose of making it clear to the masses that though the Congress was a national party, it was incapable of delivering the goods. The party represented a particular class dominated by bourgeois reactionary leadership. In a letter dated 2 March 1922, Roy advised Dange to draw up a programme that would help expose the policy of the Indian National Congress and its reactionary bourgeois leadership. 'It is needless to point out to you the object of such tactics', wrote Roy, 'we want to liberate the movement from the domination of reactionary leadership. But it should be done by putting the present leadership to a test. The programme we intend to bring forward will be such as to demand a certain revolutionary outlook on the part of those subscribing to it. Therefore, it is a foregone conclusion that the Congress as constituted will not adopt this programme. And this failure of theirs will expose their true character. This will open before us the way for launching the call for a new party of the masses with its own leadership and our programme having for its object the capture of the Congress, the traditional organ of the national struggle.'[56]

Temporarily, the propaganda had its desired effect, at least on C.R. Das. On 1 November 1922, at a political conference held in Dehradun, Das made a startling statement. 'I do not want the sort of *swaraj* which will be for middle class alone .... I want *swaraj* for the masses not for the classes. I don't care for the bourgeoisie, how few are they?'[57] This was simply an emotional outburst in tune with the trend of that time.

On the whole, however, Roy's literary thrust failed to have the desired effect on bourgeois leaders of the Congress, though it had considerable influence on the Indian press. Being enamoured of the new ideology, quite a few newspapers made free use of marxian phraseology and gave vent to their revolutionary sentiment to the discomfort of the colonial ruler. The lead was taken by *The Socialist* of Bombay, followed by *Amrita Bazar Patrika* of Calcutta, *Independent* of Allahabad, *Navayuga* of Guntur, *Vartaman* of Cawnpore, and a few others. This influence, though limited, brought a section of the educated middle class closer to marxism. To exploit this growing sentiment, but fully aware of the capacity of Indian marxists, Roy appealed to the Communist Party of Great Britain in August 1922 to depute two emissaries to work in India to help Indian marxists.

Roy promised to meet their passage money and provide necessary funds for their upkeep in India.[58] The appeal bore fruit. The Communist Party of Great Britain, without loss of time, selected Charles Ashleigh, an experienced comrade, to go to India to help Indian marxists.[59]

Towards the close of August, Ashleigh left for Berlin to meet Roy for instructions. Roy gave Ashleigh a few letters of introduction, as he was unknown to Indian marxists, and passage money for Indian delegates to attend the fourth congress of the Comintern, which was scheduled to meet in November. Ashleigh's journey, a closely guarded secret, was known to the British intelligence before he reached Bombay. Ashleigh reached Bombay on 19 September and was served with a deportation order on the same day. But as there was no ship bound for Europe before 23 September, he was allowed to stay in a hotel under surveillance. During his short stay in Bombay, Ashleigh eluded the police and managed to contact Dange. What transpired between Ashleigh and Dange is only a conjecture. It is said that apart from delivering a verbal message, Ashleigh paid Dange £800 as passage money for four Indian delegates to attend the fourth congress of the Comintern.[60] Besides this, Ashleigh could not do anything. His plan to go to Calcutta under the pseudonym 'Nandalal' and stay in the country to help organize the nascent movement remained abortive. He was put in a ship bound for Marseilles on 23 September 1922.[61]

However, as always, the failure of the Ashleigh mission did not perturb Roy. The only thing that made Roy a bit apprehensive was the possibility of the presence of Indian delegates at the fourth congress of the Comintern, where he earnestly desired to prove his credibility.

The fourth congress of the Comintern met in Petrograd on 5 November 1922, and its subsequent meetings were held in Moscow up to 3 December. The congress was attended by 408 delegates from 66 parties and organisations of 58 countries. India was represented by only Roy. According to the information of the credential committee, the Communist Party at that period had a total membership of

1,253,000, of which 825,000 were from capitalist countries.[62] Lenin did not attend the first meeting, but sent a message asserting the ultimate victory of marxism over capitalism and the task before the Communist International.[63]

The fourth congress, after thoroughly analysing the state of national liberation movements in colonial and dependent countries, came forward with the slogan of a united anti-imperialist front. Roy the only delegate to represent India, made a speech in the plenary session of the congress in support of a draft thesis on the colonial question prepared by him and other Asian delegates. In his speech, Roy made it clear that 'unless the bourgeoisie comes into existence and becomes the leader of the society, the national struggle cannot take place with all its revolutionary possibilities. So, in all these (Asian) countries, in proportion as the bourgeoisie is developing, the national struggle has become intensified. From this point of view, although we know there is danger of the colonial bourgeoisie always compromising with the imperial bourgeoisie, we must always, on principle, stand for them; the bourgeois national movement in the colonial countries is objectively revolutionary, therefore, it should be given support; but we should not overlook the fact that this objective force cannot be accepted as unconditional, and that particular historical reasons should be taken into consideration. The bourgeoisie becomes a revolutionary factor when it raises the standard of revolt against the backward, antiquated forms of society, that is, when the struggle is fundamentally against the feudal order, the bourgeoisie leading the people. Then the bourgeoisie is the vanguard of the revolution.'[64]

The above analysis was made keeping in view the recent developments in Turkey. The victory of the Turkish people did not come to its logical consequence due to the interference of the feudal military clique that stood at the forefront of the revolution. The political and economic liberation of the Turkish people was compromised to safeguard the interest of the small feudal military clique. This did not let the people enjoy the fruits of the revolution. 'We know,' said Roy, that 'while two or three months ago the revolutionary elements all over the world were hailing the victories of Mustafa Kamal Pasha, we now have the news that Kamal in a free Turkey, freed by the efforts of the revolutionary workers and peasants, is brutally persecuting the latter.'[65]

Roy wanted to prove through this example that an *entente* between the bourgeoisie and the feudal-military clique might assume the leadership of the nationalist revolutionary struggle, but a time would come when these people would betray the movement and become a counter-revolutionary force, unless 'the other social element', objectively more revolutionary, is trained politically and assumes leadership of the movement. In fact, the whole exercise of Roy was aimed at attracting the attention of the Comintern leaders towards 'the other social element' in India, which was objectively more revolutionary than the bourgeoisie fighting for political independence under Gandhi. But the Comintern leaders were not convinced by Roy's analysis. The thesis, as finally adopted on the colonial question, stated that the Comintern would 'support all national revolutionary movements against imperialism'.[66]

Though the Comintern did not accept Roy's analysis of the role of bourgeoisie vis-à-vis the revolution in colonial countries, yet, it appreciated his role in propagating marxism in India. Speaking at the fourth congress, Zinoviev, the chairman of the Comintern, said in no uncertain terms that 'we have had valuable results in India, the works of our comrades during the past few months have been crowned with success, Comrade Roy, with a group of friends issuing a periodical whose task is to smooth our ways in India. Our comrades have been able to gather together the communist elements in India. They have found entrance into the newspapers; they have entered the trade unions. I believe this is a great step forward.'[67] Though Karl Radak, the secretary of the Comintern, echoed the same sentiment as that of the chairman, he took a more cautious view of the situation when he said, 'We have not taken the first step as a political party and all this means that it is a long way to tipperary.'[68] The support to Roy is further adduced from the fact that he was elected as a candidate-member of the executive committee of the Comintern. In fact, the absence of delegates from India at the fourth congress did not affect Roy's position. He continued to enjoy the confidence of the Comintern leaders and prepared his plan accordingly. As soon as the congress was over, Roy wrote to Dange, 'The Communist International thinks that the time has come for the organisation of our party in India. We expected to begin the work by taking the delegation to the fourth congress as the basis. Therefore, we were very anxious to have such a delegation come ... but for various difficulties none of you could come to the congress, so it was decided that we should have a conference here as early as possible. In this conference should be called representatives from all the groups in agreement with our programme and feeling the need for a new start in the movement. There are already several such groups in existence in India, and we are in touch with them. This conference will be held under the auspices of the Comintern whose representatives will be present in it, besides representatives from the British and other principal continental parties. The questions of the programme and organisation of a revolutionary party of the working class will be discussed.'[69]

Apart from the formation of a revolutionary party of the working class, Roy had another task to fulfil – to get a foothold in the Congress, which he had been trying for the past two years, but without success. An opportunity came following the failure of Gandhi's 'magic formula', *swaraj,* within a year, and the abrupt withdrawal of the Khilafat non-cooperation movement. But Roy and his comrades in India failed to take advantage of the situation.

The withdrawal of the Khilafat non-cooperation movement led to certain distinct tendencies in Indian politics. The underground revolutionaries who had veered around Gandhi to try his method of struggle were disappointed and decided to return to the old path, while a few of them, more progressive in their outlook, started groping their way towards socialism. The middle class bourgeoisie, which was supporting Gandhi's movement, became suspicious of his method of struggle and turned towards a constitutional approach, but a few radicals, who disagreed with certain aspects of the programme and tactics adopted by Gandhi, turned left. The fundamentalists who, in spite of their obscurantism, supported Gandhi and took part in the Khilafat non-cooperation movement, raised their voice to the discomfort of the colonial ruler. Only marxists, though insignificant in number, remained firm in their objectives and were not swayed by the changed circumstances.

The leaders, particularly Das, took exception to Gandhi's unilateral decision and threw a challenge. A showdown between Das and Gandhi became inevitable at the Gaya session of the Congress. Hopeful of a split in the Congress, Roy put forward a radical programme for the consideration of the bourgeois national leaders, particularly Das, to fight Gandhi.

The Indian National Congress met at Gaya on 26 December 1922. A little over a month before the meeting, in November, Roy issued a leaflet from Switzerland, *A Programme for the Indian National Congress*. The leaflet reached India in the middle of November, but was promptly prohibited by the government before it could reach the people. Yet, undaunted by the government action, Roy, in the 1 December issue of *The Advance Guard*, published a summary of the programme and sent it out to India, along with the leaflet, on the eve of the Congress session. Surprisingly, though the copies of *The Advance Guard*, along with the leaflets, were intercepted, Reuters, the semi-official news agency, cabled Roy's entire programme to the subscribing Indian press, identifying it as the work of a bolshevik. The summary of the programme, as despatched by Reuters, was published in all the imperialist and national dailies of India of that time.[70]

The programme was a comprehensive document and set forth under three headings – national liberation and reconstruction programme, social and economic programme, and action programme. In a nutshell, it called for complete national independence, free from all imperial connection and foreign supervision; election of a national assembly by universal suffrage; confiscation of estates; abolition of indirect taxation; compulsory education; abolition of standing army; and establishment of a national mass militia, as part of which every citizen would be obliged to undergo a certain period of military training. To achieve this goal, Roy urged the organization of militant peasant unions, through which the rebellious poor peasantry would wage its struggle against the excesses of landlordism and high prices; countrywide mass demonstrations under the slogan of non-payment of rent and taxes; mass strikes to back up these demands, eventually leading to the declaration of a countrywide general strike; and countrywide national volunteer corps.[71]

Since Roy's literature was proscribed in India, bourgeois national leaders started wondering why the semi-official news agency Reuters gave such exposure to the programme. The reason was obvious: to frighten bourgeois national leaders by labelling the programme bolshevik. British authorities were apprehensive that at a not-too-distant time, Roy's programme would first attract the attention of bourgeois national leaders, and then the downtrodden masses, to the detriment of imperialist rule in India. The Reuters propaganda had its desired effect. C.R. Das, the president-elect for the Gaya session, on whom Roy counted most, was frightened and did a volte-face. He not only retracted his earlier stand, but took on an anti-marxist tone. Gone were the days when Das said '*swaraj* for the masses'.

In the presidential address, Das declared, 'I cannot refuse to acknowledge that there is a body of Indian opinion within the country as well as outside according to which non-violence is an ideal abstraction incapable of realization, and that the only way in which *swaraj* can ever be attained is by the application of force and violence. I do not for a moment question the courage, sacrifice and patriotism of those who hold the view. I know that some of them have suffered for the cause which they believed to be true. But may I be permitted to point out that apart from any question of principle, history has proved over and over again the utter futility of revolution brought about by force and violence. I am one of those who hold to non-violence on principle.'[72] Further, in the same address, he cautioned the National Congress against the concentration of power in the hands of the middle class and urged the Congress to organize the workers and peasants. 'If the Congress failed to do its duty', said

Das, 'you may expect to find organisations set up in the country by labourers and peasants detached from you, dissociated from the cause of *swaraj*, which will eventually bring within the arena of the peaceful revolution, class struggle and the war of special interest.'[73] Not only Das, but to the surprise of Roy, Singaravelu, the professed marxist who attended the Congress along with Dange and Manilal Shah, was also frightened and endorsed non-violence in his speech. However, in the showdown between Gandhi and Das, Gandhi reigned supreme. Das was obliged to play second fiddle and consoled himself by forming the Swaraj Party within the Congress. In fact, at the Gaya Congress, Roy was disillusioned by Das. That the Congress in general would reject the marxists' programme was expected, but that Das would bow down before Gandhi and profess to follow the exclusive path of non-violence was beyond Roy's expectations. Roy expected Das to play a better role in Indian politics from within the Congress, if not from outside, by aligning with the marxists in opposition to Gandhi. However, because of his ignorance of the Indian political scenario, Roy could not comprehend that, at that time, it was extremely difficult to oppose Gandhi and his idea of non-violence in India. A few weeks before the Gaya congress, Roy wrote, 'We have repeatedly said and still say that premature resort to violent tactics may be playing into the hands of the enemy. But it is altogether erroneous to think that there can be such a thing as a "non-violent revolution", no matter how "peculiar and abnormal" the situation in India may be. The cult of non-violence is inseparable from an anti-revolutionary spirit. Those who do not want a revolution in India can pin their hopes on non-violent methods. Strictly non-violent methods are hardly distinguishable from constitutional agitation, and no people on the face of earth have ever made a revolution by constitutional methods.'[74] Not only Roy, the leaders of the Comintern were also ignorant of the Indian political scenario. They were unaware of the fact that under the leadership of Gandhi, non-violence had become an accepted creed in India to fight British imperialism. The ignorance of the Comintern leaders becomes clear from the message the Comintern sent to the Congress at the Gaya session. The message eulogised violence and asked the people of India to take the path of violent revolution to overthrow British rule from India. In unambiguous terms, it said, 'British rule in India was established by force and is maintained by force; therefore, it can and will be overthrown only by a violent revolution. We are not in favour of resorting to violence if it can be helped; but for self-defence, the people of India must adopt violent means, without which the foreign domination based upon violence cannot be ended. The people of India are engaged in this great revolutionary struggle. The Communist International is wholeheartedly with them.'[75]

The emphasis on violence proved unproductive. Instead of bringing bourgeois national leaders closer to marxism, as Roy had envisaged, it frightened them to the detriment of marxists in India. Roy accepted the fact. Writing in the *Inprecor,* he said, 'We sought to strengthen the hands of the left wing, but only succeeded in frightening it.'[76] In the process, the only achievement of Roy was that he succeeded in exposing bourgeois national leaders as *unrevolutionary*. Yet, Roy did not give up hope and continued his efforts to influence Das for quite sometime. As late as June 1923, in a letter from Berlin, he invited Das to come to Europe and advised him to 'rally all the available revolutionary elements within and without the Congress, thus making the beginning of a revolutionary mass party, which is the crying need of the day and which alone will save the Congress'.[77] Das, as usual, did not respond.

Towards the close of December 1922, Roy's adversary, Abani Mukherjee, reached India from Berlin and headed for Gaya to attend the Congress session. Abani came to India as an emissary of the Indian Independence Party with the sole purpose to denigrate Roy in the eyes of the Indian marxists and, if possible, to get recognition for his party from the Indian National Congress. To establish credibility, he came to India armed with a letter of recognition signed by B.N. Dutta and Maulvi Barkatullah. The letter dated 13 October 1922 stated that Abani was a member and the first secretary of the Indian Committee for Russian Relief.[78] Though not a forgery, the letter was a clandestine move on the part of Roy's adversaries to enhance the credibility of Abani. A few days earlier, on 2 October, Kuusinan, the Finnish member of the executive committee of the Comintern, released an official warning against Abani, informing all concerned that he had no connection with the Communist International. 'We have absolutely no confidence in him', wrote Kuusinan, 'and, therefore, we earnestly request you to have no dealings with him.'[79] Kuusinan's letter was sent to the communist parties of Great Britain, Italy and Germany. The marxists in India came to know of Abani's expulsion from the party and the Comintern, through Roy. Roy communicated this information to Muzaffar, with a hint that Abani might come to India to jeopardize the nascent marxist movement.[80]

At the Gaya congress, Abani met Dange, Singaravelu, Manilal Shah and a few others, and seemed to have become friendly with Manilal.[81] From Gaya, sometime in January 1923, Abani reached Calcutta to fulfil his mission, i.e., to denigrate Roy and, if possible, to seek recognition for his party.

Abani had no political acquaintance in Bengal. But on reaching Calcutta, he searched out his old friend, one Santosh Kumar Mitra, who had some political connections. Santosh introduced him to the marxist circle and a few underground revolutionaries. However, his attempt to discredit Roy in the marxist circle proved futile. Marxists gave him the cold shoulder as they were already aware of his expulsion from the party. But he developed a rapport with the underground revolutionaries, who knew very little about Abani and were floored by his flamboyance. They took him as a marxist revolutionary and a true representative of the Comintern. However, Abani's limited success was short-lived. The underground revolutionaries soon came to know about him and shunned his company.

Having failed in his attempt to get recognition for his party or to come closer to the marxists and the underground revolutionaries, Abani, in sheer desperation, made an abortive attempt to execute his nefarious plan of running down the marxists in Bengal. He drafted a letter addressed to Zinoviev, the chairman of the executive committee of the Comintern, which gives an inkling of his inner self. He called the marxists of Bengal 'unscrupulous, swindlers, and government agents', who had taken to marxism anticipating that a great deal of money would be forthcoming from the Comintern, and were going to Moscow with forged documents as representatives of organizations that in reality did not exist. He warned Zinoviev that Roy, who was given the responsibility to propagate marxism in India on behalf of the Comintern, was associating himself with these 'swindlers and spies', ignoring the revolutionaries who wanted to come near and work with him.[82] To add credence to the letter, Abani, through his accomplice Santosh Kumar Mitra, sent the draft to Abdur Razak Khan to get it typed on the letterhead of the Bengal Provincial Khilafat Committee with which Khan had some acquaintance. Khan, to the misfortune of Abani, handed over the draft to his close associate Muzaffar for comments. Muzaffar, in turn, sent the same to Roy for information.[83]

After the Gaya congress, Roy wrote an editorial titled 'Ourselves' in *The Vanguard*. The editorial began with an appraisal of the Congress and went on to outline the new policy to be followed by marxists in India. The Congress, wrote Roy, 'with all its desire to enlist the support of the masses, and with all its virtuous schemes of uplifting the downtrodden … will never be able to lead the workers and peasants in the revolutionary struggle for national freedom…. Therefore, the organisation of a party of the workers and peasants has become an indispensable necessity…. It is only under the banner of the communist party that the masses can be organised and led into the national struggle as the first stage of a great revolutionary movement for liberation. So, those who sincerely stand for the interests and welfare of the toiling masses must swell the ranks of the communist party, the leader of the workers and peasants – the vanguard of national revolution … we will fight as part of the National Congress ….'[84] In the same issue, in an open letter to Chittaranjan Das and his followers, Roy wrote, 'There is room for only three parties in the Congress. Two are already in the field. You have to be either the third, that is, the political expression of the working masses, or nothing.'[85] According to Roy, the two other parties within the Congress were the 'reformists' and the 'reactionaries', and he wanted the communists to be the third.

The idea to form a communist party within the Congress was a rash and momentary decision. Within a span of three months, Roy changed his mind and returned to his original plan of two parties – an open party for the workers and peasants, and a secret communist party. This becomes clear from his correspondence with the marxists in India and the memorandum he prepared for the guidance of the proposed all-India conference of the marxists to launch a workers and peasants party.

As desired by Roy, in February 1923, Singaravelu issued a manifesto in preparation for an all-India conference and sent copies of it to Dange, Manilal Shah, Ghulam Husain and Roy. Manilal, in collaboration with Abani, made a few changes in the manifesto and reissued it to Dange, Ghulam Husain, Roy, International Press Correspondence, and even to Singaravelu. Nobody took any notice of Singaravelu's manifesto, but Manilal's plagiarised manifesto was taken note of by Dange and Ghulam Husain. On receipt of the manifesto, Dange announced in *The Socialist* of 23 April 1923 that the congress of the first workers and peasants party would be held in July, the venue and the exact date to be specified later, and requested comrades from all the provinces to attend it.[86] Like Dange, Ghulam Husain took to the idea enthusiastically and, exactly four days later, on 27 April, he sent out a circular addressed to individual marxists, including Roy, calling for a meeting at Lucknow on 30 June to organize a workers and peasants party.

On receipt of Ghulam Husain's circular, Singaravelu sent a note of protest to Husain saying, 'What you call Manilal's manifesto was our draft manifesto originally framed by us some time in February last, and it was put in circulation among a few of us through Manilal.'[87] Ghulam Husain surrendered and withdrew his call for a conference in favour of Singaravelu, but nobody took any notice of Singaravelu's call. Singaravelu then brought Manilal's plagiarism, as well as the disregard by Indian marxists to his call for a conference, to the notice of Roy. The complaint had its desired effect. On 7

May 1923, Roy wrote to Dange, 'I request you very urgently to get in touch with Singaravelu without delay.... I am convinced he is the best man available to be the figurehead of the legal party.'[88] Roy also instructed Muzaffar and Usmani to get in touch with Singaravelu.[89] In his letter to Muzaffar dated 15 May 1923, Roy put forth a plan of action. 'In the first place we shall have to organise small parties secretly among labourers and peasants in different places.... For the present, work ought to be done secretly, but along with it an open party is also to be organized .... This party will be styled "people's party" or "workers' and peasants' party".... As a matter of fact, you will have to organise two parties side by side – firstly, our communist party, but for the present a secret organisation ... secondly, the open mass party in which will have to be collected all the revolutionists and nationalists.' The letter then explained that the open work was to be concentrated on nationalism, i.e., the ejection of the British, and that 'the dictatorship of the proletariat was to be kept in the background, to be openly preached only after the first objective had been attained.'[90]

Roy, in anticipation of the conference, had prepared a memorandum for its guidance. 'Now we must adopt a programme of action,' wrote Roy in the memorandum, 'a programme which will rally the working class in the present struggle against foreign domination and prepare them for the future struggle.... The only international proletarian organisation that stands unconditionally for the freedom of the subject people and the liberation of the working classes from class domination is the Communist International.... Therefore, I propose that the central executive committee be entrusted by this conference to send as soon as possible a delegation of three to the Communist International.... The willingness, rather the eagerness, of the Communist International to help the growth of a revolutionary working class party is well known.... While believing firmly that legal existence is necessary for the growth of a mass party, I must urge upon you the necessity of an illegal apparatus which should be built as a parallel organisation .... The communist party of India ... should continue as the illegal apparatus of the legal mass party ....

The workers and peasants are to be organized, not to face suffering, but to develop the will and power to fight for freedom .... I wish you success in the task you have undertaken and put myself at the service of the workers' and peasants' party of India.'[91] In the same memorandum, Roy suggested the formation of a commission to elaborate the programme of the party, whose personnel would be Ghulam Husain; Manilal; Singaravelu; Dange; Sampurnanand; Muzaffar; and Sunder Singh, the Akali leader.[92] Roy's memorandum was followed by a congratulatory message from Kolarov, a member of the executive committee of the Comintern. Kolarov, on behalf of the Comintern, promised all assistance to the revolutionary party of the workers and peasants of India and wished it success in its effort to lead the toilers of India to their final emancipation.[93]

All these hectic activities of Roy and the marxists in India were in vain though. The proposed all-India conference failed to materialize. Instead, Singaravelu, to the surprise of marxists in India, formed a new party – the 'Labour and Kisan Party of Hindustan'. Singaravelu himself became the president of the party and one M.P.T. Velayudham, its secretary.[94] The claim of Singaravelu that the new party should be the centre, and all the others merely provincial branches, was ignored by marxists in India.[95] The party, therefore, existed only on paper, it had no *locus standi*. Personal rivalry, scramble for leadership and thoughtless action on the part of Roy and the Indian marxists were some of the factors that marred the first attempt to form an all-India peasants and workers party.

In the entire drama, the most interesting part was that Roy extended unqualified support to Singaravelu, without having a look at his manifesto. The copy of the manifesto, which Singaravelu was supposed to have sent, did not reach him.[96] Nor did he receive the manifesto of Manilal. He saw Manilal's manifesto only when some German comrades, to whom it was sent for publication, brought it to his notice. From the wordings of the manifesto, Roy could see the *evil hand* of Abani in its drafting and promptly denounced it.[97] As for his reason for supporting Singaravelu, he said that he had cracked up his manifesto in advance, on the basis of what he had been told about it, but on reading it, he realized that he had been wrong.[98] Much to the annoyance of Roy, both the manifestoes were identical and denounced 'bolshevik and foreign agents', making it difficult for him to get funds from the Comintern for the party.[99]

Abani left India frustrated and reached Berlin around the middle of 1924. The failure of his mission led to the disintegration of Chattopadhyaya's group and left the field open for Roy. Bhupendranath Dutta returned to India in 1925, Barkatullah left for America at the invitation of the Ghadar Party, Virendranath Chattopadhyaya joined the Communist Party of Germany and became a Joint Secretary of the League Against Imperialism and for National Independence, and Abani took up a job at the Statistical Institute of Moscow. After a long time, Muzaffar received a letter from Abani from Moscow: 'I am now working in the Statistical Institute, I have no connection with the party, i.e., with Roy. I have translated Bukharin's *ABC of Communism* in Bengali. You can publish it, if you want.'[100] The letter remained unanswered. Muzaffar did not respond.

Six months after the drama was over, Roy again made an abortive attempt to organize a mass party of workers and peasants in India. In a letter from Zurich dated 25 January 1924, addressed to Velayudham, secretary, Labour and Kisan Party of Hindustan, Roy first lamented at length over the ill-conceived manifesto and the attempt to form a mass party, and then put forward a new plan. 'If you are willing to reconsider the whole position and begin all over again,' wrote Roy, 'I will be very glad to join hands. But we must rise above *amour propre*. One should admit that a wrong start has been made. This brings me back to the necessity of a preliminary conference. I have insisted on this repeatedly. All these misunderstandings and political blunder could have been avoided had the party been launched after proper deliberations. It was a hasty undertaking. Adequate preparations were not made.... Can you undertake the task of organising the delegation to the preliminary conference here? I am ready to render all help to this end. See if four or five comrades can come. We will have a thorough discussion of all the questions in detail, elaborate the programme, draft a new manifesto, arrange about the party press, organisation, communication, etc. Then the delegation will return to call a large conference which will be a communist party and which will embrace revolutionary national elements besides socialists. The draft will be adopted by this Congress and the party will be launched publicly not on paper, neither in a small group, nor again as an exclusive sect, but as a powerful revolutionary mass organisation.'[101] The plan remained on paper. The marxists in India failed to come up to his expectations.

Apart from sending literature and help to form a few marxist groups, Roy failed to make any appreciable achievement. His attempt to gain a foothold in the Congress by motivating a few bourgeois national leaders failed, and efforts to form a peasants and workers party fizzled out. But for this miscarriage, Roy alone cannot be blamed. Sitting at a distance of a few thousand miles from the field of activity, Roy faced immense difficulty in assessing the political situation in India. He had to rely solely on the information supplied by his contact men and some scrappy news that reached him through censors. His close contacts, excepting Muzaffar, Dange, Sharma and Usmani, who were able subordinates, lacked political acumen and intelligence.

The achievement of the marxists was limited, yet the authorities were apprehensive, rather scared, of the potential of marxism in India. In a confidential note dated 2 June 1923, J. Crarar, secretary to the governor-general of India, stated with concern, 'The immediate and potential dangers of the communist movement in India even as an isolated factor are sufficiently obvious. But there is evidence of what is [a] still more dangerous development in the establishment of contacts between the bolshevik and communist agencies. On the one hand, there have been communications with the representatives of the old Bengal revolutionaries, many of whom are personal friends of M.N. Roy, and who since the failure of [the] non-cooperation movement have been moving towards the resumption of their former activities. On the other hand, C.R. Das and the extreme left of the Congress have not concealed their intention to 'organise the proletariat' and to resort to 'direct action'. Between these two groups, Roy's communists occupy a dangerously convenient tactical position. Action will have the effect of discrediting Roy and putting some of his active agents out of action ...'[102]

As a follow-up of this note and as a precaution, in June 1923, Muzaffar, Usmani and Ghulam Husain were taken into custody under Regulation III of 1818 and censorship was tightened. In the month of June alone, no less than 2,609 copies of *The Vanguard* were intercepted.[103] The French Government of Pondicherry, on being requested by the British, interned R.C.L. Sharma, Roy's main communication agent in India, in a small village near Pondicherry, and disrupted Roy's communication link with India.[104] French authorities also prohibited the entry of *The Vanguard* and *The Inprecor* in Pondicherry, and confiscated a mass of literature, along with a list of the addresses of persons to whom it was to be distributed.[105] All these actions were a setback to Roy. In sheer desperation, Evelyn wrote to a revolutionary in Bengal that economic and industrial movements were futile. The right method would be to impress upon the upper class the idea of British tyranny in such a way as to 'goad a few of them into fanaticism who will begin [the] desolatory act of bloodshed. This will demoralise the whites ... let there be chaos; even that is better than the lifeless existence of the people'.[106]

Besides intercepting Roy's correspondences and confiscating marxist literature, the government prepared detailed but brief identities of all persons connected with Roy, directly or indirectly, to proceed against them in a court of law. The list contained the names of 155 persons, but only 13 were selected to face trial and their cases were sent for legal opinion. The legal adviser dropped five names and advised the government to proceed against eight.[107]

In February 1924, a complaint was filed in the Court of the Magistrate at Cawnpore. Of the eight persons named in the first information report, Roy and R.C.L. Sharma could not be apprehended. The former was in the Continent and the latter was a political refugee in French Pondicherry. Ghulam Husain made a confession, became a state witness and was pardoned.[108] The case against Singaravelu was withdrawn on grounds of health.[109] Only four persons – Muzaffar, Dange, Usmani and Gupta[110] – were put up before the Magistrate at Cawnpore to face trial.

The trial began on 15 March 1924 and on 21 March, on behalf of the working class of India, Roy in an 'open letter' reminded Ramsey MacDonald, the then prime minister of Great Britain, of his duties and responsibilities. He said, 'You are a government of the working class pledged to support the interests and welfare of the working class whenever these are jeopardised. As a party you have always proclaimed the international solidarity and brotherhood of the workers. As a government, you are bound to protect the rights of the Indian workers to freedom of political association for economic ends.'[111] But the appeal failed to have the desired effect. MacDonald refused to take cognisance of the letter. The Cawnpore Conspiracy case proceeded as scheduled. The case against the accused stated they had conspired to establish throughout British India a branch of the revolutionary organization known as the Communist International with the objective of depriving the King Emperor of the sovereignty of British India.

The Magistrate at the lower court, after a brief trial, committed all the accused to sessions. The sessions trial began on 22 April and was concluded on 20 May. All the accused were found guilty of the charges and each of them was sentenced to four years' rigorous imprisonment. The accused made an appeal before the High Court but it was turned down.[112]

Like the Peshawar Conspiracy cases, the Cawnpore Conspiracy case was also contrived. The word conspiracy hardly deserves any merit. Yet, the case was instituted and the accused were punished, simply to prove to the people that the Soviet Union, through the Communist International, was trying to destabilize the established order in India. In a significant judgement, the appellate judges of the Allahabad High Court put on record that though the accused 'carried on this conspiracy with each other and with Roy in the most serious spirit, their aspirations were absurd and unbelievable'.[113] The observation of the appellate judges was further corroborated by the director of intelligence bureau, Government of India, stating that in point of time, the marxists in India accomplished but little when the Cawnpore prosecution cut short their activities.[114]

It is surprising that the marxists failed to engage a lawyer for their defence at the lower court due to paucity of funds[115] and were left to their own wit. In the sessions court, the accused were defended by two mediocre lawyers – Manilal Shah and Kapildev Malaviya. Attempts to engage Mohammad Ali Jinnah failed because he demanded Rs 30,000 as his fee.[116] In the high court, the case was defended by only Kapildev.

In spite of poor defence, the Cawnpore Conspiracy case attracted a great deal of attention both at home and abroad, particularly in Great Britain. Such was not the case with the Peshawar Conspiracy cases, which went unnoticed. In 1924, for the first time, a Labour government came to power in England and raised hopes among workers and peasants, whose support had helped it come to power. The question haunting the minds of people was, how could the Labour Party, having come to power with the support of the working class, sanction the prosecution of Indian marxists for organizing a working class party? This question remained unanswered. However, the working classes of various European countries took up the cause of the Indian marxists and extended a helping hand. The *Workers Weekly*, an organ of the Communist Party of Great Britain, not only gave wide publicity to the trial in all its issues from March to May 1924, but also formed a committee to collect funds for the defence of the Cawnpore accused. J. Lansbury became its chairman; and J. Maxton, Shapurji Saklatvala and A. MacManus, its members.[117] In India too a defence committee was formed for the collection of funds. It was headed by V.H. Joshi, the self-styled private secretary of Dange; T.V. Parvate; and K.N. Joglekar.[118] Though the amount collected did not go beyond a couple of thousand rupees, it boosted the morale of marxists in India.

About the time the law was being invoked against the marxists in India, things were moving against Roy in Germany. In 1921, after the failure of the marxists to bring about a revolution in Germany, it became apparent to Roy that, sooner or later, communist activities in Germany would be curtailed and he may have to shift to some other country. Apprehending the danger, Roy made a trip around Europe in search of a place where he could establish his headquarters and continue his activities, i.e., maintain contact with India and issue his journal. For this purpose, he visited Zurich, Marseilles, Paris, Genoa, Amsterdam, and Annecy. In 1924, when the Germans did expel him, he first shifted to Zurich and from there to Annecy and then to Paris, where he established his headquarters and started issuing his journal. From Zurich, Roy addressed a letter to Ramsey MacDonald explaining his political views and hoping that the Labour government, which rested on the power of the working class, would allow him to return to India to organize a working class party. 'What I solicit,' wrote Roy, 'is an amnesty from the alleged charges made against me in the past .... I should draw your attention to the fact that my political views have undergone a radical change since I left India in 1915 .... I will appreciate it very much if I am given the passport to come to England, there to discuss with the India Office the question of my return to India.'[119] The letter dated 21 February 1924 was addressed a month before the institution of the Cawnpore Conspiracy case. The institution of the conspiracy case changed the situation. Roy realized the futility of his appeal and did not pursue the matter any further.

While Roy was trying to regain his contact with India, the fifth congress of the Comintern met in Moscow from 17 June to 8 July 1924. The Congress was attended by 504 delegates representing 49 communist and workers' parties and 10 international organizations. At the time of the congress, the communist parties had a membership of 1,319,000.[120] It was the first congress of the Third International without its founder comrade, Lenin. The death of Lenin took away the wisdom of the Comintern and its future seemed bleak. Squabbles between Trotsky and Stalin, which had remained dormant during the life-time of Lenin, surfaced and divided the organization into two warring camps, to the detriment of the working class movement.

A few days before the congress met, the executive committee of the Comintern prepared a report for discussion within its various branches. For the Indian marxists, it set forth three tasks – (1) restoration of the national liberation movement on a revolutionary basis, (2) formation of a peoples' party and (3) launch of the trade union movement under its influence.[121] After discussion, the report was placed before the fifth congress in the form of a resolution. It was further emphasized that the Comintern, through its executive committee, should establish direct contact with the national movement for the emancipation of the working class.

At the fifth congress, Roy had to face a more difficult situation. The resolution on the national and colonial question, passed by the executive committee, was not to his liking. He opposed it on the ground that it was 'totally mistaken when considered in the light of the events that have taken place since the second congress. The resolution says, that in order to win over the people of colonial and semi-colonial countries, there must be a further direct contact of the executive committee with the national movement for emancipation. It is true that we must always have a connection with these movements but it seems to have been overlooked that these connections have not always been successful … a movement which might have had a revolutionary significance in 1920 is not in the same position in 1924. Here is the danger of rigid formula and the cause of our inefficiency … we must rectify this error … we must have direct connection with the masses, but the resolution says that we must have direct connections with the national liberation movements. These include all sorts of classes and aims. We shall never progress if we stand by this vague formula; our failure hitherto has been due to theoretical confusion'.[122]

Roy's indignant appeal failed to find takers. The resolution, finally adopted, included the phrase that Roy wanted to expunge. It emphasized not only the necessity of establishing 'direct contact between the executive committee and the national emancipation movements of the orient, but also very close contact between the sections in the imperialist countries with the colonies of those countries'.[123] The resolution was an encroachment on Roy's authority, a threat to his position. His differences with the Comintern leaders became apparent when Dimitri Manulsky, the chairman of the colonial commission, was provoked to say, 'In regard to the colonial question, Roy reflects nihilism of Rosa Luxemburg.'[124] But in spite of adverse criticism, Roy succeeded in maintaining his position in the Comintern. At the fifth congress, he was made a member of the executive committee and a candidate-member of the presidium. The colonial question with which Roy did not agree was referred to a commission for review and preparation of a report with recommendations for consideration at the fifth plenum of the executive committee.[125]

After the congress, Roy returned to Paris in August 1924 to resume his work. He was a dejected man. The Comintern gave him a tough time, his mentor Lenin was dead and the Cawnpore Conspiracy case dispelled his illusion about the capacity of his comrades in India. Further, the French government prohibited the sale and circulation of *The Vanguard* in France and slapped an order of expulsion on Roy, Evelyn and Paul Snef, a German comrade who had come to Paris to help the Roys.[126] In pursuance of the order, Roy was expelled from France, but the order against Evelyn and Paul Snef was withdrawn due to the intervention of French intellectuals, viz., Henri Barbusse, secretary of the *Comite' Pro-Hindou,* and others. The group *Comite' Pro-Hindou* did some propaganda work in favour of Indian independence, but failed to secure the reversal of the expulsion order on Roy. Evelyn and Paul Snef stayed back and, aided by a small group of Indians, notably G.A.K. Luhani and Mohammad Sipassi, and a few French intellectuals belonging to *Comite' Pro-Hindou*, tried to intensify the work, but achieved little because of the repressive measures adopted by the French government. Their only success was that they continued to publish the journal by changing its name from *The Vanguard of Indian Independence* to *The Masses of India.*[127]

About two months before Roy was expelled from France, in November, the news of the failure of the Cawnpore Conspiracy case appeal reached him and in the same month he wrote to R.C.L.

Sharma in Pondicherry: 'We had not expected anything better, poor fellows! If they could only have put up a better defence, four years in jail would have been worthwhile. We must have better communists than this lot; and the defending council (sic).... With a better lot in the dock and less stupid heads at the Bar, the Cawnpore case could have been an epoch-making event in our political history.' In the same letter, after lamenting over the drawbacks of the Cawnpore trial, he looked at the positive side of it. 'Now that the panic caused by the Cawnpore case and other prosecutions has well-nigh subsided, it is necessary to take up the threads of our work .... The organisation of the party must be pushed vigorously. The Cawnpore case has had its good effects too. People have got used to hearing things which simply terrified them before.... We must reap the benefit of the situation.'[128]

Shortly after the conspiracy case, 'to reap the benefit of the situation', Roy changed his strategy and decided upon three things – his old dictum of an open political party, the induction of communist elements into the all India congress committee and the publication of an English weekly named *The Republican* to propagate marxism under the cover of nationalism. The weekly published from India became a necessity, as his journal published from abroad had practically ceased to enter India due to the stringent surveillance of the government ever since the institution of the Cawnpore Conspiracy case. Roy promised at least two articles a week for the paper, but these were to be published without the author's name. The reason for this anonymity was the fear of detection and consequent action by the government against the marxists. Roy was not prepared to take the risk of sending his comrades to jail prematurely.[129] The Cawnpore Conspiracy case made him realize that a premature exposure would go against the movement. In July 1925, he wrote to D.P. Sinha: 'This misfortune (Cawnpore Conspiracy case and his expulsion from France) has affected me rather seriously and has dislocated our business ... but I am gathering up the threads with great difficulties.'[130]

As a follow-up action, Roy sent a manifesto to the Belgaum congress to apprise the people of the new political situation so as to prepare the ground for the proposed party. The manifesto titled 'Appeal to the Nationalists' began with an attack on the Indian National Congress for its failure on all counts, as well as internal bickering, and then dealt with the establishment of a revolutionary nationalist party for the masses, with radical programmes aimed at national independence and complete break from the Empire, abolition of feudalism and landlordism, nationalization of land, modernization of agriculture, development of modern industries, protection of workers, minimum wages, eight-hour working day, abolition of child labour, insurance and other advanced social legislation, free and compulsory primary education, freedom of religion and worship, and rights to minorities.[131]

In a short span, the manifesto brought home a new crucial point that revolution and constitutional agitation are synonymous and supplement each other. 'Revolution,' wrote Roy, 'is not an unconstitutional affair. In fact, practically all the modern constitutional states owe their origin to some sort of revolution. India has no constitutional government. When one talks of constitution in India, one has in view the British constitution. This latter has for its foundation the "Magna Carta" which was the product of a revolution. Then every successive period in the evolution of the British constitution is equally marked by events of a revolutionary nature. The same process can be read in the history of any other modern nation .... Once we have this correct concept of revolution, it becomes clear that nationalism in a given period of history, is revolutionary force, whose manifestations are not "criminal"! This force operates through a series of historical events, which will separate the India of tomorrow from the India of yesterday. This process cannot take place within the framework of a superimposed constitution, which by its very nature is meant to prevent this epoch-making break. Indian nationalism cannot, therefore, be "constitutional". Its object is to establish a constitutional government of the people for the people by the people of India.... The struggle of the Indian people for freedom is an integral part of the struggle of the international proletariat against capitalist domination, in that its success will break down one of the strongholds of world capitalism. The revolutionary nationalists of India should, therefore, not only join hands with the Indian workers and peasants, but also should establish close relations with the advanced proletariat of the world. In the age of monopolist imperialism, the subject people in their struggle for freedom must have the cooperation of the international organisation of the revolutionary proletariat. The communists will fight side by side with the revolutionary nationalists and will be found always in the front ranks.'[132]

As promised, Roy sent his first article titled 'Towards Democracy' for publication in the first issue of *The Republican*. The article merely stated the objective of the new paper – propagation of republicanism within the ranks of the nationalists – and avoided all reference to communism in order to have an innocuous appearance.[133] Roy was apprehensive that the word 'communism' may unduly frighten the nationalist bourgeoisie to the detriment of the formation of an open political party of the masses. So he tactfully avoided the word. Neither the paper, nor the article was published in India. But an abortive attempt was made to organize an open political party and induct communist elements into the all-India congress committee. The initiative was taken by Hasrat Mohani, Arjunlal Sethi, Janki Prasad Bagerhatta and a few others.[134]

Towards the close of January 1925, Roy, having been expelled from France, shifted to Luxemburg, but did not stay there for long. By March, he reached Moscow to attend the meeting of the fifth plenum of the executive committee of the Comintern, scheduled to meet from 21 March to 6 April. After analysing the global situation, the plenum made a number of recommendations on programmatic and tactical questions for the guidance of communist parties in colonial and dependent countries to help them intensify the liberation struggle. It drew 'special attention to the necessity of raising the ideological and theoretical level of the communist parties as a decisive means of strengthening and improving their fighting efficiency. It set before each party the task of mastering Leninism which represented a new stage in the development of Marxism

...'[135] For India, it set to resolve two important issues – the attitude of the Comintern towards the Indian National Congress and the type of 'direct contact' to be established between the Congress and the executive committee of the Comintern. Both these issues were of prime importance to Roy, but remained unresolved at the fifth congress, which met in the previous summer.

Before taking up the questions, the plenum had threadbare discussions on the political situation in India and the experience of Indian marxists vis-à-vis the national liberation movement. It observed that the repressive policy of the British imperialist on the one hand, and the contradictions within the national movement on the other, temporarily weakened the organized resistance of the Indian masses to British imperialism. It was neither defeat nor breakdown of the struggle for national liberation, but merely a temporary crisis within the existing national parties. Therefore, the general consensus was that marxists in India would work within the Indian National Congress to wage a determined and more vigorous political struggle for liberation and support the Congress in each of its acts of resistance to imperialism, on the basis of a united anti-imperialist front. But side by side, the marxists in India would be required to unite the various communist groups and elements into a strong party of the working class, i.e., the communist party.[136]

The plenum, having agreed upon the course of action to be followed by the marxists in India, concretized the decision through a resolution, stating, 'It is necessary for the communists to continue work in the Indian National Congress and in the left wing of the Swaraj Party. All nationalist organisations should be formed into a mass revolutionary party, an all-India anti-imperialists bloc. The slogan of the peoples' party, having for the main points in its programme: separation from the Empire, a democratic republic, universal suffrage and the abolition of feudalism – slogan put forward and popularised by the Indian communists – is correct.'[137] In the same resolution, the plenum further instructed Indian marxists 'to direct their effort towards securing leadership of the peasantry and to facilitate and encourage the organisation and amalgamation of trade unions and to take over the leadership of all their struggles'.[138] The resolution, as it appears, rejected Roy's strategic formulation, but endorsed the formation of a mass revolutionary peoples' party made up of all nationalist organizations.

By 1924, the Comintern appeared to have developed doubts about Roy's ability to deliver the goods. The fifth congress of the Comintern, therefore, resolved to pay special attention to the colonies to intensify communist activities there. In a resolution on the colonial question, it said that there should be 'very close contact between the sections (of the Comintern) in the imperialist countries and the colonies of those countries'. Acting on this resolution, the Communist Party of Great Britain sent Percy F. Glading, alias R. Cochrane, to India to survey the political situation before the formation of a labour party.[139] Glading, a member of the national minority movement of England and a prominent member of the British bureau of the Red International of Labour Union, arrived in India on 30 January 1925. On reaching India, he first attended the fifth session of the all-India Trade Union Congress at Bombay and then left for Delhi. He stayed for a month in Delhi and then went to Calcutta. From Calcutta he came to Bombay again, before leaving for London on 10 April. During his short stay in India, he met quite a few people but his discussions with them about the modalities for the formation of a labour party left him disappointed.[140]

Apart from sending Glading to India, the Communist Party of Great Britain took the initiative to set up a colonial committee, also known as the colonial department, to help propagate marxism in colonies. But no sooner had the colonial committee been formed, than there arose dissension between the Indian marxists residing in London and the Communist Party of Great Britain, because of the bureaucratic attitude of the latter, manifested in its refusal to admit Indians into the inner conclave of the colonial committee. Hurt and humiliated, A.C. Banerjee, a confidante of Roy, wrote to Evelyn, suggesting the formation of a colonial bureau of the Communist Party of India, with a request to forward the proposal to Moscow.[141] Evelyn responded: 'Whether you can call the organisation a colonial bureau and get separate representation for it before the Communist International, I do not know. The heads do not like the duplication of efforts and much wrangling. They would refuse to recognise it on the ground that there already existed a colonial bureau of the party. I imagine you will have to function through the latter for your representation at the centre. This does not, of course, mean that you cannot agitate for fuller and better representation, and that you should not fight against party bureaucracy if it manifests, itself in an unreasonable form.'[142] In the course of the same letter, Evelyn referred to the constant friction between Roy's group and the local communist parties on the Continent and said, 'We occupy ourselves a somewhat independent position, and have to struggle against either complete neglect, or bureaucracy, as well as a sense of rivalry. But we are a party organisation directly affiliated to the centre.'[143] The upshot of this correspondence was that the Comintern finally approved Banerjee's suggestion and allowed the Indian marxists in London to form an Indian bureau. A.C. Banerjee, P.C. Naidu, N.J. Upadhyaya, C.P. Dutt and a few others became its members. The Comintern instructed the Communist Party of Great Britain to accord recognition to the Indian bureau and put an end to the dispute.[144] For proper coordination, David Ramsey of the Communist Party of Great Britain was included in the Indian bureau as the representative of his party, while A.C. Banerjee was given a place in the colonial committee.[145]

Besides these two groups, a third group, the European bureau, also known as the Foreign bureau of the Indian marxists, sprang up in the continent under the auspices of the executive committee of the Comintern. The chief protagonist of this bureau was Roy and, to a lesser extent, Sipassi and C.P. Dutt. The idea behind setting up the European bureau was to bring together Indians residing in Europe and imbue them with the ideology of marxism, and thereafter establish a link between the bureau and the marxists in India. C.P. Dutt became the link between the Comintern, the Communist Party of Great Britain, the Indian bureau of London and the European bureau of Roy.[146] The Communist Party of Great Britain decided to call an oriental conference to coordinate the work of these groups, rather than to establish authority.

To discuss the oriental conference, but more to clear certain issues that had cropped up due to a multiplicity of groups, the Communist Party of Great Britain called a meeting at Amsterdam on 11 and 12 July 1925. Present at the meeting were Percy F. Glading, R.W. Robson, Clemens Dutt, Gertrude Hessler, H. Sneevliet, N.J. Upadhyaya, M.A. Khan, M.N. Roy, Evelyn Roy and a few others.[147] To the discomfort of Roy, the meeting opened with a report from Glading concerning his visit to India. In the report, Glading first gave the names of the places he had visited and the people he had met.[148] Thereafter, he said, 'that he had not met a single convinced communist during his visit to India'.[149] And that 'those with whom he had come in contact were useless'.[150] Roy considered the report a challenge to his claim that under his stewardship, marxists had established a foothold in India and that they were genuine marxists. He refused to accept Glading's observation and asserted: 'Glading had not had an opportunity of meeting the genuine communist workers in India, and that his visit was too short.'[151] A sharp difference of opinion arose when Roy criticized the Communist Party of Great Britain for its enthusiasm to control the marxist movement in India and said that it 'smacks of imperialism'.[152]

Soon after the Amsterdam meeting, Roy reached Moscow and met the Comintern leaders. What actually transpired is difficult to ascertain, but subsequent events show that he succeeded in thwarting the Communist Party of Great Britain's attempt to direct the marxist movement in India. By September, through the facilitation of the Comintern, a settlement was reached that, from now on, the Indian bureau in London would carry on its activities in consultation with the colonial committee of the Communist Party of Great Britain, but politically it would be guided both by the European bureau of Roy and the colonial committee.[153] A little later, the decision was again reassured by the Comintern, when it said that 'until we can legalise ourselves in India, the centre of our work must be in England for technical and as well as political reasons.'[154] The Comintern further emphasized the need to create special cadres for work in colonies and advised the Communist Party of Great Britain to put some of its best members in it.[155]

The Comintern's decision did not establish clear lines of authority, but simply directed the Communist Party of Great Britain not to work independently of Roy. Though not satisfied, Roy accepted the verdict. He appeared to have realized the importance of the services of the Communist Party of Great Britain, particularly in matters of recruiting seamen as couriers and sending experienced comrades as emissaries to India. Thus, peace was restored and both the groups worked in harmony, at least for some time to come. C.P. Dutt, a prominent member of the Communist Party of Great Britain, and a good friend of Roy, possibly played a major role in this settlement. Both Roy and the Communist Party of Great Britain jointly decided to send Dutt as an emissary to India, unlike the case of Glading, who was sent to India without consulting Roy. Dutt agreed to the proposal, but his application for a passport was turned down by the secretary of state for India.[156]

Notes

1 *Memoirs,* p.494.
2 Bernard Isaacs, op. cit., p.115.
3 *Documents*, Vol. I, p.262.
4 ibid., p.266.
5 *Memoirs*, pp.525-6.
6 ibid., p.526. About this time the Soviet Union signed a trade agreement with the British Government. One of the conditions of the agreement was that hereafter the Soviet authorities would stop all propaganda directed against the British Empire.
7 ibid., p.528.
8 ibid.
9 Fazal Ilahi Qurban, The Eastern University in Moscow, *The Vanguard of Indian Independence*, 1 April 1923.
10 J.V. Stalin, *Works*, Vol. VII, Moscow, 1954, p.138. Lecture delivered on the occasion of the fourth anniversary of the University of the Toilers of the East.
11 ibid., p.153.
12 Cecil Kaye, op. cit. p.5.
13 *Memoirs*, p.529.
14 Cecil Kaye, op. cit, p.6. Letter from Roy to B.K. Sarkar, 13 August 1921.
15 *Memoirs*, p.541.
16 ibid., p.542.
17 ibid. p.545.
18 ibid.
19 *Documents*, Vol. I, pp.343 and 354. For the full text see: pp.341-54.
20 *Memoirs*, p.547.
21 Cecil Kaye, op. cit, p.7.
22 Muzaffar Ahmed, ibid., pp.134-5. The appeal was printed in India by one Dattatreya Parasuram Pandeya belonging to Ajmer and distributed at the Congress session by Kalicharan Dutta, Gopinath and few others.
23 R. Palme Dutt, *India Today*, Calcutta, 1947, p.347.
24 For the full text of Nalini's statement before the police, see: Dwijendra Nandi, *Some Documents Relating to Early Indian Communists and Controversies Around Them*, New Delhi, 1971, pp.66-102.
25 Muzaffar Ahmed, op. cit., pp.86-7
26 ibid., p.259. Letter from Roy to Muzaffar Ahmed, 19 March 1924
27 *Memoirs*, p.552.
28 ibid., p.552

29 ibid.
30 ibid., p.553.
31 M.N. Roy, *India in Transition* (Reprint), Bombay, 1971, pp.16-17.
32 M.N. Roy, *What do we want*, (Reprint), Bombay, 1971, p.32.
33 Dwijendra Nandi, op. cit., pp.94-5.
34 *Memoirs*, p.548.
35 Shaukat Usmani, *Historic Trip of a Revolutionary-Sojourn in the Soviet Union*, New Delhi, 1977, p.69.
36 ibid., p.71.
37 ibid.
38 Bhupendranath Dutta, op. cit pp.301-2
39 Cecil Kaye, op., cit., p.11.
40 Cecil Kaye, op. cit., p.57.
41 *Memoirs*, p.379.
42 ibid., p.544.
43 *Memoirs*, pp.499-500.
44 ibid., p.500.
45 Cawnpore case evidence, exhibit No. 5
46 *Documents*, Vol. II p.27.
47 For details see: *Documents*, Vol. II, pp.40-41.
48 M.N. Roy, 'Manufacturing Evidence', *Inprecor*, 31 May 1923.
49 *Documents*, Vol. II, p.37.
Letter from Roy to S.A. Dange, 25 December 1922
50 A.K. Hindi, *M.N. Roy - The man who looked ahead*, Ahmedabad, 1958, pp.122-4.
51 ibid. p.125.
52 Muzaffar Ahmed, op. cit, p.261.
Roy addressed a letter to Subhas around the middle of 1922 and sent the same to Muzaffar for delivery. Muzaffar, who had no communica¬tion with Subhas, handed over the letter to Bhupendra Kumar Dutta, a classmate of Subhas for doing the needful. Subhas refused to accept the letter on the plea that it should have come to him directly by post instead of by hand.
53 Cecil Kaye, op. cit., p.23.
Letter from Usmani to Roy, 12 October 1922.
54 *The Vanguard of Indian Independence*, 15 July 1922
55 ibid.
56 Cawnpore case evidence, exhibit No. 5.
57 *The Tribune*, Lahore, 4 November 1922.
58 Cecil Kaye, op. cit., p.16.

59 ibid., p.17.
Charles Ashleigh was a fairly well-known comrade. In 1918 he was sentenced to 10 years' imprisonment on a charge of fomenting riots following the strikes of the industrial workers in America. He was released in 1922 and deported to the United Kingdom where he joined the Communist Party of Great Britain.
60 Muzaffar Ahmed, op. cit., p.319.
61 Cecil Kaye, op. cit., p.159.
62 Bernard Isaacs, op. cit., p.159.
63 V. I. Lenin, *Collected Works*, Vol. 33, p.417.
64 *Inprecor*, 22 December 1922
65 ibid.
66 *Resolutions and Thesis of the Fourth Congress of the International*, (A publication of the C.P G.B.), London, 1923, p.55.
67 ibid.
68 ibid., p.224.
69 Cawnpore case evidence, exhibit No. 20.
Letter from Roy to S.A. Dange, 19 December 1922
70 *Documents*, Vol. I. pp.561-2.
71 Cecil Kaye, op. cit., p.42.
72 P. C. Ray, Life and Times of C.R. Das, Oxford, 1927, pp.267-8.
73 ibid. p.288.
74 *The Advance Guard*, 1 December 1922.
75 The message was signed by Humbert Droz, secretary of the presidium of the fourth congress of the Comintern. It was later published in the 1 January 1923 issue of *The Advance Guard*.
76 M.N. Roy, 'The Indian National Congress', *Inprecor*, 1 March 1923.
77 Cawnpore case evidence, exhibit No. 10.
78 Cecil Kaye, op. cit., p.57.
79 ibid., p.58.
80 Muzaffar Ahmed, op. cit., p.225.
81 Cecil Kaye, op. cit., p.58.
82 Cawnpore case evidence, exhibit No, 18A.
83 Muzaffar Ahmed, op. cit, pp.226-7.
84 *The Vanguard of Indian Independence*, 15 February 1923.
85 ibid.
86 Cecil Kaye, op., cit, p.62
87 ibid., p.53
88 ibid., p.63.
89 ibid.

90 David Petrie, *Communism in India*, 1924-1927 (Reprint), Calcutta, 1972, p.42.
91 Cecil Kaye op. cit., pp.60-1.
92 ibid p.61.
93 ibid.
94 ibid., p.62
95 ibid., p.63
96 ibid., p.64.
97 ibid.
98 ibid.
99 ibid.
100 Muzaffar Ahmed, op. cit., p.243.
101 Subodh Roy, *Unpublished Documents, Communism in Indian* (1919-1924), Calcutta, 1971, p.306
102 *Documents*, Vol. II, p.274.
103 Cecil Kaye, op. cit., p.75.
104 ibid, p.82
105 ibid.
106 ibid., p.73
107 ibid., p.94

(i) M. N. Roy
(ii) Muzaffar Ahmed
(iii) Gulam Husain
(iv) Shaukat Usmani
(v) S.A Dange
(vi) R.C.L. Sharma
(vii) Nalini Gupta
(viii) Singaravelu Chettiar

108 ibid., p.66.

Ghulam Husain admitted his guilt in a petition for mercy and made a formal statement before the Magistrate acknowledging his receipt of bolshevik money, though urging that he had spent the money on himself and his friends and not for the furtherance of bolshevism. He gave details of his stay in Kabul and his relations with Mohammad Ali (Khushi Mohammad), Zafar Husain Abdullah and Mohammad Shafiq. In consideration of his confession, and his consent to give evidence against Shafiq, (who had been arrested in Baluchistan in November 1923 and sent to Peshawar for trial in which he was sentenced to 3 years' R.I.) Ghulam Husain was pardoned and released.

109 ibid., pp.97-8.

Singaravelu produced a medical certificate stating that he was physically unfit to travel to Cawnpore to stand trial and was released on bail pending recovery. But the recovery was so slow that it was eventually decided to withdraw the charge against him.

110 As an emissary of Roy this was Nalini's second visit to India. On this occasion he came to recruit young men with political background to study marxism at the University of The Toilers of the East. He recruited one Gopendra Krishna Chakravarty, a member of the *Anusilan Samiti*, and sent him to Roy. Nalini left Moscow on 16 December, and reached Karachi via Iran on 9 June 1923. From Karachi, via Bombay and Madras, he arrived at Calcutta in July. He was taken into custody on 20 December under Regulation III of 1818.

111 *Inprecor*, 27 March 1924.

112 All the accused were released before the expiry of their term of impri¬sonment. Nalini was released on 3 July 1925; Muzaffar on 12 September 1925; Dange on 24 May 1927 and Usmani on 26 August 1927. Nalini and Muzaffar were released earlier on health ground.

113 David Petrie, op. cit., p.63.

114 ibid., pp.65-6

115 Muzaffar Ahmed, op. cit., p.350.

116 ibid., p.358.

117 *Documents*, Vol. II, p.289.

118 ibid., p.292.

119 Subodh Roy, op. cit., pp.263-6.

120 Bernard Isaacs, op. cit., p.210.

121 *From the Fourth to the Fifth World Congress* (A publication of the C. P. G. B.), London, 1924, p.68.

122 *The Vanguard of Indian Independence*, 15 August 1924.

123 *Inprecor*, 29 August 1924.

124 ibid., 12 August 1924.

125 *Inprecor*, 29 August 1924.

126 Cecil Kaye, op. cit., p.104.

127 David Petrie, op. cit., p.86

128 ibid., p.89.

129 ibid., p.90.

130 ibid., p.94.

131 *Documents*, Vol. II, p.446.

132 The manifesto dated 1 December 1924 was printed as a supplement to *The Vanguard* of 15 December. In a slightly modified form it was reprinted in India by K.N. Joglekar and Janki Prasad Bagerhatta and distributed at the Belgaum congress. For the full text of the original manifesto and the changes made therein see: Documents, Vol. II, pp.437-8.

133 David Petrie, op. cit., p.93.

134 ibid., p.97.
135 Bernard Isaacs, op. cit, p.227.
136 Bernard Isaacs, op. cit, p.227.
137 *Inprecor*, 18 April 1925.
138 ibid.
139 David Petrie, op. cit., pp.95-96
140 ibid., p.260.
141 David Petrie, op. cit., p.232.
142 ibid., p.233.
143 ibid.
144 ibid.
145 ibid., pp.233-4.
146 David Petrie, op, cit, p.237.
147 For an account of the proceedings of the Amsterdam meeting, see: R. W. Robson Report, *Documents*, Vol. II, pp.579-89.
148 David Petrie, op. cit., pp.260-1.
Glading met Lajpat Rai and Deoki Prasad Sinha in Delhi; I.B. Sen in Calcutta ; F.J. Ginwala, secretary of the Textile Union and R.B. Lotvala, secretary of the Free Press of India in Bombay.
149 ibid., p.96.
150 *Documents*, Vol. II, p.579.
151 David Petrie, op. cit, p.96.
152 *Documents*, Vol. II, p.583.
153 Horace Williamson, *India and Communism* (Reprint), Calcutta, 1976, p.145.
154 ibid., p.146.
155 ibid.
156 *Documents*, Vol. II, p.498.

4

India Accepts Marxism

Early in 1923, one Satya Bhakta arrived in Cawnpore from Central Province (now Madhya Pradesh) and opened a bookshop – Socialist Book Depot. Though he was not a professed marxist, he was in touch with Dange through correspondence and, on arriving at Cawnpore, he developed acquaintance with Usmani. In the same year in December, when Usmani was taken into custody, Satya Bhakta became a self-styled marxist. He began contributing articles to newspapers and issuing occasional leaflets with a marxist stance. From the proceedings of the Cawnpore Conspiracy case, he came to the conclusion that it was no offence to have faith in communism itself as long as there was no conspiracy to deprive the King Emperor of the sovereignty of British India. With this conclusion, Satya Bhakta, in August 1924, in an article for the *Aj*, a Hindi daily of Benaras, defined socialism as the panacea of all ills and proposed the formation of an Indian communist party. In the same article, he communicated a message to all persons interested in socialism to correspond with the manager of the Socialist Book Depot and announced that a public meeting would be convened to launch the party as and when sufficient numbers would be enrolled.[1] The quantum of response received is difficult to ascertain but, as proposed, on 1 September 1924, Satya Bhakta formally launched the Indian Communist Party, the first of its kind in India.[2]

The formation of the Indian Communist Party by Satya Bhakta was duly communicated to Roy by one J.P. Bagerhatta, a member of the all-India congress committee. Why and how Bagerhatta got interested in communism is anybody's guess, but soon after Satya Bhakta launched his party, he established contact with Roy. In an open letter to Roy, he expressed concern about the prospect of marxism in India and raised doubts as to the method adopted by him. 'I learn from the vernacular press of India,' wrote Bagerhatta, 'that you and your party have decided to propagate communism by illegal secret societies. I have always maintained that secret parties can do no real good to the country and that communism cannot be preached without open propaganda.... By secret method we can approach only a few educated men worth nothing in any political or economic activity.'[3] Roy appreciated the letter. He found its content interesting and wrote back, 'I will take liberty of publishing it in our paper over your signature. This will go to prove that we are not partisans of secret organisations, if the chance of open and legal activities is available.... The vernacular press from which you gather your information about the methods of our work must be badly informed. We do not propose to organise our party as a secret society.'[4] Following Bagerhatta's letter to Roy, Sipassi, a member of Roy's European bureau wrote in the same month to Hasrat Mohani, 'We are very desirous to know what is the status of the "Cawnpore Party". Is it, in reality, a revolutionary organisation or is it only so nominally?' Further, in the same letter, he assured Hasrat Mohani, 'If that party accept your leadership, assistance of every kind can be given in your name.'[5]

The news of the formation of the Indian Communist Party made Roy suspicious. In this modest attempt of Satya Bhakta, he found the support of the police. To know the real state of affairs and, if possible, to despatch a few youths to Moscow to study marxism, he sent Gopendra Krishna Chakravarty to India in June 1925.[6] Gopen, an active member of the *Anusilan Samiti*, was sent to Moscow by Nalini on his second visit to India.[7] The idea was to train Gopen in the marxist-leninist tactics of revolution and arrange his study of marxism at the University of the Toilers of the East. However, on grounds of mere suspicion, he could not be admitted to the university. No sooner did he arrive in Moscow, than a letter from the Dacca *Anusilan Samiti* reached the office of the Comintern, stating that he was not a trustworthy person and should not be granted any 'privileges or opportunities'. The letter was taken seriously and his admission to the university was barred. Cut off from everything, he was allowed to stay on in Moscow for nine months under observation and thereafter sent back to India.[8]

On his way back, Gopen stopped in Paris and met Sipassi, a member of the European bureau of the Indian marxists. Sipassi advised him to build an organization on his return to India and report to the European bureau.[9] As advised, on reaching India, Gopen re-established his contact with underground revolutionaries, particularly those belonging to the *Anusilan Samiti*, to propel them towards marxism in the hope to form a communist party under his aegis.

Soon after, the executive committee of the Young Communist International – the youth wing of the Comintern, addressed a special manifesto to the youth of India belonging to the underground revolutionary movement. The manifesto asked the revolutionary youth to shun individual terrorism and take the path of marxism-leninism to achieve a revolution. 'In spite of your heroic effort you have not been able to drive the foreign capitalists, you have not been able to obtain any considerable concession … It merely shows you have not yet learnt the proper methods to apply in the fight, you have not yet properly understood what social classes must conduct this fight to a victorious finish …. The role of the students is of exceptional value, you will fulfil your historic mission by carrying revolutionary ideas among the masses of the toilers, by developing their revolutionary consciousness, and by establishing a political organisation, which will include workers and peasants, i.e., the elements of the real struggle for the emancipation of India … We would advise you to adopt the programme drawn by comrade M.N. Roy for the national revolutionary movement in India.'[10] How far the manifesto helped Gopen or motivated the underground revolutionaries towards marxism-leninism is only a conjecture. But subsequent events show that a large number of underground revolutionaries did make an attempt to give effect to the manifesto. They first formed the Hindustan Socialist Republican Association and, thereafter, some of them joined the Communist Party of India, while continuing individual terrorism for quite some time.

Gopen did not fully come up to Roy's expectations. He could not send the promised report on the state of affairs in India, but succeeded in sending a youth, Akshay Kumar Shah, to Moscow to study at the University of the Toilers of the East.[11] Roy, thereupon, sent Jatin Mitra to India in November 1925, with instructions 'to expedite the matter of the despatch of the youths from India' and 'to find out everything about Satya Bhakta's party'.[12] Jatin let down Roy on both the counts. On reaching India, he not only forgot his mission, but also became rather hostile to Roy.

Bhakta's Indian Communist Party did not attract much attention, though he regularly published articles in newspapers and issued leaflets to propagate the party. At the annual session of the Congress at Belgaum, Bhakta distributed a leaflet giving an outline of the objectives of his party, its programme of work and its methods and principles, but nobody seemed to take any notice of it. After remaining dormant for about six months, Bhakta, as secretary of the Indian Communist Party, again issued a leaflet in June 1925, *The Future Programmes of the Indian Communist Party.*[13] The programmes included, among other things, the organization of the Indian peasants, labourers and other working class; total abolition of landlordism, fixing of minimum wages and maximum hours of labour; opening of a communist reading room in every city; and regular propaganda through the medium of newspapers. In the same leaflet, he justified the formation of the Indian Communist

Party on the grounds that the parties in existence would never be of any benefit to the masses, for they were all under the control of capitalists. If India achieves independence through the effort of these parties, it would be no better for the poor. The only difference would be that Indians would take the place of Englishmen and it was not certain that they would prove any better than their predecessors.[14] Soon thereafter, Bhakta decided to hold an open conference of the Indian Communist Party. He convened a meeting of his associates to select a president and decide the venue and time of the conference. The meeting was chaired by Hasrat Mohani. It decided to hold the conference at Cawnpore during the Christmas week, simultaneously with the annual session of the Indian National Congress, and sent a request to Shapurji Saklatvala to become the president. The question of affiliation of the party with the Third International also came up, but opinions differed and no decision could be taken.[15]

The conference, as scheduled, was held in Cawnpore, but not in the Congress *pandal*. The bloc of delegates with supposedly communist sympathies frightened the Congress authorities. To save the Congress from the communists, the authorities refused permission to hold the conference in the Congress *pandal*. The communists thereupon held their conference on a plot of land 'in an old tent of miserable dimension dimly lit by a few oil lamps'.[16] Saklatvala could not come but sent a message stating, 'Although owing to programme of business on this side I shall not be at your conference, I shall be with you in spirit and hope that the conference will be the beginning of a large and stable communist movement in India.'[17]

In the absence of Saklatvala, Singaravelu became the president and Hasrat Mohani, chairman of the reception committee. In his presidential address, Singaravelu made a startling observation, 'Indian communism is not bolshevism, for, bolshevism is a form of communism which the Russians have adopted in their country. We are not Russian bolsheviks and bolshevism may not be needed in India …. We are one with the world communists but not with bolsheviks.'[18] Hasrat Mohani, in his speech, not only echoed the same sentiment, but also went a step further when he said, 'Our organisation is purely Indian. It is necessary to mention that at least for the present the work for our party will be restricted to India alone. Our relations with similar parties of other countries will be only that of sympathy and mental affinity to all these in general and to the Third International in particular. We are only fellow travellers in our paths and not their subordinates.'[19]

The session of the Indian Communist Party was held for three days from 25 to 27 December 1925. It was attended by about 500 delegates, of whom ninety per cent were of the labouring and cultivating classes.[20] The conference was not a smooth affair; dissensions arose from the very outset. Satya Bhakta and his associates considered the conference as their achievement, which Muzaffar Ahmed, S.V. Ghate, K.N. Joglekar, J.P. Bagerhatta and others of their group refused to accept. The matter came to pass when on the second day of the conference, Muzaffar and his group mooted the suggestion to change the name of the Indian Communist Party to the Communist Party of India, much to the annoyance of Satya Bhakta and his associates. Finding himself in a minority, Satya Bhakta left the conference in a huff, followed by his group. Singaravelu tried to mediate, but to no avail. Muzaffar and his group called it a day.

After the voluntary exit of Satya Bhakta and his group, the proceedings of the conference became smooth. Without opposition, the name of the party was changed as proposed; a provisional constitution was adopted; a central executive committee was formed; and the headquarters of the party was shifted from Cawnpore to Bombay.[21] The only question that remained undecided was the affiliation of the party with the Communist International.

Though Satya Bhakta left the conference in the midst of the sessions, his name was included in the central executive committee, which might be an act of pacification. But the honest gesture did not make any difference. Satya Bhakta resigned from the party and, within four days, formed a new party of his own, the National Communist Party, supported by his group comprising Hasrat Mohani and Radha Mohan Gokulji.[22] A few days later, Satya Bhakta wrote to Singaravelu,

'The reason of my resignation is a fundamental one. I am of the opinion of keeping Indian communists separate from international communists and had always vigorously opposed all such proposals favouring international connections coming from any quarter.'[23] Satya Bhakta's National Communist Party was a party in mere name. By 1927, for all intents and purposes, it was defunct.[24] Satya Bhakta thereafter ceased to be active in politics. Long afterwards, while writing his autobiography, Satya Bhakta remembered the day when he was obliged to quit the communist conference at Cawnpore: 'In reality I felt least dissatisfaction or regret when the communist party was captured by others. Though I had taken up the work inspired by my inner urge, the lack of resources and continual obstacles placed in my way by the government was a great strain on me, I felt exhausted. I was against securing financial aid by irregular means either in the country or from abroad. I myself wanted that some others should take up the responsibility of the work and relieve me.'[25]

Roy came to know all about the Cawnpore conference and the manoeuvres of the communists through a communication from Bagerhatta. He was taken aback. In his opinion, it was a premature move on the part of the comrades to form an open communist party in India. He firmly believed that in the given circumstances, no genuine communist party could legally be formed in India. He was still harping on his original idea of two parties – a peoples' party with radical programmes to fight for national liberation as a partner of a united front and an illegal communist party within it. But from the report of Bagerhatta, he could see that all the four major communist groups in India from Calcutta, Bombay, Madras and Lahore attended the conference and occupied key positions in the central executive committee of the party. He developed an ambivalent attitude towards the new party. However, he thought it prudent not to neglect or remain indifferent to the matter. He accepted the new party as *fait accompli*. In his letter to Bagerhatta, he asked his Indian comrades to affiliate the new party with the Communist International and send a delegation at the next congress of the Comintern.[26] In the same letter, after extending the usual advice regarding programmes and tactics to be followed by communists, he expressed his concern about the new party and asked the comrades to remain vigilant. 'It is only on consequence of accidental combinations of events,' wrote Roy, 'that attempts to organise a legal communist party are tolerated by our rulers. We must not have illusion on that score. We must be prepared for the attack any moment and organise the party in such a way that an attack on legality will not destroy the party.'[27] While appreciating the manoeuvre of his comrades, Roy took up for no reason a cudgel against Satya Bhakta for his conception of an Indian Communist Party. Satya Bhakta retaliated and the matter ended in mudslinging, each calling the other a government agent.

Like Satya Bhakta, Gopen Chakravarty, after doing some spade work among the underground revolutionaries and with the help of Jatin Mitra, Dharanikanta Goswami and a few others, sat in a meeting at Calcutta from 16 to 18 April 1926 and declared it a conference of the Communist Party of India.[28] The idea behind the move was to impress upon the European bureau that a party had been formed, as well as to secure financial assistance. Those present in the conference expressed anguish and indignation at Roy's failure in sending money and decided to write a 'stiff letter'. Accordingly, Jatin Mitra wrote to Sipassi: 'You people do not realise our difficulties here .... The boss (Roy) and family are living as princes... and the boys here – real, sincere workers – are starving. You hypocrites mean no business; you are simply exploiters. Your behaviour has created such a bad atmosphere against you that now, except a few of us, all in the Punjab, U.P., Bombay and Bengal are losing confidence in you.'[29]

After perusing the letter, Roy regretted the creation of this atmosphere of 'disgust and mistrust'. In a letter to Mitra, he assured continued cooperation for ideological and tactical guidance, but gave a cold shoulder with regard to financial assistance. 'We consider our relation is and must be primarily political. It would be a great mistake on your part to look upon us as your financial agents.... It will lead to endless misunderstanding and mistrust, which will only harm the work in which we are interested.'[30] He then went on to say that the Indian communist group abroad was a body for making political and ideological contribution to the proletarian movement in India and should not be regarded as a reservoir from which funds could be drawn. Lastly, he advised Mitra that, henceforth, with regard to financial matters, all correspondence should be addressed to the Communist International.[31]

Interestingly, when the marxists in India formed the Communist Party, in Europe, Roy and the Communist Party of Great Britain were vying with each other for the privilege of directing the communist movement in India. Since the Amsterdam meeting, Roy and the Communist Party of Great Britain had maintained an uneasy truce. But by the beginning of 1926, disagreements cropped up once again over the strategy to be followed by the communists in India. Roy and the Communist Party of Great Britain opened the campaign by publishing their views in their respective journals, as well as in the official Comintern publication till such time they concretised their conceptions in two books: *The Future of Indian Politics* by M.N. Roy and *Modern India* by R. Palme Dutt, representing the views of the Communist Party of Great Britain. Both the books were published in 1926, almost simultaneously, and made an attempt to analyse the class process in India and outline the strategy to be followed by the communists.

In *The Future of Indian Politics*, Roy resumed his attack on the Indian bourgeoisie by exposing its dubious role in the freedom struggle. He asserted: 'The bourgeois bloc seeks to make a united front with the imperialist forces of law and order to make the country safe against any possible revolution. The middle class, which still makes the show of parliamentary fight, is in hopeless political bankruptcy.... The future of Indian politics will, therefore, be determined by the social forces which still remain and will always remain antagonistic to imperialism even in the new era dominated by the higher ideals of *swaraj* within the Empire. These social forces are composed of the workers, peasantry and the petty bourgeoisie.'[32] With the change of the social base, Roy envisaged that a new class alignment would take place, and change both the leadership and the organizational form. 'The social elements that will henceforth compose the movement for national liberation,' wrote Roy, 'are petty intellectuals, artisans, small traders, peasantry and the proletariat. In the existing condition of Indian society, these all belong to the oppressed and exploited class. The movement for national liberation will take place on the basis of the struggle between the exploiting and the exploited classes. Henceforth, the fight for national freedom in India will become class struggle approximating to the final stage.'[33]

After having dealt with the strategy, Roy turned to tactics. He argued that the Indian National Congress would not serve the purpose of liberating the country from foreign yoke. It was, therefore, necessary to form a mass party wherein all anti-imperialist elements minus the bourgeoisie would rally for the struggle for independence. 'The people's fight for freedom,' wrote Roy, 'must be led by the party of the people – a party organisation which will be broad enough for all the forces of national revolution. The proletariat will be in it, but it will not be a proletariat party, nominally or essentially. In this party, the proletariat will stand side by side with the petty bourgeois and peasant masses, as the most advanced democratic class.'[34]

R. Palme Dutt's *Modern India* was, in many ways, similar to Roy's *The Future of Indian Politics*. But unlike Roy, Dutt was not prepared to write off the bourgeoisie as an *unrevolutionary* class. He agreed with Roy that 'The Indian bourgeoisie is today a counter-revolutionary force: They fear the social revolution that would follow on national independence more than they desire independence; and, therefore, they have made their terms with the imperialists and are all supporters of the Empire.'[35] Yet, while advocating for a united front, Dutt included the bourgeoisie. 'The fight for national liberation,' wrote Dutt, 'is a fight for many social strata – of workers, of peasants, of the lower middle class, of the intelligentsia and even of a section of the bourgeois.'[36]

With regard to tactics too, Dutt differed from Roy, but only marginally. He also preferred a people's party, but not immediately, as demanded by Roy. Dutt was prepared to wait for the development of a new situation. 'When the time comes,' wrote Dutt, 'the new forces will have to find their form of organisation and expression.

It is a matter of indifference how this will arise, whether through the existing forms of the Congress and the Swaraj Party or by a combination of these and other elements.'[37] But he agreed with Roy that 'only a new national movement, based on the workers and peasants, and with a political and social programme expressing the interest of the masses, can bring new life'.[38]

The duel between Roy and the Communist Party of Great Britain was a futile exercise. Both the parties were trying to seize the booty before the battle had begun. The Communist Party of India at that time was in its embryonic stage, consisting of hardly a dozen people.

Along with *The Future of Indian Politics*, Roy, on behalf of the Communist Party of India, prepared a manifesto to be distributed at the Gauhati session of the Congress. In the manifesto, Roy criticized the Congress and the Swaraj Party for their policies and programmes, as well as their incapacity to lead the country to independence. Once again, he emphasized the formation of a people's party as the panacea for national liberation. 'The movement for national liberation,' said Roy, 'can be led to victory only by a party of the people. Unless it is led by a party which acts according to a clearly defined programme, the nationalist movement will be floundering like a rudderless ship.... The nationalist movement loses all meaning if its object is not to secure national freedom.'[39] The manifesto failed to have any impact on the bourgeois leaders. Roy's advice to the Congress to adopt a mass-oriented programme to come closer to the people fell on deaf ears.

Though the manifesto failed to have the desired effect, the speech delivered by Bhupendra Nath Dutta as president of the political sufferers' conference, held simultaneously with the Congress session, gave a fillip to communist activity in India. In the course of his speech, Dutta criticized the Congress as a worn-out organization, representing only a small section of people, and emphasized the need to organize the masses on the basis of socioeconomic programmes, while urging the poor middle class to give up the petty bourgeois mentality and cast its lot with the fate of toilers.[40] Dutta was a marxist but not a member of the Communist Party of India. His speech was hailed by communists for its marxist overtones. Roy appreciated the speech too. In his opinion, it was 'far in advance of anything said by other political leaders'.[41]

When Roy and the Communist Party of Great Britain were at loggerheads, George Allison, alias Donald Campbell, arrived in India on behalf of the Communist Party of Great Britain to organize labour unions along revolutionary lines and get Indian communists in touch with their British counterparts. For a few months, Allison worked silently, establishing contact with communists and trade union leaders, but by August, he came into the open and published a few articles on trade unionism in the *Indian National Herald*, Bombay, edited by B.G. Horniman. In November, he left Bombay for Calcutta with a letter of introduction from K.N. Joglekar addressed to Muzaffar Ahmed.[42] In Calcutta, just when he came into prominence as a trade unionist, he was put under arrest on the charge of forgery and breach of passport rules. On the expiry of his detention term, he was deported from India and sent to Marseilles.[43]

Within two years of Allison's visit, a host of emissaries came to India, either on behalf of the Communist Party of Great Britain or on their own, to help the communists organize the proletariats as a viable group, in the form of trade unions, and workers and peasants parties for national liberation, either within the Congress or outside it. Prominent among them were Philip Spratt, Sapurji Saklatvala and Benjamin Francis Bradley.

Philip Spratt, a young man in his mid-twenties, landed in Bombay on 30 December 1926 on behalf of the Communist Party of Great Britain as a representative of a firm of booksellers. His job, as he said, 'was to be that of a messenger and reporter'.[44] But, actually, his mission was to help Allison in his attempt to form trade unions, and workers and peasants parties, and advise the communists on organizational matters. On reaching India, he established contact with communists without delay and set to work. The arrest and deportation of Allison did not matter much to him. An able and dedicated worker, he brought new enthusiasm to the trade union movement and party work.

Within a few days of Spratt's arrival, Sapurji Saklatvala arrived in India and took the urban elite by storm, much to the discomfort of British authorities and bourgeois national leaders. Saklatvala, a member of the British Parliament on a communist ticket, came to India not as an emissary of the Communist Party of Great Britain, but on his own. His visit was not so much to spread communism, but to convince labour leaders to adopt an international outlook. During his short stay in India, he addressed large meetings in Bombay, Calcutta, Madras, Delhi and a few other places, advocating 'communism as the panacea of India's multifarious ills and repeatedly lauded the Soviet Union as a model of good government and an example of the success of the proletariat's effort to manage their own affairs'.[45] Saklatvala's campaign stirred the imagination of the intelligentsia, but his frequent, contemptuous reference to Gandhi proved somewhat unproductive. He entered into a lengthy correspondence with Gandhi in an effort to convince him that his economic theories were reactionary and his spiritual leadership was degenerative. He told Gandhi that by playing the role of a *mahatma*, he was ruining the mentality and psychology of the people, particularly of the villagers. 'Politically this career of yours is ruinous,' said Saklatvala, 'and from a humanitarian point of view its degenerating influence appears to me to be a moral plague.'[46] Saklatvala made a good impression in the political circle. His speeches were extensively reported in the press and he was accorded a hearty welcome wherever he went.

Though himself a communist, he did not get on well initially with the communists in India and treated them somewhat cavalierly, because the Communist Party of India was not affiliated with the Comintern. In his opinion, it was 'an unrepresentative body infested by spies and agents-provocator'.[47] His attitude towards the Communist Party of India created a lot of ill feeling among the comrades. But before he left India, his attitude had changed and he summoned the Indian comrades to Delhi, discussed party matters with them and came to a working understanding. Interestingly, the meeting of the communists in Delhi was held at the Arya Samaj Temple in Chawribazar, presided by Muzaffar Ahmed.[48] Saklatvala sailed for England on 9 April 1927, carrying with him an overall view of the Indian political situation. Much impressed, he intended to return to India the following October to take active part in Indian politics, but he was refused visa by the British government. He was a communist; besides, he was known for his frequently uncharitable remarks. Once in the course of a discussion, he scornfully commented that the Union Jack was a 'wretched rag' and an 'emblem of slavery'. It created an uproar in the British parliament.[49]

In September 1927, the Communist Party of Great Britain sent Benjamin Francis Bradley as an emissary. This was Bradley's second visit to India. Earlier, around 1921-22, he had come to India as a government employee to work in an arms factory in Peshawar and had stayed for nine months. But this second visit was for a different mission: to help Spratt in his work under the guise of a representative of his brothers' firm – The Crab Underdrain Tiles and Company. Bradley stayed in India for eight years and worked mainly in trade unions, as along with taking part in the formation of workers and peasants parties, in close cooperation with his comrades in India.

Apart from the above emissaries, a few others, viz., Hugh Lester Hutchinson, Fazal Elahi alias Qurban, J.F. Rayn and J.W. Johnson, also came to India and did useful work. Under their able guidance, particularly that of Spratt and Bradley, the movement gathered momentum. The impact was felt in the organization of workers and peasants parties and the trade union movement.

About the time the Communist Party of Great Britain sent Spratt to India, the Comintern sent Roy to China as the head of a delegation to implement its China policy, framed at the seventh plenum of the executive committee.

The absence of Roy from Europe gave the Communist Party of Great Britain a free hand in Indian affairs. Under its guidance, the communist movement gathered momentum in India. From a group of barely a dozen people, it grew into a party under the cover of workers and peasants parties, and youth and trade union organizations.

About two months before the Cawnpore conference of Satya Bhakta's Indian Communist Party, on 1 November 1925, a workers and peasants party was formed in Bengal, in conformity with Roy's ideas. It was named *Bharatiya Jatiya Mahasamitir Shramik-Praja-Swaraj Dal* or the Labour Swaraj Party of the Indian National Congress. The persons who took the initiative were not all marxists, but had sympathy with the peasants and workers. Prominent among them were Qutubuddin Ahmed, Qazi Nazrul Islam, Shamsuddin Hussain, Abdul Halim and Hemanta Kumar Sarkar.[50] The aim of the new party was to organize the peasants and workers of Bengal to make them conscious of 'their political rights and wrest freedom from unwilling hands of vested interest by their own right and for their own interest'.[51] Within four months from the date of its foundation, the party changed its name to Peasants' and Workers' Party of Bengal at a conference of the *Nikhil Bangiya Praja Sammelan* held at Krishnanagar on 6 February 1926 and, still later at the third conference from 31 March to 1 April 1928, the name of the party was finally changed to Workers' and Peasants' Party. To propagate the ideology, the party brought out a weekly in Bengali, *Langal*, whose name was later changed to *Ganavani*.[52]

The news of the formation of the Peasants' and Workers' Party and the issue of the Bengali weekly reached Roy in due course. In this modest achievement, he found the crystallization of political ideas and ideologies, and considered it an epoch-making incident. In his journal, *The Masses of India*, he wrote: 'Nothing is more important than to give an adequate and faithful political expression of the grievances and demand of the peasantry.... The objective demand of the peasantry is not reform but revolution.... We are anxious to see that *Langal* creditably discharges its historic mission.'[53] Roy's hopes did not come true. The Workers' and Peasants' Party of Bengal failed to come up as a political force in India. It was confined to Calcutta, with only one branch at Mymansingh. 'Its membership at any point of time, did not exceed more than forty.'[54] The reason for its failure was the inability of its leaders to forge ahead, as well as the paucity of funds. But from 1927 onwards, the movement started growing and workers and peasants parties were set up in Bombay, the Punjab and the United Province, and they finally crystallized into an all-India Workers' and Peasants' Party.

As in Bengal, in Bombay, a party of peasants and workers evolved out of the Congress Labour Party, which had been in existence since 1925. In February 1927, at a meeting of the Congress Labour Party in Bombay, the name of the Congress Labour Party was changed to the Workers' and Peasants' Party of Bombay.[55] Dhundiraj Thangdi became its president and S.S. Mirajkar, its secretary; S.V. Ghate, S.H. Jhabvala, Lalji Pande, K.N. Joglekar, R.S. Nimbkar and J.B. Patel formed the executive committee.[56] The aim of the party was 'to free the Congress from the narrow shackle of class interests, and to yoke it to the task of attaining national freedom from the imperialist bondage, as a step towards complete emancipation of the masses from exploitation and oppression'.[57] The work of the party was confined to organizing industrial workers and appealing to the Congress to adopt a radical programme. To propagate the ideology, the party brought out a weekly in Marathi, *Kranti*, under the guidance of an editorial board.

In the Punjab, the initiative was taken by Abdul Mazeed, Santokh Singh, Sohan Singh Josh, Bhag Singh Canadian, Feroz Mansoor and a few others. Their party, *Kirti-Kishan Party*, was formed in December 1927. Subsequently, its name was changed to the Workers' and Peasants' Party of the Punjab and it had its first all-Punjab conference in April 1928. The aim of the party was to liberate workers and peasants from exploitation of every kind and establish a socialist republic. By and large, the activities of the party were limited to organizing peasants and pressing for their demands, including the abolition of intermediaries and the reduction of rent. The party brought out a bi-monthly, *Kranti*, published simultaneously in Punjabi and Urdu. The editor of the Punjabi edition was Sohan Singh Josh, while that of the Urdu one was Feroz Mansoor.

In the United Province, around 1925, two parties were formed almost simultaneously to take care of workers and peasants' demands. One was founded by B. Mukherjee, *Kishan and Mazdoor Sabha;* while the other was formed by Gauri Sankar, *Mazdoor and Kishan Sangh*. Both the parties worked under the Congress and had hardly any independent view. In October 1928, Gauri Sankar and his associates convened a conference of the *Mazdoor and Kishan Sangh* at Meerut, in which, besides Spratt, Muzaffar, Abdul Majid, Sohan Singh Josh and K.N. Sehgal, members of the *Kishan and Mazdoor Sabha* also participated. It was at this conference that both the parties combined and formed the Workers' and Peasants' Party of the United Province, with branches in Delhi, Jhansi and Gorakhpur. B. Mukherjee became the president and P.C. Joshi assumed the role of the secretary of the party. To popularize its views, the party brought out a monthly in Hindi, *Krantikari*.

The workers and peasants' parties in different provinces did not have a centralized leadership or coordinated action. The leaders often corresponded with one another to formulate a common policy for unified action with vague and diffused ideas, but never acted in a concerted way. Initially, they began their work from within the Congress as its left wing, with little or no say in policy matters. They preferred collaboration with the Congress to acting independently. But soon there came a change. Gradually, for all practical purposes, the workers and peasants' parties became the political projection of the Communist Party of India. All appeals, manifestoes and literature prepared by the communists were projected through the workers and peasants' parties. 'What we used to decide in the Communist Party,' writes Muzaffar, 'was actually put into practice from the platform of the workers' and peasants' parties. The leaflets of the party were all drafted by the central committee of the communist party.'[58] In fact, the communists failed to draw a line of demarcation between the workers and peasants parties and the Communist Party of India.

About the time workers and peasants parties were coming up in different provinces, Roy returned from China. He addressed a letter to his comrades in India to reopen his suspended contact.[59]

The letter, among other things, gave an outline of his plan of action. It laid down in brief the aims and objectives of the workers and peasants parties; how they should be organised; what should be their relationship with the communist party and the Comintern; and lastly, broached the topic of their affiliation with the League Against Imperialism.

From the letter it appears that Roy, though away in China, was aware of the activities of communists vis-à-vis workers and peasants parties in India. 'There seems to be some confusion,' wrote Roy, 'about the existence of two parties. Some comrades at home appear to think that the formation of WPP [workers and peasants parties] means liquidation of CP [Communist Party]. It is not true. We do not propose the liquidation of the CP .... The WPP is not and should not be merely a legal cover of CP .... We proposed the formation of WPP as a much broader organisation. It should be the rallying ground of the exploited social elements (proletariat, peasantry and petty-bourgeois) which must unite themselves in a revolutionary struggle against foreign and native reaction .... The communists should be in the WPP and, by virtue of their being the conscious vanguard of the working class, will be the driving force of the party .... The WPP is distinct from the CP in that its programme is not a communist programme, its programme is the programme of domestic revolution which includes realisation of the minimum political and economic demands of the workers and peasants.'[60] After expressing his views on the aims and objectives of workers and peasants parties and their proposed relationship with the communist party, Roy reminded his comrades in India,: 'It is high time for the WPP to have a national organisation and a national CC [central committee]. The situation is very favourable to convene a congress for the formation of the WPP on national scale' and that the party 'should affiliate itself with the League Against Imperialism.'[61]

Coincidentally, in December 1927, at the Madras session of the Congress, the leaders of the various workers and peasants parties gathered together and decided to hold an all-India conference in

Calcutta some time in 1928 to launch a workers and peasants party on a national scale, as envisaged by Roy.

The all-India conference of the Workers' and Peasants' Party was held in Calcutta from 21 to 24 November 1928 under the presidentship of Sohan Singh Josh.[62] The conference was attended by about 300 delegates from all over the country. Spratt, Bradley and Rayan, who had come to India as emissaries to help communists in their attempt to form a mass party of the people and turn the trade union movement towards revolutionary nationalism, were also present.

However, the all-India Workers' and Peasants' Party failed to come up to the expectations of the communists. Though the party was formed on a pan-India scale with a national executive committee, the provincial parties maintained their separate identities and continued to work as before, ignoring the national executive.[63] Along with the Workers' and Peasants' Party conference, the communists, on the second day of the session, sat in a separate meeting to discuss the party programme, but without any result. Muzaffar Ahmed, Dharani Goswami, Gopen Chakravarty, Shamsul Huda – all started quarrelling on personal issues. The only tangible decision taken was that the party headquarters should be shifted from Calcutta to Bombay.[64]

Meanwhile, along with the formation of workers and peasants parties, the communists took the initiative to organize the youth. Underground revolutionaries brought youth into revolutionary politics, but never made any attempt to build a mass youth organization. The dare-devilry of underground revolutionary youth was often admired, but no one had thought of organizing an open mass political party of the youth. It was the communists who introduced the youth to the marxist-leninist theory of revolution and organized it into a party.

The first youth organization seemed to have come into existence in Bengal in 1927 under the name All Bengal Youths Association. It was an organization with a nationalist orientation, confined to paper, with little or no impact on the politics of the country. But early in 1928, the young communists in touch with the Workers' and Peasants' Party of Bengal organized the youth into a party, the Young Comrades League – a name supposed to have been suggested by Saklatvala."[65] The initiative was taken by Gopal Basak, Gopen Chakravarty, Dharani Goswami and a few others. From its very inception, the league was closely associated with the Communist Party of India and the Workers' and Peasants' Party of Bengal. Four out of the seven members of the executive committee of the league were members of the Workers' and Peasants' Party of Bengal.[66] The objective of the league was to organize a radical and militant movement of the youth on the basis of marxist-leninist ideology to help the people, i.e., workers and peasants, in their struggle against the existing capitalist order and establish an independent republic of India on the basis of the socioeconomic emancipation of the masses.[67]

As in Bengal, the left-oriented youth part of the underground revolutionaries in Punjab, and inspired by Sardar Bhagat Singh, formed a youth organization – *Naujan Bharat Sabha* – in 1926. Till 1927, it functioned as a debating society of the revolutionary youth of the Punjab, but in 1928 when the *sabha* came in contact with the Workers' and Peasants' Party of Punjab, it became a broad-based organization of the youth. In April 1928, it called its first conference and opened a few branches in Punjab, mainly to recruit youth for underground revolutionary work. The aim of the *sabha* was to imbue a sense of patriotism and a spirit of sacrifice among the youth, as well as to propagate socialism as propounded by Marx and Lenin.

A youth organization also came up in Bombay. In January 1928, the Workers' and Peasants' Party of Bombay adopted a resolution 'to support such youth organisations consistently participating in militant mass activities'.[68] Soon thereafter, an organization – Bombay Presidency Youth League – was formed by the youth of Bombay with left leanings, but little to do with the left movement. It was towards the close of 1929 or at the beginning of 1930 that the communists in Bombay succeeded in organizing a youth organization of their own

– Young Workers' League – which drew the youth of Bombay to the arena of politics, inspired by marxist-leninist ideas of revolution.

Along with workers and peasants parties and youth movements, the communists in India made some headway in the trade union movements too. Before the First World War, there was no trade union movement worth its salt in India. Only individual humanitarians made some attempt to ameliorate the inhuman conditions of industrial workers.[69] The first philanthropist to take up the cause of industrial workers was S.S. Bengalee, who around the 1870s started an agitation to draw the attention of the authorities towards the pitiable condition of industrial workers. Bengalee was followed by N.M. Lokhande, who was himself an industrial worker. In 1890, Lokhande formed an association of the Bombay mill workers called the Bombay Mill Hands Association, with himself as president and one D.C. Athalye as secretary. After that, quite a few associations sprung up under different leaderships, but none of these organizations, in the proper sense of the term, can be called a trade union. Loosely organized, they lacked radicalism, as they relied more on peaceful methods than on an agitational approach. Trade unionism became an organized movement with the formation of the all-India Trade Union Congress in 1920, but its method of working remained the same as before. Lala Lajpat Rai, Dewan Chaman Lal, V.V. Giri and the new leaders occasionally resorted to the use of militant phraseology but, when necessary, they did not go beyond peaceful or constitutional methods. Though Dange, Singaravelu and a few other marxists had joined the movement by then and had attended the first conference of the all-India Trade Union Congress, their presence was not discernible. Marxists were still very few in number and were not too clear about their role in the trade unions. There came a change when the fourth congress of the Comintern sent a telegram to the Lahore session of the all-India Trade Union Congress, asking it not to restrict the working class movement to 'a fair day's wage for a fair day's work', but to bring the trade union movement under marxian influence; organize it on class basis and 'purge it of all alien elements'. Following this telegram, Roy made it known to the marxists that 'The task before the trade union congress is not reform but revolution. It is not conservative trade unionism based upon [the] bankrupt theory of "collective bargain", but revolutionary mass action involving the pauperised peasantry as well as the city and rural wage-earners and led by those who want to see that India enter upon a period of social progress. The trade union congress must free itself from the leadership which believes in piecemeal reform.'[70] Roy further said, 'Our object is the economic freedom of the producing classes. This ultimate goal will be attained after a long and bitter struggle. Therefore, our primary task is to organise the masses and lead them in the struggle for economic freedom.'[71]

In the dictum of communists, the trade union movement ought to be based on the principle of class struggle. The struggle of the working class should not be confined to mere economic interest of the workers, it must be extended to the social and political life of the country. In fact, trade unions are not merely organizations of the working class, but organized bodies of all the oppressed people for the abolition of the capitalist system, with the working class in the forefront. On the other hand, non-communists believed that the purpose of the trade union movement was to defend the economic interest of the working class through collective bargain, for which the unity and solidarity of the working class was essential, but there was no place for class struggle.

The communists failed to come up to Roy's expectations. The trade union movement continued to be guided by conservative leaders who believed in collective bargain for economic betterment of the working class, keeping them away from nationalist politics. But from 1926 onwards, with the arrival of foreign emissaries, the communists, as planned, made inroads into trade union movements to give it a new direction. 'We felt,' wrote Bradley, 'that if the workers' position was to be improved and a sound trade union movement built up, it was essential to attack and overthrow the leadership of the reformists in the trade unions.'[72]

The communists started their work in right earnest. In 1927, there were eleven registered unions with 45,253 members, but by 1929, the number of registered unions rose to forty-two with 1,53,463 members.[73] Along with the increase in the number of unions and membership, the number of strikes in the industrial establishments also rose. Though the chief centre of the strikes was Bombay, they spread all over the country. The issue was usually wage cut and unemployment in the name of rationalization.

With the growth of the trade union movement, the question of its affiliation with an international organization also came up. At the Cawnpore conference of the all-India Trade Union Congress, the question of international affiliation became an important one. The moderates wanted the trade union congress to affiliate with the International Federation of Trade Unions, but the communists, who had become sufficiently strong by then, wanted the trade union congress to affiliate with the Red International of Labour Unions. A deadlock ensued and after several skirmishes, the idea of international affiliation was dropped for the time being.[74]

The growing influence of communists on the trade union movement worried the colonial rulers. To stem the tide, in May 1927, the government prohibited the import into India of any publication or documents issued by or emanating from the Communist International or any organization affiliated to or connected with it.[75]

As stated earlier, in 1925, the Communist Party of Great Britain had planned an oriental conference and sat in a meeting at Amsterdam to discuss the modalities for it. But as it happened, the meeting was a fiasco. Roy opposed the proposal and showed resentment towards British interference in Indian affairs. Taking advantage of Roy's absence in China, the Communist Party of Great Britain revived the plan once again. They called a conference of colonized countries at Brussels to organize an anti-imperialist front with branches all over the world to protect colonial people from imperialist oppression.[76] Towards the end of 1926, the Communist Party of Great Britain sent invitations to prominent political leaders, newspaper editors and trade union activists all across the colonial world, including India. The Indians who took part in the planning of the conference included, among others, Chattopadhyaya, Roy's old rival, and Saklatvala. The proposed oriental conference, then named 'the Congress of the Oppressed Nationalities', was held at Brussels with great fanfare from 10 to 15 February 1927. It was attended by 175 delegates from 37 countries.[77]

The high hopes with which the conference was organized remained unfulfilled. But out of the deliberations, an organization – the League Against Imperialism – emerged.[78] The impact of the conference on the imperialists was minimal, and as far as the oppressed people of India were concerned, it was of no utility. Indian and Chinese delegates decided to fight imperialism jointly and to open branches in each other's country for better coordination, but nothing came out of it.[79]

A few months after the Brussels conference, around May 1927, Soumendranath Tagore, a member of the executive committee of the Workers' and Peasants' Party of Bengal left for Europe to explore the possibility of establishing direct contact with the Comintern to end the via-media of Roy. Tagore arrived in Moscow in June and, shortly thereafter, met Ossip Piatnitsky, the treasurer of the Comintern. In the course of his discussion, Tagore dispelled Piatnitsky's illusion about the communist movement in India. He contradicted Roy's supposed claim that there were hundreds of communists in India; in his opinion, there were not more than a dozen. Tagore lamented that the communist movement could not take off in India due to the lack of funds and literature.[80] He also made two allegations against Roy: that he had misled the Comintern about the reach of the communist movement in India and that he had embezzled Comintern's funds to the detriment of the communist movement in India.

There might have been some truth in Tagore's allegation about the scope of the communist movement in India, but the allegation that he had embezzled Comintern's funds was a mere conjecture, based on hearsay. There is no evidence to show as to how much money was sanctioned and released by the Comintern to propagate marxism in India. The only evidence available with us is a letter of March 1924, wherein Roy informed Evelyn that 'almost unlimited funds have become available'.[81] The letter of March 1924 seems to have been based on a proposal made by the Third International to the politburo in December 1923 that the adjoining Central Eastern Section should be allotted a sum of 10,000,000 gold roubles for propaganda, out of which 5,000,000 should be set apart for India.[82] But there is no evidence to show that the proposal was given effect, or if so, how much of the sanctioned amount was released and placed in the hands of Roy. Roy's lifestyle in India or the assets left behind by him on his death did not speak of his affluence. Nevertheless, Tagore succeeded in making a dent in Roy's political career.

While Tagore was appraising Piatnitsky about the failure of Roy, communists in India met in a conference in Bombay from 29 to 31 May 1927 to adopt a new constitution and form a presidium and an executive committee.[83] The party also adopted a programme whose objectives included achieving complete national independence, abolishing landlordism, striving for a democratic republic based on adult suffrage, nationalizing public utilities, limiting work to eight hours a day and fixing minimum wages as a basis for cooperation with radical nationalists.[84] As a matter of strategy, the communists resolved to work from within the Indian National Congress as its left wing, and to cooperate with the radical nationalists so as to force the Congress to adopt programmes based on democratic principles suited to the needs of the toiling masses of India.[85]

Soon after Tagore met Piatnitsky, Roy returned to Moscow from China. There he met Tagore and came to know all about his discussion with Piatnitsky. Though alarmed, he did not react adversely, except asking Tagore to return to India, while he himself left for Berlin. In Moscow, Roy found the situation grave. The long-drawn struggle between Stalin and Trotsky was reaching its climax. He and Borodin had come back from China with disgrace, but the circumstances helped them salvage their political career at least for the time being.[86] Stalin defended the China policy of the Comintern and put the blame on the Communist Party of China for the debacle. On the roles of Roy and Borodin, Stalin maintained diplomatic silence. He neither accused nor exonerated them for their failure.

Stalin's cool and calculated move gave Roy the illusion of exoneration from the responsibility of the China debacle. Despite Tagore's accusations and his failure in China, Roy was confident of his future. Stalin was his friend and, in his estimation, he had reciprocated the friendship well. This was a miscalculation. In politics, friendship is a matter of convenience, always transitory and never perpetual. Roy, with all his experience in politics, failed to understand this reality of political friendship. He arrived in Moscow to attend the ninth plenum of the executive committee of the Comintern. This was his last visit to the dreamland of marxist revolutionaries across the world.

Roy arrived in Moscow on 4 February 1928 and attended the opening session of the plenum on 9 February. On 22 February, he developed a serious infection in his ears and had to be in bed under medical advice. He could not attend the subsequent plenum meeting. His absence from the meeting gave rise to rumours that his illness was politically motivated. However, his friends in Berlin were worried. One of them came over to Moscow and secretly rescued him to Berlin. Under proper medical care, Roy recovered from the illness.

In 1920, when Roy had arrived in Moscow, he was given a hearty welcome, received with respect and escorted to the 'Gutchkov Mansion' in a large black limousine – he was a state guest. But in 1928, when he left Moscow stealthily, being scared for his life, he became a *persona non grata*.

No sooner did Roy leave Moscow than the Comintern began to veer around his views. It all started with an article by Eugene Varga, who dismissed Roy's assertion of the industrialization of India and argued that the British industrial policy in India in the post-war years sought to arrest industrialization, which it had allowed to grow during the war. From this premise, Varga's conclusion about the role of the Indian bourgeoisie in the nationalist movement came closer to Roy's. He pointed out that the Indian bourgeoisie had joined the nationalist movement to improve its own position within the Empire and not to fight British imperialism. The mantle of the nationalist movement therefore rested with the Indian proletariat.[87] It was the same idea that Roy had been trying to make the Comintern understand all along – the bourgeoisie was *unrevolutionary*.

Varga's formulations were challenged by the Communist Party of Great Britain when they came up for discussion at the Comintern's Indian commission. Soon thereafter, R. Palme Dutt in an article first tacitly agreed and then explicitly disagreed with Varga. He accepted Varga's contention that in the post-war period there had been some change in Britain's industrial policy in India and that there was a noticeable change with respect to 'concession and conciliation' towards the Indian bourgeoisie. But he insisted that this did not mean that there was no industrialization or that industrialization had stopped. The British policy of industrialization in India was to secure industrialization under British control.[88] 'From every sign of what is going on at present,' said Dutt, 'we can build with confidence on our diagnosis of the continuing capitalist and industrial evolution in India, with the accompanying political revolutionising consequences, and, in particular, on the growth, both in numbers and consciousness, of the industrial proletariat, alongside the intensifying agrarian crisis.'[89] The polemic was beside the point. The main question was: Under the given circumstances, what should be the Comintern's attitude towards the national bourgeoisie and the Indian National Congress? 'In general and on all fundamental questions,' said Dutt in his article, 'the role of the Indian bourgeoisie since the collapse of the non-cooperation movement has evolved in the direction of becoming more and more clearly counter-revolutionary.... But at the same time, within this general framework of capitulation, there takes place a process of friction and antagonism which has recently grown sharper.... Thus the role of the bourgeoisie in the national struggle is not yet exhausted, and may even extend under certain conditions, but it remains permanently limited in scope by its fear and hostility towards any wider mass revolutionary movement, and, therefore, very dangerous to the real struggle against imperialism....

But if we turn to the rank and file of the nationalist movement, representing in the main the various elements of the petty bourgeoisie, the sharpening of opposition is much more conspicuous. Here an actual process of revolutionisation is at work among a considerable section, following on the disillusionment after the collapse of Gandhi and non-cooperation, and on the economic hardship of the present period.'[90]

Following these articles, the executive committee of the Comintern prepared a report as a basis for discussion at the sixth congress of the Comintern. The report, besides dealing with organizational problems in general, discussed communist activities in all the major countries of the world, including India. In the report, the executives of the Comintern noted with concern the aspiration of the Indian bourgeoisie to control the masses through the petty bourgeoisie in a bid to utilize their revolutionary orientation for its reformist policy. 'By keeping the leadership over the petty bourgeoisie and the intelligentsia in its hands,' the report said, 'the bourgeoisie is endeavouring to establish a connection with the upper strata of the proletariat and the peasantry which it hopes to draw into its struggle. Organisationally unseparated from the bourgeois political parties and politically led by them, the nationalist left wing, with its slogans of independence, social equality and socialism, has evolved into an instrument in the hands of the bourgeoisie, for the penetration and vicarious leadership of the broad working masses.'[91]

That this observation of the Comintern executives had a direct bearing on the Workers' and Peasants' Party in India became apparent in the report. It said: 'The Workers' and Peasants' Party cannot develop into a party of mass national revolutionary struggle unless it emancipates itself entirely from the influence of bourgeois politicians and becomes transformed into a bloc of the working class with all the exploited masses under the leadership of the proletariat. On the other hand, it is entirely out of question that the Workers' and Peasants' Party should be a substitute for the Communist Party, the organisation of which is absolutely necessary.'[92] The academic exercise finally concentrated on a single point – whether the Comintern should support the Workers' and Peasants' Party or the Communist Party. The leadership of the Workers' and Peasants' Party was predominantly petty bourgeois, unreliable and subject to the influence of the bourgeoisie. Support to such a party would mean helping the petty bourgeoisie to extend its sway over the proletariat – an un-marxian course of action. The sixth congress of the Comintern met to decide this and other related issues as far as India was concerned.

The sixth congress of the Comintern met in Moscow from 17 July to 1 September 1928. It was attended by 532 delegates from 57 countries and 7 organizations. According to the information of the credential committee, there were 1,799,000 communists in the world, of which 1,211,000 were members or candidate-members of the Communist Party of the Soviet Union.[93] In this world congress, India was represented by six delegates, but none of them was accredited by the Communist Party of India.[94] They attended the congress in their personal capacity. Roy, who could speak for the communists of India, made his absence from the congress conspicuous, leaving the field open for the so-called representatives of India. Roy's absence was a great loss to the communists, particularly those from India. It was at this congress that the Comintern shifted its stand on the colonial revolution – from broad-based mass action to ultra-left consolidation. The Indian delegates were not only welcomed and given the right to vote[95] by Stalin, but one of them, Shaukat Usmani, was also elected to the presidium. It was a miscalculation on the part of Stalin. Usmani was a poor substitute for Roy. Twenty-five years after the congress, Usmani made a frank confession, 'I did not deserve such an honour – I was pushed into the presidium of the Comintern congress and found myself seated third from Stalin.'[96] The congress discussed a number of issues of international importance. India was primarily concerned with one issue – the revolutionary movement in colonial and semi-colonial countries, out of which emanated the imperialists' policy of industrialization in the colonies and the theory of *decolonization*.

The report on the revolutionary movement in colonial and semi-colonial countries was placed before the congress by Bukharin, who, after the exit of Zinoviev, became the general secretary of the Comintern. On this issue, the Comintern had already taken a decision in its 'draft programme'. Bukharin simply presented it before the congress for the appraisal of the delegates. With regard to the revolutionary movement, it was stated that the revolution in colonial and semi-colonial countries was 'in an embryonic stage… inadequate for independent socialist construction. Feudal medieval relationships predominate in the economic as well as in their political superstructure, and important industries, commerce, banks and principal means of transport, etc., are concentrated in the hands of the foreign imperialist groups. The most important task in such countries: peasant revolution on the one hand, and to fight for national independence against the foreign imperialists on the other'.[97] This assessment of the level of capitalist development in the colonies and the emphasis on agrarian revolution was a blow to what Roy had envisaged. Roy believed that in countries such as India, capitalism had reached a stage where proletariats were in a position to take up the leadership of the nationalist movement. The British and Indian delegates were hesitant to share his views. Yet they criticized Bukharin for not taking into account the changed industrial policy of the imperialists in the colonies, particularly in India after the world war. Bukharin refused to accept the contention of both the British and the Indian delegates, that the imperialists had embarked upon a new policy of industrialization in colonial and semi-colonial countries and had laid emphasis on an 'agrarian peasant revolution' for their emancipation. He observed that the bourgeoisie would play a revolutionary role for any length of time and would manoeuvre against imperialism, but an armed struggle against imperialism, as staged by the class in China, was a far cry.[98] Bukharin's analysis provided an inkling of the Comintern's views on the revolutionary movement in colonial and semi-colonial countries.

The main report on this and other questions was placed before the congress by O.V. Kuusinan. Kuusinan's report primarily focused on India because, as he said, the 'enormous importance of India among the colonies, because of the class character of the colonial monopoly which is particularly noticeable in India, and because I hold the view that a serious revolutionary crisis will develop in India in the not far distant future'.[99] Kuusinan began with an attack on the industrial policy of British imperialism in India and the consequent development of the theory of decolonization. He argued, 'To assume that the British policy is following an entirely new course in regard to the industrial development in India, I must say that they [Roy and R.P. Dutt] have gone too far. A semblance of this was possible in the boom years of 1921-23. Actually no change has taken place in the course of the British colonial policy. Some of these comrades went even (to) the length of holding out the prospect of "decolonisation" of India by British imperialism. This was a dangerous term.'[100] Talking about the bourgeoisie, he said, 'The national bourgeoisie is raising a hue and cry is quite true. But it is important to understand the political character of the Indian bourgeoisie, *its nationalist reformist policy*. That this policy is directed against the proletariat is as plain as that the bourgeoisie is bourgeoisie. That the policy of Indian bourgeoisie is not revolutionary, is also quite clear.'[101]

Both the British and the Indian delegates challenged the observation of Kuusinan. British delegates pointed out that under British control, industrialization in India was growing, as was the working class, i.e., the proletariat. A failure to recognize this would tantamount to misrepresenting the role of the working class.[102] While summarising the British point of view, C.P. Dutt added that 'the Indian bourgeoisie is a counter-revolutionary force, but that does not mean that we cannot use it even in the development of mass revolution'.[103] The most scathing remark came from Luhani: 'I repudiate the interpretation which comrade Kuusinan has given.... I have not the possibility here of raising the question whether the point of view is right or wrong or whether it is right or left.... I want you delegates to the conference to take note of the fact that the point of view has been presented to you, not in original, but in its travestied form.... I must register my energetic protest against the method of controversy as, to put it mildly, unfair both to the delegates of the congress and those whose point of view is being criticised.'[104] The debate finally converged on a single point, whether industrialization in the colonies and semi-colonies was growing under imperialism and, if so, what role would the bourgeoisie play in the national liberation movement. In fact, the disagreement was both strategic and tactical, and focused on what came to be known as the theory of decolonization.

Roy said that the term decolonization was first used by Bukharin. While summarizing the debate on the report of the Indian delegates, Bukharin suggested that the commission set up for examining the question should report on the process of such decolonization.[105] The term was used in a purely tentative and relative sense. However, on the basis of the preparatory work done by the commission, Roy, on his return from China, was asked to draft a resolution. In the draft resolution, after analysing the economic condition and the new tendencies of post-war colonial exploitation, Roy stated that the post-war crisis of capitalism would abolish old, antiquated forms and methods of colonial exploitation in favour of new forms and methods. The forces of production that were so far denied the possibility of normal growth, would become unfettered and change the basis of the national economy. Imperialism, forced by its inner contradiction, would permit, even encourage, partial industrialization of a colonial country and narrow down the basis of antagonism between the native bourgeoisie and foreign imperialists. Old class relations would be replaced by new ones. The existing nationalists' united front would break up and a new united front of the native bourgeoisie and foreign imperialists would be formed, to the detriment of the working class. Basic industry and agriculture would be revolutionized, and the native bourgeoisie would acquire an ever-increasing share in the control of the economic life of the country. In order to stabilize the economic base and strengthen its position in colonies, imperialists would be obliged to adopt a policy of 'concession and conciliation' towards the native bourgeoisie in the form of gifts. The imperialists would take the native bourgeoisie more and more into partnership, and together they would exploit the masses; the bourgeoisie would be brought nearer to running their own affairs. But in exchange for the concession, the bourgeoisie would have to dampen the revolutionary zeal of the masses and help imperialism retain its foothold. The implication of this new policy would be gradual decolonization, i.e., from a state of dependency to 'dominion status'.[106] Roy used the term decolonization by way of indicating a tendency purely and relatively hypothetical, only in connection with the national bourgeoisie, which constitutes a minuscule portion of the entire population. But nowhere did he state that the tendency would affect the entire populace and India would be free with the sanction of imperialism. The only thing he asserted was that the process would improve the status of the colonial bourgeoisie and intensify the exploitation of the nation as a whole. The draft resolution was never formally accepted because of the waning interest in the subject. Yet, the adversaries of Roy concluded at the sixth congress that Roy's draft resolution objectively implied defence of the social democratic theory of decolonization. According to this theory, imperialism plays a progressive role in colonies by forcing capitalist development and converting the colonies into capitalist countries. The congress came to the conclusion that the theory of decolonization was formulated by Roy to justify the imperialist policy in colonies and weaken people's struggle against imperialist oppression.

After speaking at length on the imperialist policy of industrialization in colonies, particularly in India, and its impact on the Indian bourgeoisie, Kuusinan took up the question of workers and peasants parties, raising serious doubts about their substitution for the Communist Party of India. 'It is now clear than before,' said Kuusinan, 'that the form is not recommended, specially in colonial and semi-colonial countries. It would be an easy matter for the labourer and peasant parties to transform themselves into petty bourgeoisie parties, to get away from the communists, thereby failing to come in contact with the masses. To consider such parties as a substitute for a real Communist Party would be a serious mistake.

We are for a bloc with the peasantry, but we will not have anything to do with the fusion of various classes.'[107]

Kuusinan's observations implied the liquidation of workers and peasants parties in India. With the exception of J.T. Murphy, the entire British delegation and a section of Indian delegates took a firm stand and opposed Kuusinan's thesis. C.P. Dutt, on behalf of the Communist Party of Great Britain, made it clear 'that the question of Workers' and Peasants' Party cannot be dismissed with a phrase.... The characteristic feature of the workers' and peasants' parties in the present stage of development in India is that they are forming an important route through which communists are finding their way to the masses'.[108] Among the Indian delegates, Usmani and Masood Ali Shah supported Kuusinan. 'The workers' and peasants' parties,' said Usmani, 'exist owing to wrong tactics and instructions of the Comintern.'[109] Masood Ali went a step further and criticized the Comintern for its policy of overseeing the organization of workers and peasants parties, while altogether ignoring the organization of the Communist Party of India. This, he considered, 'as absurd as to put the cart before the horse', and advised the Comintern to revise its policy.[110] On the other hand, Tagore defended the existence of workers and peasants parties. He criticized Kuusinan, Usmani and Masood Ali. 'It seems to me,' said Tagore, 'that the comrades are scared with the nightmare which is the result of their own irrational fantasy that the Workers' and Peasants' Party is a substitute for the Communist Party. Nobody has ever put forward that the Workers' and Peasants' Party would be a substitute for the Communist Party....'

'The petty bourgeois intelligentsia, the urban petty bourgeoisie, have to play a role in the revolutionary movement in the colonies.... The Communist Party of India should utilise the revolutionary energies of the petty bourgeoisie. I think it is clear that this anti-imperialist front can only take the organisational form of a Workers' and Peasants' Party composed of urban intelligentsia and the petty bourgeois elements, under the leadership of the proletariat.' The proposed liquidation of the workers' and peasants' parties, said Tagore, 'is pure and simple professional dogmatism...'[111]

Though Tagore was one with the Communist Party of Great Britain in criticizing Kuusinan, particularly on the question of the liquidation of workers and peasants parties in India, he resented the hegemony of the Communist Party of Great Britain. 'Nobody will deny,' said Tagore, 'that in the organic structure of British imperialism, India and England are closely connected with each other for carrying out the proletarian revolution in these two countries, but this on no account means subordination of the colonial party to the leadership of the imperialist home country.'[112]

After prolonged discussion, the colonial thesis that finally emerged reflected in the main the Chinese experience. The communist parties were advised to keep away from the formation of any bloc with the bourgeoisie, particularly, the trading bourgeoisie who serve the interest of imperialist capital. The communists can make temporary alliance with the bourgeoisie with definite anti-imperialist demonstration, but 'demarcate themselves in the most clear-cut fashion, both politically and organisationally, from all the petty bourgeoisie groups and parties'.[113] Regarding workers and peasants parties, the communists in India were advised to liquidate them and instead form a 'union of all communist groups and individual communists scattered throughout the country into a single, illegal, independent and centralised party'.[114] The Comintern further imposed great responsibility on the communist parties of imperialist countries to build the party in colonial and semi-colonial countries and assist 'in the matter of working out correct political line, accurate analysis of experiences in the sphere of organisation and agitation' and to look into the 'systematic education of the party workers; the publication of a certain minimum of marxist-leninist literature and its translation into languages of the different colonial countries'.[115]

The thesis adopted at the sixth congress on the strategy and tactics to be followed in the national liberation struggle and the role of the bourgeoisie in colonial and semi-colonial countries had a 'sectarian character'. The folly was detected at the twentieth Congress of the Communist Party of the Soviet Union. Kuusinan accepted that the thesis adopted at the sixth congress of the Comintern on the role of the national bourgeoisie in colonial and semi-colonial countries 'bore a definite shade of sectarianism'.[116] Interestingly, it was for his 'sectarian' views that Roy had all along been accused by the communists in India. But when at the sixth congress, the Comintern adopted the same views, Indian delegates dared not raise their voice and accepted the decision of the Comintern with grace. Roy, who by now had drifted towards the right, was at Berlin and noticed the difference. He lamented and accused Indian delegates of meek submission. In 1928, Roy wrote, 'The sixth congress of the Communist International advised its Indian section to adopt a course of action which, in my opinion, was erroneous. It was the result of a wrong estimation of the social character and the perspective of the development of the Indian revolution. The majority of the Indian communists, labouring under a false notion of discipline, accepted the resolution of the Communist International.... The mechanical acceptance of the resolutions of the Communist International blinded the Indian communists to the realities of the situation, and compelled them to commit tactical mistakes which isolated them from the anti-imperialist mass movement and even from the labour movement. Thanks to those mistakes, they could never be more than a small sect with no influence on the political life of the country.'[117] The observation had some truth in it, but the communists in India were too weak to rectify the mistake.

The decision of the sixth congress took some time to reach the communists in India. Meanwhile, the political situation in India took a new turn. To the discomfort of the colonial ruler, a section of bourgeois national leaders, including Jawaharlal Nehru, started appreciating socialist programmes, though not socialism. Nehru's appreciation of socialist programmes and sympathy for communists developed from the time he took active part in the Brussels conference of the League Against Imperialism. With his socialist stance, Nehru emerged as the leader of the Congress radicals in 1927 at the Madras session of the Indian National Congress, and with their support, succeeded in carrying through almost all the resolutions put forward by him. 'This all-round support,' said Nehru, 'was gratifying, but I had an uncomfortable feeling that the resolutions were either not understood for what they were or were distorted to mean something else.'[118]

Nehru was supported by the communists here. Philip Spratt, K.N. Joglekar, R.S. Nimbkar and a few others who attended the Congress were elated to find that Nehru was a radical and extended their cooperation. They did not claim equality with him and were happy to play second fiddle. Ironically, their own resolution on the anniversary of the socialist revolution and the protest call against the projected visit of the Indian statutory commission headed by John Simon were turned down.

The Congress, to the satisfaction of Nehru, unanimously passed a resolution for complete independence of India. When this was brought to the notice of Gandhi, he expressed his displeasure by criticizing the resolution as 'hastily conceived and thoughtlessly passed'. To reclaim lost ground, Gandhi took to ruse and outmanoeuvred his adversaries in a subtle way.

Soon after the Congress session, a controversy arose regarding the meaning of the independence resolution. It looked as if the Congress would split again, but the situation was saved. Advised by Gandhi, the working committee appointed Motilal Nehru to draft a constitution for independent India. The Nehru Report, as it was called, recommended dominion status as against full independence. Thereupon, the young radicals headed by Jawaharlal Nehru, Srinivasa Iyengar and Subhas Chandra Bose formed the Indian Independence League. The league in its first meeting held in Delhi on 3 November 1928 declared its objectives as 'the achievement of complete independence for India and reconstruction of Indian society on a basis of social and economic equality'.[119] Nehru envisaged that the league would be a permanent body with a definite policy and programme and would cooperate with all organizations with 'the same objects in common with it'.[120]

When a small section of bourgeois nationalist leaders was taking a radical posture, communists in India were making steady progress in their projected path. Guided by foreign comrades, viz., Spratt and Bradley, they established their leadership in the trade union movement and made sufficient progress in organizing workers and peasants parties. To put a stop to this spurt of radicalization, the government, in September 1928, introduced the Public Safety Bill in the Central Legislative Assembly. The bill was primarily an anti-communist measure, designed to strengthen the position of the government to expel foreign communist emissaries from India through legal means and to create fear among the newly emerged radicals. Nationalists of all shades opposed the bill, both from within and outside the legislature. The bill was defeated. For the communists, things looked bright as never before.

The thesis adopted at the sixth congress was communicated piecemeal to the communists in India. It started tricking in from December 1928, when G.M. Adhikari arrived from Europe with a letter from the Comintern to the Workers' and Peasants' Party. Complete instructions were communicated only towards the close of 1929, after the tenth plenum of the executive committee of the Comintern iterated the thesis adopted at the sixth congress. The delay was mainly caused by the indifferent attitude of the Comintern bureaucracy. Spratt explained that 'by 1928 the Comintern had ceased to matter, except as a field for the intrigues of the Russian party faction, and the swing to the left in that year bore no relation to world politics but was merely an outcome of these factional quarrels. Probably the Comintern bureaucracy in Moscow realised this and saw that it did not matter whether the Indian party followed the new line or the old'.[121] However, in December 1928, when the different workers and peasants parties met in a conference in Calcutta to form an All-India Workers' and Peasants' Party, the letter from the Comintern reached. After congratulating the workers and peasants of India for their 'heroic struggle against imperialist oppression and feudal reaction', it advised them to dissociate from 'the organisations and groups of prominent petty bourgeois intellectuals' (i.e., the

Indian Independence League), 'the main obstacle to the victorious organised struggle against British imperialist and its feudal allies'.[122] The Comintern's observation was resented by a section of the party leadership: K.N. Joglekar, D.R. Thengdi and S. Kumaranand moved a resolution to stall the implementation of the Comintern's advice.[123] The resolution was defeated, but the thesis adopted amounted to a virtual rejection of the Comintern's instruction. It agreed that the objective of the Indian Independence League was, to a great extent, to prevent the independent growth of the mass movement. The members of the Workers' and Peasants' Party cannot, therefore, be the members of the Indian Independence League. But the Workers' and Peasants' Party can 'work with the Independence League in a united front, on the basis of its propaganda for independence which in spite of its frivolous character has objectively some value. But it is necessary continually to expose the League's faults of programme and policy, and its fundamentally bourgeois even fascist character, and ultimately counter revolutionary role'.[124] Thus, the Workers' and Peasants' Party, in contravention of the Comintern's instructions, decided to work for independence as a united front with the Indian Independence League, while reserving the right to criticize and expose its counter-revolutionary character.

The decision of the communists in India was tacitly accepted by the Communist Party of Great Britain. In a pamphlet, R.P. Arnot, the head of the British Party, maintained that though the sixth congress of the Comintern preferred the liquidation of the Workers' and Peasants' Party, in a real sense, it was a 'conscious mass movement for the first time in India, a real proletarian awakening'.[125] He therefore advocated the continuance of the Workers' and Peasants' Party. The Communist Party of Great Britain was, however, opposed to the alliance between the Workers' and Peasants' Party and the Indian Independence League. In its opinion, the league did not represent revolutionary socialism but reformist social democracy.[126] In fact, the Communist Party of Great Britain advised communists in India to continue organizing the Workers' and Peasants' Party in opposition to the Comintern's advise, but at the same time asked them to avoid any alliance with the Indian Independence League, as desired by the Comintern.

Roy's views during the period were not only at variance with the Comintern, but often also self-contradictory. This contradiction became apparent ever since he returned from China and took up the pen in support of Stalin to justify the Comintern's China policy, while opposing the same policy in India. The real confusion began when even after his exit from the Comintern, his articles continued to be published in the *Inprecor*. In an article in the *Inprecor*, while analysing class differentiation in the nationalist movement, Roy wrote, 'The petty bourgeois rank and file breaking away from bourgeois leadership, owing to treachery of the latter, is still remote, because they are "largely under the control and influence of the treacherous reformist bourgeois leaders".'[127] And then he contradicted himself by saying, 'The development of independent political action by the working class is splitting the petty bourgeois radical nationalists into two ever-diverging tendencies. One advances towards revolutionary alliance with the working class in Workers' and Peasants' Party; and the other moves rapidly toward fascism. This regrouping of class forces is a precondition for a revolutionary anti-imperialist fight for national liberation.'[128] The article in the *Inprecor* provides an inkling of his vacillating mind with no commitment to move in either direction. But gradually his choice became clear. He moved towards the right of both the Comintern and the Communist Party of Great Britain.

Besides doctrinal confusion and conflicting advice, there was also a communication gap. As late as March 1929, Spratt wrote to C.P. Dutt, 'I should say, by the way, that I have heard practically nothing yet of the British Party affair, not even anything of value about the International.'[129]

This pervading confusion and contradiction stood in the way of the communists. They could not make full use of the favourable situation created by the radicalization of Indian politics. Attempts to organize the Workers' and Peasants' Party into a mass party of the proletariat failed. The little that was done was of no political utility. It was organized in isolation, away from the masses. But as far as the trade union movement was concerned, the communists made headway. By 1928, they secured a definite hold over the workers of Bombay and Calcutta and, to some extent, in upper India. The impact of communists on the trade union movement became evident with a spate of strikes, particularly in Bombay and Bengal. The strike of the cotton mill workers of Bombay and the railway employees of Lillooah in Bengal unnerved the government. It is recorded in the confidential government report that by 1928, transport workers, industrial workers, agricultural workers, colliers and scavengers, all came under the influence of the communists.[130] To put a stop to this growing influence, the government thought of instituting a conspiracy case. In a letter to Stanley Jackson dated 18 January 1929, the Governor of Bengal, Irwin, wrote, 'We have, however, at present a reasonably good hope of being able to run a comprehensive conspiracy case against these men (communists). If we could do this, it would in our opinion deal a severe blow to the Indian communist movement than anything that could be effected through further special legislation, and we are not in favour at present of taking any new powers.'[131]

The die was cast. The communists were unaware of this plan. To discuss the existing political situation and to reorganize the party, the communists held a meeting at Bombay from 17 to 19 March 1929. G.M. Adhikari, who had recently arrived from Berlin, presented concrete proposals for the reorganization. According to his plan, the party was to be organized into five departments – trade unions, peasants, propaganda, organizational and political control, and the secretariat.[132] The matter relating to the Workers' and Peasants' Party was also discussed, but no decision could be arrived at about its future. Mirajkar opposed the dissolution and was supported by Usmani, though at the sixth congress of the Comintern, Usmani had favoured its liquidation. However, to discuss the details of the reorganization and thrash out the question of the continuance of the Workers' and Peasants' Party, a sub-committee was formed. However, it could not meet. The government, as planned, struck the communists on 20 March 1929, a day after the Bombay meeting. Thirty-one persons were taken into custody and sent to Meerut to face trial on charges of conspiracy to deprive the King Emperor of the sovereignty of British India.[133] About two weeks later, another person, Lester Hutchinson, was put under arrest and his name was added to the list of those to be prosecuted. Out of these thirty-two persons, about fifty per cent were communists, while the rest were either trade unionists or members of the Workers' and Peasants' Party.[134] Besides, the government submitted a supplementary list of another fifty persons who were in some way connected with the conspiracy, but could not be apprehended. Prominent among them were M.N. Roy, George Allison, Khushi Mohammad alias Sipassi, J.F. Rayan, C.P. Dutt, Shapurji Saklatvala, V.N. Chattopadhyaya and R.C.L. Sharma.[135]

The lower court concluded its trial on 14 January 1930. An accused named Dharambir Singh was discharged, while the rest were committed to sessions. The sessions trial continued for nearly three years and the judgement was delivered on 16 January 1933. All but four of the thirty-one accused were sentenced. The highest sentence was awarded to Muzaffar Ahmed – transportation for life – while the rest were sentenced to various terms of imprisonment, ranging from three to twelve years. On appeal to the high court, all except four – Spratt, Muzaffar, Dange and Usmani – were released. Spratt was released in September 1934; and Muzaffar, Dange and Usmani, in the autumn of 1935. While delivering the judgement, the judge observed, 'The conspiracy was impracticable one might even say impossible of achievement. The steps taken by the accused till their arrest were in one sense utterly puerile and could not be conceived to lead to any such serious consequences as the accused dreamt of.'[136] To prove this 'utterly puerile' conspiracy, the government collected 3,000 exhibits as evidence; presented 320 witnesses; and spent about 15 lakh rupees of public money.[137]

Apparently, the Meerut trial was a setback to the communists, but it went in their favour eventually. The vacuum created by the arrests was soon filled by a set of energetic young men. Abdul

Halim, B.T. Ranadive, S.V. Deshpande, Suhasini Nambiar and R.D. Bhardwaj, among others, came to the fore to build the party once again. Spratt recalls, 'The revelation of our secret methods caused people to admire us[;] we had done what most young men wanted to do…we had our opportunity in the sessions court to make political statements and these were widely published in the press…most of what can be said in favour of communism was said.'[138] This was no exaggeration. During the period, socialist ideas had become fashionable among the young educated elite of India. Even the bourgeois leaders who had no love for communism came forward in support of the Meerut accused. Gandhi rushed to Meerut to meet the prisoners; the working committee of the Congress passed a resolution and condemned the arrests; bourgeois nationalist leaders of all shades formed a defence committee and issued an appeal for collecting funds.[139] Outside India, the Workers' Welfare League of India, London, took the initiative to constitute a defence fund and issued appeals to the workers of Great Britain to condemn the arrests and contribute to a fund for the defence of the Meerut accused. Similar efforts were also made in the Soviet Union. For the first time, the communists in India came in the limelight.

While the Meerut Conspiracy case was in progress, the political situation in India was tense. On 8 April 1929, Bhagat Singh threw a bomb on the floor of the Central Legislature as a mark of protest against the passing of the Trade Dispute Bill, an act directly affecting the labour movement in India.[140] This was followed by the Chittagong uprising and the civil disobedience movement. It was expected that the communists would exploit the situation and come up as a viable political force, but they failed. At this crucial hour, without taking into consideration the prevailing political climate in India, the Comintern, at the tenth plenum of its executive committee, reiterated the decision of the sixth Congress and advised the communists in India to turn their back on the mainstream liberation struggle. The instruction was obeyed and the communists, cut off from the mainstream, went into isolation.

The tenth plenum met at Moscow from 3 July to 19 July 1929. Kuusinan, the spokesman of the Comintern for India, said in his report, 'Our greatest weakness [is]... that we are not yet firmly enough established as a communist party... [and] hardly any practical revolutionary work has been done yet among the peasantry.'[141] Soon after the tenth plenum, the *Inprecor* published an open letter from the Young Communist International. In unambiguous terms, the letter asked the youth, workers and peasants of India to dissociate themselves from the Indian National Congress and the Independence for India League, while continuing to 'disclose their falseness and treachery'.[142] About the Workers' and Peasants' Party, P. Schubin, a Russian delegate, lamented, 'when they cease to live they refuse to die, clinging to the shell of their existence hindering the development of sound forms of organisation.'[143]

The tenth plenum, apart from asking communists in India to go into isolation, took another decision. It settled the fate of Roy, which had been hanging in the balance for quite some time. Musso, the Indonesian delegate, announced at the plenum, 'Roy is no longer our comrade. He is rather the comrade of Gandhi or at best a comrade of Brandler and Thalheimer.'[144] Though he was denounced, his expulsion from the Comintern was formally announced in the *Inprecor* of December 1929. It said, according to the decision taken by the presidium of the executive committee of the Comintern on 19 December 1929, 'Adherents of the Brandler organization cannot be members of the Communist International, the presidium of the EECI declare that Roy by contributing to the Brandler press and supporting the Brandler organisation, has placed himself outside the ranks of the Communist International, and is to be considered as expelled from the Communist International.'[145]

After the expulsion of Roy, the Comintern sent a few of its emissaries to ascertain whether communists in India were actually following its directions. Except for one, all the others were either deported or had left the country before they could achieve anything tangible. The first of the emissaries to arrive was one Prem Lal Singh, an ex-student of the Lenin Institute, Moscow. He came to India in early 1930, stayed for a few months and returned to Moscow. His only achievement was that he could visit Meerut and meet the under-trials of the Meerut Conspiracy case.[146] Then, an American, William N. Kweit, and his wife, Helen Bowlen, arrived in India. They were soon joined by another American, Harry Somers, in July 1930. They established contact with the Bombay group and helped publish a few news sheets. By September, they were detected and deported from India.[147] Close on the heels of their deportation came another American, Henry G. Lynd. Lynd stayed in India for about a year and fared a little better than his predecessors. He also established contact with the Bombay group; attended a few of their secret meetings; and helped them issue a pamphlet, *Programme of the Communist Party of India*. Besides, he made an abortive attempt to overhaul the existing party machinery to free itself from the influence of the Congress and reformist elements. But contrary to the Comintern's directive, he advised the communists to retain the Workers' and Peasants' Party to utilize it as a reservoir for the recruitment of new members to the Communist Party. Whether the communists gave any credence to his advice cannot be asserted with any degree of certainty; at least it did not reflect in the working of the party. However, by December 1931, he was detected and deported from India.[148]

The most successful of these emissaries was Amir Haider Khan, an absconder accused in the Meerut Conspiracy case. Haider arrived in India in March 1931 and selected Madras as his base of activity. Within a year of his arrival, he succeeded in forming communist groups in at least three important cotton mills of Madras. He organized a Young Workers' League with a branch in Bombay and established contact with the Bombay group of communists. He was detained on 7 May 1932, and tried and sentenced to imprisonment for two and a half years.[149]

Communists in India followed the ultra-left policy of the Comintern until the summer of 1932. During this period, V.N. Chattopadhyaya emerged as the Comintern expert on India. He, together with C.P. Dutt and Karl Radek, contributed a few articles to the *Inprecor*. The main thrust of their argument was opposition to

Gandhi, Nehru and Bose by branding the Congress as a bourgeois counter-revolutionary party. This ultra-left policy of the Comintern was further intensified when the *Inprecor* carried a message from the all-China Labour Federation to the working people of India. The message reflected the Chinese experience of the bourgeois Kuomintang and drew a parallel between it and the Indian National Congress. 'The Indian National Party under the direction of Gandhi,' said the message, 'is just like the Kuomintang of China. We must not have the slightest illusion towards Gandhi. On the contrary, we must oppose him in order to guarantee the victory of the revolution.'[150] The most ultra-left document of the period was the 'draft platform of action' of the Communist Party of India.[151] The 'platform' began with an attack on imperialist Britain for exploiting Indian masses in all spheres of activities. It denounced Gandhi for his counter-revolutionary attitude and depicted the Congress as an 'organisation of the capitalist working against the fundamental interests of the toiling masses of our country'.[152] But the most scathing attack it made was on the left elements of the National Congress. 'The most harmful and dangerous obstacle to the victory of the Indian revolution,' said the 'platform', 'is the agitation carried on by the "left" elements of the National Congress, led by Jawaharlal Nehru, Bose, Ginwalle and others. Under the cloak of revolutionary phraseology they carry on the bourgeois policy of confusing and disorganising the 'revolutionary struggle of the masses and help the Congress to come to an understanding with British imperialism.'[153] The emancipation of India will, therefore, come, the 'platform' said, through the revolutionary armed insurrection of the widest possible masses of the working class, the peasantry, the poor of the towns and the Indian soldiers, around the banner and under the leadership of the Communist Party of India.'[154]

The 'draft platform of action' received mixed reactions from the communists. While the old guards sitting in the Meerut prison were worrying about the dissociation of the communists from the civil disobedience movement, on the plea that it was not a real struggle and that the Congress was a bourgeois party, the newly emerged leaders were fighting among themselves over the tactics to be followed. Despite the Comintern's instruction to build an illegal party, Abdul Halim and S.V. Deshpande decided to play safe and worked within the framework of law. Deshpande formed a Marxian Students' Club and brought out two journals – *Workers' Weekly* and *Kranti*. Besides, he published a few pamphlets with 'vague fulminations than of tangible revolutionary scheme'.[155] B.T. Ranadive, on the other hand, preferred to follow the militant Comintern line with strikes and demonstrations. In fact, at that point of time, factionalism raised its head once again, resulting in chaos, confusion and disorganization. In this, the main casualty was the party. The unity achieved on the eve of the Meerut Conspiracy was disrupted, damaging the trade union movement, the main arena of the communists.

To redress the sorry state of affairs, the Meerut prisoners, between 1931 and 1933, prepared three memoranda and smuggled them out of jail.[156] These memoranda were intended for communist emissaries who had come to India soon after the institution of the Meerut Conspiracy case, as well as for Comintern leaders, to apprise them of the state of the communist movement in India. In these memoranda, the writers lamented over the poor state of communist activity in India and requested the Comintern to issue an 'open letter' to set the mistake right. The writers admitted that the offensive launched by the government, the advent of the 'Roy group' and the civil disobedience movement presented before the party a tactical problem – they 'deplored the mismanagement and lack of activity which had allowed things to reach a stage where practically all the unions over which the party had previously held control had passed into the hands of the adversaries, the "Roy group"'.[157] As desired, the Comintern published in the *Inprecor* an 'open letter' signed by the communist parties of China, Great Britain and Germany. The letter began with the accusation that the development of the communist movement in India was being thwarted by a state of discord and the separate existence of party groups, and then stated that 'it must be thoroughly realised that the leading organs of the party and the kernel of its organisations must be in an illegal position … while developing the illegal organisation in everyway measures must be taken for preserving and strengthening the conspirative (sic) kernel of the party organisation. For this purpose all kinds of open activity (in the press, meetings, leagues, trade unions, etc.), special groups and commissions, etc., should be formed which, working under the leadership of party committees, should under no circumstances injure the existence of legal nuclei'.[158] The 'open letter' cautioned communists that mixing of the open and conspiratorial apparatus of the party organization would be fatal.

An attempt to give effect to the suggestions put forward in the 'open letter' was made by the Indian comrades after the first batch of the Meerut prisoners was released. The most active of the released prisoners were G. Adhikari and P.C. Joshi. Soon after being released, Adhikari left for Bombay and Joshi, for the United Province. In Bombay, Adhikari first made an abortive attempt to revive the Young Workers' League of Amir Haider and the Marxian Students' Club of Deshpande. Having failed in this attempt, around November 1933, Adhikari left for Calcutta accompanied by S.G. Patkar, a member of the Deshpande faction. In Calcutta, Adhikari met Joshi and established contact with the different factional groups of the communists to form a central committee. He succeeded in his effort. The period of chaos and confusion, which began with the institution of the Meerut Conspiracy case, came to an end. In a meeting in Calcutta, attended by the representatives of different groups, a provisional central committee of the Communist Party of India was formed, with Adhikari as secretary, pending an all-India convention of the party. To give a concrete shape to the discussion, it was decided to draw a political and organizational thesis for consideration at the all-India convention.[159]

Adhikari's achievement was noticed by the Communist Party of China. In an 'open letter', the central committee of the Communist Party of China lauded his success and advised Indian comrades to form a mass communist party with strict discipline, like the Communist Party of the Soviet Union, and not a peaceful but militant, bold revolutionary party. In the same letter, it warned

Indian comrades about the slow progress of the communist movement in India.[160]

The proposed thesis for the Calcutta meeting was ready by February 1934 and its cyclostyled copies were distributed to different centres of communist activities all over India. After dilating at some length on the iniquities of imperialism and the inadequacies of the politics of Roy, Nehru, Bose and Gandhi, the thesis discussed the role of the petty bourgeoisie, the peasantry and the working class in the revolutionary struggle against imperialism. In a nutshell, the plan advocated the transformation of individual strikes into a general strike, and spontaneous peasant movements against rents and debts or taxes into an all-India movement; fostering a nation-wide agitation in favour of complete independence; and the spread of revolutionary propaganda among the police and the army. The next step suggested was the overthrow of British imperialism, the princes and the landlords through an armed mass insurrection of workers, peasants and soldiers, under the leadership of the working class and its party, i.e., the Communist Party of India.[161] To realize this aim, the communists were asked to work in unison, to win over the rank and file of terrorist groups and especially those who were inclined towards marxism. The communists were also advised to join every trade union and fight from within for the execution of class programmes and for revolutionary leadership and politics.[162] The thesis finally concluded with a note that the 'Communist cadres have considerable experience of open mass work, but they still have to learn to devise methods to combine legal and illegal activity. Without this it is impossible to organise and bring the toiling masses to the revolutionary battles. Without this it is impossible to create a mass communist party.'[163]

The communists threw their lot with Adhikari and came to a temporary understanding with the 'Roy group' to exploit the growing general dissatisfaction in the industrial centres of India. In January 1934, a month before the distribution of cyclostyled copies of the thesis, the combined group met in a conference at Bombay, formed an action committee and decided to stage a strike of textile workers.

At the call of the action committee, the strike began in April with the Bombay textile mill workers, and soon spread to other areas. The government took to the usual method of repression through mass arrests, but failed to stem the tide. Finding no other alternative, in July 1934, the government declared the Communist Party of India and its subsidiaries, such as the Young Communists League, the Marxist Students' Club and Red Trade Union Congress, illegal – a status that was not changed until 1942.

The ban failed to have the desired effect, however. The communists went underground and, through a network of activities, continued to flourish and grow in strength, by adopting a more practical line. The disownment of the ultra-left policy and the return to united front tactics were appreciated by the Comintern. In an article in the *Inprecor,* Indian communists were advised to forge relations with the petty bourgeois rank and file of the Indian National Congress and cooperate with leftist forces.[164] To give effect to the Comintern's directive, the Communist Party of India made a feeble attempt to establish contact with the newly formed Congress Socialist Party – a party that emerged in May 1934 from within the Congress to counter Gandhi's vacillating policy.[165] The objective behind the new party was the formation of a state based on socialist principles, as against the bourgeois democratic state envisaged by Gandhi.

Changes in the Comintern's views sought to counter the rise of fascism in Germany. The fascists in Germany grew in strength with the tacit support of the imperialists. In their bid for power, the imperialists saw in fascism a strike force aimed at the proletarian movement – a movement that Hitler described as the 'cancerous disease of democracy'. In a quandary, the Comintern gave up its ultra-left policy and advised communists in colonial and semi-colonial countries to adopt united front tactics and act as a pressure group on the imperialists to save the proletariat movement from fascist interference. This fascist menace and other related questions were discussed at the seventh congress of the Comintern, which met in Moscow from 25 July to 21 August 1935. It was attended by

513 delegates representing 65 countries and a number of industrial organizations affiliated to the Comintern.[166] There was no official delegation from India to represent the Communist Party of India, though in 1933 the party was affiliated with the Comintern.[167] S.V. Deshpande and S.S. Mirajkar, who were supposed to represent the Communist Party of India at the congress, were taken into custody at Singapore *en route* to Moscow.[168]

The congress discussed a number of issues, but the focus was on the fascist offensive and the task before the Comintern. Georgi Dimitrov was the main spokesperson on this issue. In his report, he urged communist parties to change their attitude towards social democratic parties and reformist trade unions, which were trying to form an effective united front in the mass struggle against fascism. He insisted on putting an end to the stock phrases used at random as substitutes for the marxist analysis of reality, which were preventing communist parties from becoming the real organizers and leaders of the anti-fascist struggle. He emphasized a basic change in the Comintern's policy, in the absence of which it was impossible to exercise effective leadership over all sections of the Comintern from a single centre. He proposed that the Comintern should modify its method of working and concentrate on providing ideological and political guidance to the communist movement.[169] The main thrust of Dimitrov's thesis was on the formation of a broad-based popular front against the fascist menace. The Comintern took due notice of this thesis. It realized that the efforts of the working class, even if united, were not sufficient to secure victory over fascism. The policy of alliance had to be extended to those social groups that were concerned with safeguarding traditional democratic freedom and fascist enslavement,[170] though they were not adherents of proletarian dictatorship.

To the Indian communists, Dimitrov's message was that while retaining the independence of the party, the communists should 'support, extend and participate in all anti-imperialist mass activities, not excluding those which are under national reformist leadership... they must carry on active work inside the organisations which take part in the Indian National Congress, facilitating the process of crystallisation of a national revolutionary wing among them, for the purpose of further developing the national liberation movement of the Indian people against British imperialism'.[171]

Dimitrov's appeal for a united front was initially opposed by Bela Kun, Lozovsky, Konorin and Wang Ming, the Chinese delegates who spoke at length on India. They defended the existing guidelines of the Comintern and agreed only to a certain change in tactics. But in the course of the discussion, they came round to the views of Dimitrov and admitted the need for a revision.[172]

The main spokesman on the policy to be adopted in the colonies was Wang Ming. While advocating united front tactics, Ming cited instances of Chinese and Brazilian communists, and urged Indian comrades to make use of both the experiences.[173] He chided Indian communists for their failure to take active part in the anti-imperialist struggle and pointed out that the sectarian error committed by the Communist Party of India helped retain Gandhi's influence. 'Our comrades in India,' said Ming, 'have suffered for a long time from left-sectarian errors; they did not participate in all the mass demonstrations organised by the National Congress.... The Indian communists must formulate a programme of popular demands which could serve as a platform for a broad anti-imperialist united front.'[174] The Indian communists failed, as Ming said, due to the absence of united front tactics.

In the absence of official delegates from India, the Communist Party of Great Britain came forward to play its usual role of the 'big brother'. Without waiting for the Comintern to communicate the new policy to comrades in India, the Communist Party of Great Britain took upon itself the responsibility to implement the new policy. To begin with, it made an abortive attempt for an alliance between the Communist Party of India and the Congress Socialist Party. Minoo Masani, one of the founder-members of the Congress Socialist Party, happened to be in Moscow at that time. Harry Pollitt, R. Palme Dutt and Ben Bradley met him and proposed an alliance between the Communist Party of India and the Congress

Socialist Party. Masani agreed to the proposal on the condition that the Communist Party of India dissolves itself to form a united socialist party, separated from the Comintern.[175] The terms were not acceptable, and the negotiations failed. The Communist Party of Great Britain thereupon proceeded to inform the Communist Party of India about the new policy of the Comintern. R. Palme Dutt and Ben Bradley prepared a formal statement in the form of a guideline based on the new policy. The Dutt-Bradley thesis, as it was popularly known, began with a polemic asserting that the Indian National Congress had ceased for the time being to direct the anti-imperialist struggle, but it had the potential to become the united front of the people of India in the national struggle for liberation. 'The National Congress,' said Dutt and Bradley, 'has undoubtedly achieved a gigantic task in uniting wide forces of the Indian people for the national struggle and remains today the principal existing mass organisation of diverse elements seeking national liberation. Nothing should be allowed to weaken the degree of unity that has been achieved.' But 'as it exists at present it is not a united front of the people of India in the national struggle. Its constitution still leaves out broadest sections of the masses. Its programme does not express with full clearance the programmes of the national struggle. Its leadership cannot yet be recognised as the leadership of the national struggle.' The National Congress would be a truly anti-imperialist people's front only when the mass organizations of the workers and peasants, the trade unions and the peasants' unions, which were outside the pale of the Congress would join it either 'in a united front agreement or by the collective affiliation of these to the Congress'.[176] When this was achieved, the National Congress would play a significant role in the building of the anti-imperialist people's front.[177]

Dutt-Bradley envisaged that the Congress Socialist Party would play a major role to achieve this goal. Though at that time, it was a poor minority in the Congress, yet, with the addition of the mass organization and the communists, it would surely constitute a majority. The communists were, therefore, advised to work for a united front with the National Congress under the cover of the Congress Socialist Party. The aim of the communists, it was suggested, should be to isolate the national bourgeois leaders from its rank and file, and transform the National Congress into a broad revolutionary party against imperialism.

The Dutt-Bradley thesis gave a new direction to the communist movement in India, but in the initial stage the communists were not favourably disposed towards it. The formation of an anti-imperialist people's front with the national bourgeoisie was considered a heresy. This became apparent when, in January 1936, the Congress Socialist Party unilaterally passed a resolution at the national executive at its second congress to admit communists into the membership of the party, but received little response from the communists. Jaiprakash Narayan, the general secretary of the Congress Socialist Party, informs that the Communist Party of India remained aloof from, if not hostile towards, the Congress Socialist Party.[178] A change in the attitude of the communists was manifested when P.C. Joshi became the general secretary of the Communist Party of India. Under Joshi's guidance, communists came to understand the proper implication of the Dutt-Bradley thesis and looked for ways to implement it.

Joshi provided a new impetus to the communist movement in India. He revamped the party's organizational apparatus; brought out a secret party journal – *Communists*; and raised and motivated a group of dedicated young men to work as a disciplined unit within the Congress Socialist Party, in the National Congress and other mass organizations, including trade unions and peasant unions.

The successful infiltration into the Congress Socialist Party and, through it, into the National Congress, gave a new boost to the communist movement in India. As members of the Congress Socialist Party, communists worked among the populace at the grassroots level, and as members of the National Congress, they acquired respect in the society. In a short span of time, communists carved a space for themselves everywhere – from the lowest village unit to the top level of the Congress. So successful was the move that by 1939 the communists could claim twenty members in the all-India Congress Committee and there was manifold increase in party membership.

However, the honeymoon of the communists and the congress socialists received a setback in the very first year of the working of the united front. Towards the close of 1936, reports began to reach the national executive of the Congress Socialist Party that the communists were disrupting the organization. This was no wild allegation. From the very day the communists started infiltrating into the Congress Socialist Party, their aim was to first capture the local units and then woo the congress socialists to convert them into communists. However, the national executive of the Congress Socialist Party responded mildly to the allegations, only spreading a word of caution among the provincial units of the party. The communists were not slow to realize the danger, so they entered into the so-called 'Lucknow agreement' with the Congress Socialist Party. The agreement raised a false hope that the two parties – the Communist Party of India and the Congress Socialist Party – would merge into a single organization.

The uneasy truce continued for a year and then, in early 1937, trouble cropped up again. In February 1937, the politburo of the banned Communist Party of India adopted a resolution stating that the anti-imperialist front must include not only the National Congress, the Congress Socialist Party, the Communist Party of India and the mass organizations of India, but also certain organizations of Indian merchants and industrialists.[179] The resolution was further elaborated in the editorial of the *Communist*, the secret journal of the party. It stated in unequivocal terms that the Communist Party of India would support 'the struggle of the Indian capitalists against the domination of British finance capital'.[180] The resolution was hailed by the communists as 'a landmark', but it created a furore in the congress socialist camp. The congress socialists termed the communists revisionists, while the communists, in turn, retaliated by calling the congress socialists left-sectarian.[181]

Despite ideological differences and occasional disputes, the communists and the congress socialists continued to function in unison on important issues pertaining to economic and social policies. But within a few months, dissension raised its head once again. In August 1937, at a meeting of the Congress Socialist Party's national executive, a secret circular, alleged to have been issued by the Communist Party of India, was brought to notice for information and action. The document, among other things, had put on record that 'the Congress Socialist Party was no socialist party and that it was to be used as a platform'.[182] The exposure of the document, as Jaiprakash Narayan said, was a 'painful shock' and caused 'great indignation'. The communists, however, manipulated the situation by pledging allegiance to the 'Lucknow agreement'. The national executive consequently took a mild view. Communists were allowed to stay in the party, only new admissions were stopped. Long after the incident, Jaiprakash Narayan confessed, 'It was a mistaken decision.'[183]

The truce continued till September 1938. In the same year, a secret circular titled *Plan of Work* came to light. The circular dated 9 May 1938 was a handiwork of the communists. It laid down in detail the tactics to be followed by the communists to capture the Congress Socialist Party. Masani got the circular published under the caption *Communist Plot Against CSP*.[184] 'For many comrades,' said Jaiprakash Narayan, 'the circular was the last straw. Yet the executive held its hand and allowed the thing to drift.'[185] The inaction of the executive gave a new lease of life to the so-called united front. It continued amidst confusion in the ranks of the congress socialists.

The communists exploited the united front to the hilt. Besides infiltrating into the Congress Socialist Party and, through it, into the National Congress, they successfully converted a large number of congress socialists into communists. To name a few, E.M.S. Namboodripad, P. Ramamurthi, P. Jeevandandan and P. Sundarayya joined the Communist Party through the Congress Socialist Party. For the success of the communists, Masani held Jaiprakash Narayan responsible, but exonerated himself, though he was one of the founder-members and the joint secretary of the Congress Socialist Party. 'The united front tactics of the communists,' said Masani, 'were greatly facilitated by the enthusiasm of Jaiprakash Narayan, the general secretary of the Socialist Party, who had become an intellectual adherent of the Comintern during his years as a student in the USA. The reason for this attitude was the same as elsewhere – lack of understanding of communist tactics and intellectual surrender to marxism.'[186] The statement cannot be dismissed. The strategy and tactics of the communists are as complicated and varied as the mysteries of the universe. No one except only a practicing communist can hope to understand them. Jaiprakash Narayan might have been a communist in his student days, but at that time he was a congress socialist. However, as partners of the united front, communists gained respect in the arena of politics: The nomenclature 'communist' ceased to be a taboo. But the communists' plan to rid the Congress of rightist elements and convert the party into a revolutionary organization, with the ultimate aim of capturing it, was a failure. When the opportunity came, the communists lost heart, making it clear that they were fit for only petty intrigues.

The strength of the united front or the left-combination within the Congress was first perceived at Faizpur, when the Congress met primarily to chalk out its plan to contest the provincial election under the new constitution. The Communist Party of India issued a manifesto titled *Gathering Storm*, addressed to 'all anti-imperialist fighters'. The manifesto stated: 'The united front is not a vague lining up of allied groups and organisations for passing pious resolutions. The anti-imperialist united front is the spearhead formation of our fighting force.'[187] In the light of the manifesto, the communists posed a challenge to the mellowed bourgeois leaders, who were keen to come to power through self-government by peaceful means. Through an amendment, the communists asserted that self-government could be achieved only by an uncompromising revolutionary mass struggle against imperialism. The amendment was defeated, but the left-combination secured 43 votes out of 128 in the all-India Congress Committee, and 262 out of 713 in the full session.[188] The not-too-bad performance emboldened the left-combination to push forward and confront bourgeois leaders at the Tripuri congress.

In 1939, at the Tripuri session of the National Congress, Subhas Chandra Bose staked his claim for the presidentship of the party for the second consecutive term. Gandhi, though not a member of the Congress, opposed the candidature of Bose, on the flimsy ground that he had fascist leanings, and placed his own candidate to oppose him. Undeterred and supported by the left-combination, Bose went ahead with his plan and defeated Gandhi's candidate. The rightist bourgeois leaders were taken aback. After overcoming the initial shock and in consultation with Gandhi, they set their strategy and threw down the gauntlet. Under Gandhi's instructions, they refused to serve under Bose and resigned *en bloc* from the working committee of the party. When the tussle between Bose and Gandhi reached its climax, the congress socialists proclaimed their dubious neutrality and the communists extended their eventually fatal support to Gandhi, leaving Bose in the lurch. The communists argued that support to Bose was sure to split the Congress. True though it was, it would have helped them capture at least half the Congress. The communists lost the opportunity to come up as a frontline independent political force to participate in the national liberation movement, along with other political parties.

The decision to support Gandhi came from abroad. Communists in India were mere pawns in the game. Harry Pollitt, speaking for the Communist Party of Great Britain, sent an instruction in the form of a message to the communists in India at the Tripuri congress, indicating that 'the question of paramount importance in India in our view is unity of all national forces under the leadership of the Indian National Congress'.[189] The communists obeyed the order. Like good communists, they did not raise any question or gave a second thought to the command. The communists were perhaps under the impression that Bose would continue to be in the Congress even after Tripuri, and they, under the cover of the united front, could exploit the situation. This was a mistake. To avenge Tripuri, Bose formed his own party – The Forward Bloc, first within the Congress and then outside it. The communists tried their best to desist Bose from forming a new party, but to no avail. Bose, by now, had come to see through communist tactics. Yet, his illusion was not over. To counter the right-wing offensive, Bose formed a 'left consolidation committee' composed of communists, congress socialists, *Kisan Sabha* and the League of Radical Congressmen.

Harry Pollitt's decision to support Gandhi was wrong. . It was the result of a lack of political farsightedness and dependence on foreign advice. After the Tripuri congress, the united front ceased to exist for all practical purposes, though officially it came to an end in 1940, when the national executive of the Congress Socialist Party expelled the communists. But by now, the rape was complete. The Congress Socialist Party was 'all but finished'.[190] In Madras, Travancore-Cochin and Hyderabad – in fact, across south India – the Congress Socialist Party was transformed into the Communist Party of India. The communists continued to be in the Congress for some more time, but only as unwanted guests. The Congress was too big an organization for the communists to make a dent.

The ill-conceived strategy adopted by the marxists at the Tripuri congress was enough provocation to bring to the surface a few splinter groups. They disagreed with the leaders on all counts and, in time, formed parties of their own, which posed a challenge to the parent body but failed to muster popular support.[191]

Notes

1 David Petrie, op. cit, p.158.

2 ibid., p.159.

3 *Documents*, Vol. II, p.377. Letter from Bagerhatta to Roy, 8 September, 1924.

4 ibid., pp.382-3. Letter from Roy to Bagerhatta, 22 October, 1924.

5 David Petrie, op. cit., p.96.

6 ibid., p.123

7 David Petrie, op, cit., p.123.

8 Muzaffar Ahmed, op. cit., p.424.

9 ibid., p.425.

10 *Documents*, Vol. II, pp.473-82.

11 David Petrie, op. cit, p.123. Besides Shah, Gopen tried to despatch four other youths to Moscow but they were detected and taken into custody at the shipping office at Calcutta where they had gone to collect seaman's certificate.

12 ibid., pp.96-7.

13 ibid., p.160.

14 David Petrie, op. cit., pp.160-61. For the full· text of the leaflet see: *Documents*, Vol. II, pp.630-39.

15 ibid., p.161.

16 ibid., p.164.

17 *Documents*, Vol. II, pp.639-40.

18 ibid, p.656.

19 ibid., p.641. For the full text, see: pp. 640-1

20 David Pavid Petrie, op. cit., p.164

21 *Documents*, Vol. II, pp.662-8.

22 David Petrie, op. cit, pp.167-8.

23 *Documents*, Vol. II, pp.618-9.

24 David Petrie, op. cit., p.168.

25 Satya Bhakta, *Krantipath-ke-Pathik* (Hindi), Mathura, 1973, p.149

26 *Documents*, Vol. II, p.626.

27 ibid., p.627.

28 David Petrie, op. cit., p.99.

29 ibid.

30 ibid., p.102.

31 ibid.

32 M.N. Roy, *The Future of Indian Politics* (Reprint), Calcutta, 1971, p.69.

33 ibid., p.72.

34 ibid., p.86.

35 R. Palme Dutt, *Modern India*, London 1927. p.17. The book was first published in India in 1926 but in the following year a revised edition was published from London.

36 ibid., p.129.

37 ibid., pp.148-9.

38 ibid., p.18.

39 *Documents*, Vol. IIIA, pp.244-5.

40 *Documents*, Vol. IIIA, pp.167-9.

41 ibid.

42 Muzaffar Ahmed, op. cit., p.460.

43 David Petrie, op. cit, p.104. It was alleged that after his request for passport and empire-wide visa was refused, Allison got hold of the passport of one Donald Campbell; affixed his own photograph and made necessary alterations complete with seal and stamp of the foreign office.

44 Philip Spratt, *Blowing up India: Reminiscence and Reflections of a former Comintern Emissary*, Calcutta, 1955, p.29.

45 David Petrie, op. cit., p.109.

46 Sapurji Saklatvala, *Is India Different?* London, 1927, p.17.

47 David Petrie, op. cit, p.110.

48 Muzaffar Ahmed, op. cit., p.441

49 *Documents*, Vol. III B, p.163.

50 Muzaffar Ahmed, op. cit., p.414

51 *Documents*, Vol. II p.84.

52 ibid., p.672.

53 *Documents*, Vol. II, pp.687-9.

54 *Documents*, Vol. III A, p.25.

55 *Bombay Chronicle*, 24 February, 1927.

56 *Documents*, Vol. IIIB, p.168.

57 ibid., p.169.

58 Muzaffar Ahmed, 'Our First Day', *New Age*, Delhi, April, 1958.

59 The letter dated 30 December 1927 is commonly known as the Assembly letter, because an intercepted copy of the letter was read out in the Central Legislative Assembly. It was placed before the Meeirut trial as exhibit. For the full text of the letter, see: *Documents*, Vol. III C, pp. 225-43.

60 *Documents*, Vol. III C, pp.227-32.

61 ibid., pp.235-7.

62 Muzaffar Ahmed, op. cit, pp.431-2. Josh, a new comer to the party, was chosen as president to stall Dange from occupying the position.

The election of Dange as president would have resulted in internal bickering. Joglekar and Nimbkar were not prepared to accept Dange.

63 S.V. Ghate, R.S. Nimbkar, K.N. Joglekar, S.A. Dange (Bombay), Philip Spratt, Dharani Goswami, Muzaffar Ahmed, Hemanta Kumar Sarkar (Bengal), Sohan Singh Josh, Bhag Singh Canadian, Firozuddin Mansoor, Kedar Nath Sehgal (Punjab), Lakshmi Kant Kedam, Biswanath Mukherjee, P.C. Joshi, Gauri Sankar (U. P.) were the members of the national executive.

64 Muzaffar Ahmed, op., cit pp.432-3.

65 *Documents*, Vol. III C, pp.95-7.

66 ibid., p.99.

67 ibid., p.96-8.

68 ibid., p.91.

69 There was no law to regulate the conditions of work, no provision for rest, no housing facilities, no Sunday and no holidays. Men, women and children had to work from 12 to 18 hours and occasionally 23 hours a day. The monthly wage varied from Rs 4 to Rs 18 depending on the industry.

70 M.N. Roy, *Political Letters*, Zurich, 1924, pp.19-20.

71 ibid., p.32.

72 B.F. Bradley, *Trade Unionism in India*, London, 1932, p.13.

73 *Studies and Report: Industrial Labour in India*, I.L.O., Geneva, 1938, p.126.

74 N.N. Mitra Ed., *Indian Annual Register*, Vol. II, Calcutta, 1927, p.119.

75 Horace Williamson, op. cit., p.284.

76 David Petrie, op. cit., p.284

77 *Labour Monthly*, London, March 1927, pp.170-85. Jawaharlal Nehru attended the conference as an official delegate of the Indian National Congress and took prominent part in the proceedings. He was also elected a member of the organising committee. In 1931 Nehru was expelled from the League Against Imperialism.

78 The League Against Imperialism was first known as the League Against Cruelties and Oppression in the Colonies. Thereafter it changed its name to League Against Imperialism and colonisation for National Liberties, and still later the League Against Imperialism.

79 David Petrie, op. cit., p.88.

80 Soumendranath Tagore, *Historical Development of the Communist Movement in India*, Calcutta, 1944, pp.10-11.

81 David Petrie, op. cit, p.72.

82 ibid., pp.71-2. Besides the above-mentioned 5,000,000 gold Rouble, Cecil Kaye in *Communism in India* has stated that to propagate marxism in

India, the Comintern sanctioned $120,000 in July 1922 (p.12); $120,000 in November 1922 (p. 40); and $2,000 in February 1923 (p.52).

83 S.A. Dange, Muzaffar Ahmed, Gour Rahman and K.S. Iyenger formed the Presidium; M. Singaravelu, K.N. Joglekar, M.A. Majid, R.S. Nimbkar, A. Halim and Soumendranath Tagore formed the executive committee.

84 *Guidelines of the History of the Communist Party of India*, (Communist Party of India), New Delhi, 1974, p.18.

85 David Petrie, op. cit., p.112.

86 Within two years from the China debacle both Roy and Borodin were expelled from the Comintern. Roy escaped to India and died in 1954. Borodin could not leave the Soviet Union and said to have died in 1951 in a labour camp in Siberia.

87 Eugene Varga, 'Economics and Economic Policy in the Fourth Quarter of 1927', *Inprecor*, 14 March 1928.

88 R. Palme Dutt, 'Notes of the month', *Labour Monthly*, June 1928, pp.326-31.

89 ibid., p.334.

90 ibid., pp.334-5.

91 *The Communist International between the Fifth and the Sixth World Congress.* (Communist Party of Great Britain), London, 1928, p.469.

92 ibid., p.476.

93 Bernard Isaacs, op. cit., p.273. 112.

94 (i) Shaukat Usmani
(ii) Soumendranath Tagore
(iii) G.A.K. Luhani
(iv) Mohammad Shafiq
(v) Masood Ali Shah
(vi) Habib Ahmad Nasim

95 The Indian delegates were allotted six votes, three deciding and three consultative.

96 Shaukat Usmani, *I Met Stalin Twice*, Bombay, 1953, p.23.

97 'Draft Programme of the Communist International as adopted by the executive committee of the Comintern', *Inprecor*, 6 June 1928.

98 *Inprecor*, 13 August 1928.

99 O.V. Kuusinan, 'The Revolutionary Movement in the Colonies', *Inprecor*, 4 October, 1928

100 ibid.

101 ibid., Emphasis Original

102 *Inprecor*, 17 October 1928.

103 ibid., 30 October, 1928.

104 ibid., 8 November, 1928.

105 M.N. Roy, *'My crime' (An open letter to the members of the Communist International), Our Differences,* Calcutta, 1938, p.30.

106 M. N. Roy, *Our Differences* pp.30-34

107 O. V. Kuusinan, 'The Revolutionary Movement in the Colonies', *Inprecor*, 30 October, 1928.

108 *Inprecor*, 30 October, 1928.

109 ibid., 8 November, 1928.

110 ibid.

111 ibid., 30 October, 1928.

112 ibid., 25 September, 1928.

113 'Thesis on the Revolutionary Movement in the Colonies and Semi-colonies', *Inprecor*, 12 December 1928.

114 ibid.

115 ibid.

116 Bernard Isaacs, op. cit., p.268.

117 M. N. Roy, Our *Differences*, p, .2.

118 Jawaharlal Nehru, *An Autobiography*, New Delhi, 1926, p, .161.

119 N. N. Mitra, Ed., op. cit., Vol. II, 1929, p.513.

120 ibid.

121 Philips Spratt, op. cit., p.43.

122 To the all India conference of Workers' and Peasants' Parties', *Documents*, Vol. III c. pp.757-8.

123 Meerut case evidence, exhibit No. 465.

124 'The Political Situation in India: Thesis of the Workers' and Peasants' Party of China', *Labour Monthly*, London, March 1929, p.160.

125 R.P. Arnot, *How British Rule India*, London, 1929, p.30.

126 C.P. Dutt, 'The India League for Independence', *Labour Monthly*, January 1929, p.27.

127 M.N. Roy, 'The Indian Constitution', *Inprecor*, 24 August, 1928.

128 ibid.

129 Meerut Sessions Judgement, p.242.

130 Horace Williamson, op. cit., p.124.

131 Subodh Roy, Ed., op. cit, p.76.

132 Horace Williamson, op. cit., p.131.

133 Although the main centres of communist activity were Calcutta and Bombay, the accused were tried at Meerut, a small district town in the United Province, to avoid trial by jury. But on appeal the government agreed for a trial by jury at the sessions court and summoned five

assessors from the rural areas of Meerut. They were shopkeepers, moneylenders and well-to-do peasants who had neither the knowledge of English nor of marxism.

134 (i) Muzaffar Ahmed (xvii) S.N. Banerjee
(ii) S.A. Dange (xviii) M.G. Desai
(iii) S.V. Ghate (xix) Ayodhya Prasad
(iv) K.N. Joglekar (xx) K.N. Sehgal
(v) G.M. Adhikari (xxi) R.R. Mitra
(vi) P.C. Joshi (xxii) S.H. Jhabwalla
(vii) R.S. Nimbkar (xxiii) D.R. Thengdi
(viii) S.S. Mirajkar (xxiv) G. Chakravarty
(ix) Shaukat Usmani (xxv) G.R. Kasle
(x) M.A. Majid (xxvi) K. Ghosh
(xi) Sohan Singh Josh (xxvii) A.A. Alwe
(xii) Dharani Gosswami (xxviii) B. N. Mukherjee
(xiii) Gopal Basak (xxix) L. R. Kadam
(xiv) Philips Spratt (xxx) Gauri Sankar
(xv) B.F. Bradley (xxxi) Shamsul Huda
(xvi) Lester Hutchinson (xxxii) Dharambir Singh

135 Horace Williamson, op. cit., p.136.

136 ibid., p.137

137 Meerut Committal Order, pp.12ff.

138 Philips Spratt, op. cit., pp.51-2.

139 The defence committee was dissolved by 1930, partly due to the difference of opinion on the line of defense to be adopted and partly due to the inauguration of the civil disobedience movement.

140 Bhagat Singh was caught, tried and sentenced to life imprisonment. While serving the term, he was tried again for the murder of one noto¬rious British police officer, Saunders, which had been committed before his arrest in the Assembly Bomb case. For this murder he was sentenced to death and hanged on 23 March 1931. Bhagat Singh was not a communist but had leanings towards communism.

141 *Inprecor*, 20 August, 1929.

142 ibid., 21 August, 1929.

143 ibid., 17 September, 1929.

144 ibid., 21 August, 1929.

145 ibid., 19 December, 1929.

146 Horace Williamson, op. cit., pp.169-70.

147 ibid., p.170

148 ibid, pp.170-71

149 ibid., pp.171-2. Besides the above-mentioned emissaries, two Canadians, John Magnus Clark and William Bennett, also came to India and Muhammad Ali alias Sepassi made an abortive attempt to come to India. Clark and Bennett stayed in India for a year. They were put under arrest on mere suspicion of being communist emissaries, but when they prayed they were allowed to leave the country on their own

150 Solidarity with the Working Masses of India', *Inprecor*, 31 July, 1930.

151 The 'draft platform of action' was first printed in the Inprecor and then in the Daily Worker of London and Pravda of Moscow. It was reprinted in Bombay and circulated at the Karachi congress. Later it was translated into Urdu and widely distributed in India.
For the full text of the 'draft platform of action' see: Horace Williamson, ibid., pp.315-33.

152 Horace Williamson, op. cit, p.316.

153 ibid., pp.320-21.

154 ibid., p.320.

155 ibid., p.157.

156 ibid., p.176.

157 ibid., p.177.
Roy, after his expulsion from the Comintern, came back to India in 1930 under an assumed name, Dr. Mahmud, and tried to build up a party to recapture the leadership of the communist movement, but failed to make headway in his projected plan. In July 1931, he was detected, taken into custody, tried as an accused in the Cawnpore Conspiracy case and imprisoned for six years. On his release, he joined the Congress, but soon after the second world war broke out, he was forced to quit the party for his pro-war policy. After leaving the Congress, to maintain his support to anti-fascist war, he formed a party – the Radical Democratic Party and a trade union organization – Indian Federation of Labour, and made a dent in the labour movement in India. After the war was over, he dissolved the party and for all practical purposes, took leave from active politics.

158 *Inprecor*, 1 June, 1932.

159 Horace Williamson, op. cit., pp.182-3.

160 *Inprecor*, 24 November, 1933.

161 Horace Williamson, op. cit., pp.185-8.

162 ibid., p.188.

163 ibid., p.189.

164 V. Basak, 'A Few Remarks on the Indian Communist Movement, Inprecor, 1 June, 1934.

165 The idea to form a Congress Socialist Party was first mooted towards the close of 1933, when a draft proposal made its appearance in Bombay. (Horace Williamson, India and Communism, p.212).

166 Bernard Isaacs, op. cit., p.371.

167 ibid., p.321.

168 S.V. Deshpande, New Age, June, 1953.
Although there was no official delegation from the Communist Party of India, the *Inprecor* of 17 August, 1935 refers to one Tambe, an Indian who attended the congress and spoke for India.

169 Bernard Isaacs, op. cit., pp.357-8.

170 ibid., p.382.

171 Georgi.Dimitrov,- 'The Offensive of Fascism and the Task of the C. I. in the Struggle for Unity of the Working Class Against Fascism"', *Inprecor*, 20 August, 1935.

172 Bernard Isaacs, op. cit., p.359.

173 The communists in China in their struggle for national and social emancipation sought temporary alliance with the militarists, national reformists and all other anti-imperialist forces under their leadership. Whereas the communists in Brazil sought to build a broad anti-imperialist front comprising political groups of all hues.

174 *Inprecor*, 11 November, 1935.
A revised and enlarged version of the speech in the form of a pamphlet entitled The Revolutionary Movement in the Colonial Countries was published from New York in 1935. It was reprinted in Bombay in 1950.

175 M.R. Masani, 'The Communist Party in India', *Pacific Affairs*, New York, March 1951, p.22.

176 R. Palme Dutt and Ben Bradley, 'The Anti-Imperialist People's Front', *Inprecor*, 29 February, 1936.

177 ibid.

178 Jaiprakash Narayan, *Towards Struggle*, Bombay, 1946, p.170.
Jaiprakash Narayan had been a communist in his student days in America. Though at a later date he renounced bolshevism, he regarded the Indian communists as good marxists and aspired for left unity under the Congress Socialist Party

179 *Communist*, March, 1937.

180 ibid.

181 ibid., April, 1973.

182 M.R. Masani, *The Communist Party of India: A Short History*, London, 1954, p.69.

183 Jaiprakash Narayan, Towards Struggle, pp.172-4.

184 M.R. Masani, op. cit., p.69.

185 Jaiprakash Narayan, *The Socialist Unity and the Congress Socialist Party*, Bombay, 1941, p.26.

186 M. R. Masani, op. cit., p.67.

187 *Guidelines of the History of the Communist Party of India*, p.50.

188 *Communist*, February, 1937.

189 National Front, March, 1939.

190 Madhu Limaye, *Communist Party: Facts and Fiction*, Hyderabad 1951, p. 38.

191 In between 1939 and 1942, based on marxian ideology quite a few parties were formed. But except the Revolutionary Socialist Party of India which somehow managed to survive, all other parties either dissolved by themselves or slipped into slumber. In 1939 Pramod Das Gupta, Sisir Roy, Biswanath Dube, Niharendu Dutta Mazumdar and others formed the Bolshevik Party of India; in 1940 Jogesh Chatterjee, Tridib Choudhury, Thakur Haribans Singh, Keshave Sharma and others formed the Revolutionary Socialist Party of India; in 1941 Inder Sen, Ajit Roy and others formed the Bolshevik-Leninist Party of India; and in 1942 Soumandranath Tagore, Sudhir Das Gupta, Pannalal Das Gupta and others formed the Revolutionary Communist Party of India.

5

War and the Indian Marxists

Upon the outbreak of the Second World War, communists all over the world were confronted with the twin tasks of defining the nature of the war and their attitude towards it. The problem became all the more acute when the Soviet Union signed a non-aggression pact with Germany to secure temporary respite from Nazi aggression and, in the bargain, gained additional territory. For the Soviet Union, it was an act of diplomacy, but for the communists outside the Soviet Union, it became a question for which answers were hard to find. Secured by the pact, Germany invaded Poland on 1 September 1939 and, two days later, France and Great Britain declared war on Germany. In India, events moved faster than expected. To the annoyance of the bourgeois national leaders, the Viceroy, the chief agent of the British Crown in India, issued a proclamation declaring India a belligerent country. While people in general wanted to take advantage of the war to free their motherland from colonial oppression, a section of bourgeois leaders, viz., Gandhi and Nehru, extended heartfelt sympathy to Britain in their individual capacities. Gandhi lamented, 'I am not, therefore, just thinking of India's deliverance, it will come, but what will it be if England and France fall? Or if they come out victorious over Germany ruined and humiliated.'[1] Nehru went a step further. He not only sympathized but also extended unconditional support to Britain. He wanted 'India to play her full part and throw all her resources into the struggle for a new world'.[2] Nehru's emotions, however, gave way to cold logic after the first flush of enthusiasm was over, but Gandhi's emotionalism continued, tinged with mysticism. However, on 14 September, the Congress working committee met and adopted a resolution asking the British government to declare its war aims and categorically assure India its independence to enable the Congress to support Britain's war effort. Having failed to get a suitable response, the Congress ministries in the provinces resigned *en bloc,* charging the political atmosphere of the country with emotion. People expected the Congress to confront the imperialist government, but they were disillusioned. As a token protest, Gandhi took to individual *satyagraha,* while keeping the doors open for a negotiated settlement for independence. He was against jeopardizing Britain's war effort. Along with the Congress, the Congress Socialist Party also changed its stand and accepted the Congress position. Only Bose and his Forward Bloc, along with the Communist Party of India, remained true to their faith to wage an immediate national struggle for independence, with or without the Congress.

Bose's radical posture was viewed by the Congress working committee as a defiance of Gandhi's leadership, which led to his suspension. After his exit, he organized the 'anti-compromise conference', hoping to gain support from communists and other left elements within or outside the Congress. But the communists refused to be a party to the anti-compromise conference, though earlier they were active members of the 'left consolidation committee' formed by Bose after the Tripuri congress. Disheartened and disgusted, Bose left India in search of new allies to fight British imperialism from abroad. After his departure, the Forward Bloc became a rudderless ship. It swayed for some time in the high seas of politics in search of moorings, but when the Quit India movement was launched, it jumped into the fray only as an appendix to the Congress Socialist Party.

However, communists in India were in a better position than communists involved in the war in other imperialist countries. In November, when the executive committee of the Comintern termed the war an 'imperialist war' and urged communist parties of all countries to oppose the war efforts of imperialists, the communist parties of France and Great Britain were put in a highly embarrassing position. They were asked to oppose the war efforts of their respective governments.[3] But this was not the case with the Communist Party of India. Being a country subservient to Britain, the Comintern policy suited the Indian communists. In a resolution in October 1939, the politburo of the Communist Party of India made it clear that the British government had no intention of granting independence to the colonies. The task of the Indian people would, therefore, be the revolutionary utilization of the war crisis for the achievement of 'national freedom' by transforming the imperialist war into a war of national liberation.[4] But as the Communist Party was not strong enough to mobilize the masses for the freedom struggle, it decided to use the Congress as a platform to achieve the goal. Soon after the politburo resolution, communists in India began intensifying anti-war propaganda, simultaneously accusing bourgeois national leaders of seeking a treacherous compromise with the British imperialist.

The communists became more and more radical as the Congress vacillated. In January 1940, on the tenth anniversary of the traditional day of independence introduced by the Congress, the Communist Party of India issued a manifesto portraying the imperialist war as the greatest crisis of capitalism. The manifesto informed the people that 'The world is on the brink of mighty upheavals. Before our very eyes the old order is tottering, shaking, falling to pieces .... Amidst chaos and carnage, amidst worldwide clash of arms, new forces are rising.... In every imperialist country engaged in war, the masses are already raising the red banner of revolt. In every country in bondage, the people are preparing for decisive battles with their enslavers .... *With the outbreak of war a new phase of our national movement has begun.*

No longer is Britain the master of the situation, master of our destiny. The war has changed the whole position.... If today, when all the conditions are favourable for a victorious advance, we falter and fail, we shall commit a crime against our national movement, a crime against humanity. History will never forgive that crime.... *Never were we as powerful as we are today. Never was our enemy so weak*.... We are today in a position to launch an attack which imperialism will not be able to resist. Let this truth be carried to the millions of our countrymen on Independence Day.'[5]

The Comintern's advice to Indian communists was to continue with united front tactics and consolidate the left as an ally of the Congress. The communists had no objection to working with the Congress, but were not too keen to waste their time on the left consolidation programme. They were cautious enough not to allow any other party to take advantage of their spadework and launch a mass movement to wrest the revolutionary initiative from them. Their main rival was the Forward Bloc and, to a lesser extent, the Congress Socialist Party. P.C. Joshi, the general secretary of the Communist Party of India, in a statement issued in early March 1940, clarified the party's policy towards the Forward Bloc. In unambiguous terms, he said, 'Workers, peasants, students have already adopted the proletarian technique of struggle.... The effort of the Forward Bloc to win over these movements... has to be resisted...not as being too left but as being the disruptive agency of the bourgeoisie.'[6]

The radicalism of the communists reached its peak at the Ramgarh congress. To make the policy clear, the communists of India issued a statement – *Proletarian Path*. In the statement, the communists advocated the conversion of the war crisis into revolution, starting with strikes in major industries, to be followed up with a countrywide no-rent and no-tax movement. After this phase, 'the national movement would enter a new and higher phase – the phase of armed insurrection'. The main features of this phase would be 'storming of military and police stations by armed bands of national militia in rural as well as urban areas...'.[7] Following the 'policy statement', communist delegates K.M. Ashraf and V.D.

Chitale, who attended the Ramgarh congress, urged for an immediate mass struggle and moved an amendment to this effect for the main resolution, though in vain.[8]

The failure to lead the Congress to the revolutionary path did not matter much to the communists. They had already chalked out their plan and set the ball rolling. Led by the *Girni Kamgar Union*, the Bombay textile workers began their strike on 5 March, involving 1,75,000 workers of 65 cotton textile mills. In solidarity with the textile workers, other sections of workers, numbering 3,50,000, went on a day's strike on 10 March 1940 in response to the call of the all-India Trade Union Congress. The Bombay strike was followed by a wave of strikes all over the country. 'Textile workers of Cawnpore, municipal workers of Calcutta, jute workers of Bengal and Bihar, oil workers of Digboi in Assam, coal-miners of Dhanbad and Jharia, iron and steel workers of Jamshedpur and workers in some other industries struck work demanding dearness allowances.'[9]

As the working class was on the move, the government came down with an iron hand and clamped down the Defence of India Rules. *National Front* and *Kranti* were banned, which was followed by a countrywide round-up of communists and other radical elements. S.A. Dange, Muzaffar Ahmed, B.T. Ranadive, S.S. Mirajkar, S.V. Ghate, R.S. Nimbkar and G.S. Patkar, among others, were taken into custody. According to the government, 'The communists by means of subversive propaganda and in other organised ways, have attempted to prejudice the internal peace of India and to interfere with the efficient prosecution of the war by impeding the supply of men and material.'[10] The arrests were also extended to cover non-communists belonging to the Congress Socialist Party, the *Girni Kamgar Union*, the all-India Kisan Sabha and the all-India Trade Union Congress. J.P. Narayan, N.G. Ranga, Swami Sahajananda Saraswati, Rahul Sankrityayana and several others were taken into custody under the Defence of India Rules and removed from the political scene. Reginald Maxwell, the home member, declared in the Central Legislative Assembly that of the 700 who were detained without trial, 'about 480 persons were almost, without exception, either acknowledged communists or else active supporters of the communists' programme of violent mass revolution.'[11]

The communists had to pay dearly for their radical posture. Although the party was banned in 1934, by 1936 the communists were working openly under the cover of the united front. The leniency on the part of the government gave the communists a false sense of impunity. Their radical posture was further encouraged by the Comintern, evidently unaware that the government would not tolerate radicalism, particularly in times of war. In an article in *Bolshevik*, Kochariants, a Soviet spokesman, approved, rather appreciated, the radical posture of the communists in India, including their tirade against the Forward Bloc. He criticized the Congress for its tendency to compromise with the imperialists, but simultaneously advised the communists to maintain unity with the Congress, neutralize the bourgeois leadership and capture the nationalist movement.[12] Encouraged by the support of the Comintern, in September 1940, when the all-India congress committee met in Bombay to discuss the war policy, the communist members stood unitedly and opposed the main resolution on the war policy vis-à-vis the Congress. It is said that Nehru flew into a rage and, in a fury, demanded that their names be recorded.[13] The matter ended there. The communist Congress *entente* practically came to an end.

Having snapped their relations with the Congress, the communists moved a step further. In October 1940, the Communist Party of India issued a statement accusing gandhian leadership of 'bankruptcy' and 'hypocrisy', and of sabotaging the liberation struggle with a view to 'manoeuvring for a suitable compromise'.[14] The tirade did not end here. At a conference of leftist students, the communists, in a resolution, challenged the right of the Congress to speak for the whole of India. Assuming that the Congress had failed to solve the communal problem, the communists recorded in the resolution that the future of India should be a 'voluntary federation of regional states based on mutual confidence'.[15] The resolution gave a fillip to the Muslim League's demand for Pakistan. However, the communists became unpopular, rather renegades, in the eyes of the people.

After years of hectic activity, the communists had failed on all counts. The expected revolution did not materialize; the attempt to capture the National Congress or convert it into a radical organization of the people failed; and the united front tactics, which brought the communists in the limelight, ended. Once again, the communists isolated themselves from the masses by their own actions. Before the communists could think of a new strategy, the German army got ready to give effect to Hitler's grandiose plan, *Operation Barbarossa.*

By the summer of 1941, practically the whole of Europe with its vast manpower and material resources came under the control of Nazi Germany. The independence of Britain hung in the balance. Confident of victory, the German army launched a massive attack on the Soviet Union and changed the character of the war. For the first time in history, an international front made up of the most diverse forces was formed. Britain, the United States and the Soviet Union joined hands to fight a common enemy – fascism. The alliance between the imperialists and the communists was within the permissible limit of communist tactics. During the civil war, Lenin had pointed out that proletarian dictatorship could, for reasons of political and military expediency, conclude agreement with a group of capitalist powers. Communists, he said, did not by any means 'in general reject military agreements with one of the imperialist coalitions against the other in those cases in which such an agreement could, without undermining the basis of soviet power, strengthen its position and paralyse the attacks of any imperialist power…'[16]

The Nazi attack on the Soviet Union was resented by the bourgeois nationalist leaders. In a resolution, the Congress working committee declared, 'The Soviet Union has stood for certain human, cultural and social values which are of great importance to the growth and progress of humanity. The working committee consider that it would be a tragedy if the cataclysm of war involved the destruction of this endeavour and achievement.'[17] Taking the resolution at its face value, the British expected that, in tune with the sympathy for the Soviet Union, the attitude of the bourgeois national leaders towards the British would also change, but they were disillusioned. The change did come, but only towards the war in general. India's attitude towards England continued to be the same as before. The bourgeois nationalist leaders stuck to their demand for independence, whatever might occur outside India.

Germany launched its attack on the Soviet Union on 21 June and on 22 June the executive committee of the Comintern sat in a meeting to discuss the war situation. The decision called for a reorganization of the entire work of the Comintern apparatus. For day-to-day management of the work, a small committee consisting of Dimitrov, Manuilsky and Togaliatti was formed and a statement issued, calling upon communist parties of all the countries fighting fascist Germany 'to support all the war efforts of their governments, as these were in the national interest of their peoples and a real aid to the Soviet Union'.[18] On the basis of this general policy guideline, *Labour Monthly*, the official organ of the Communist Party of Great Britain, published an article reminding communists of all the countries involved in the war about their duties and responsibilities. 'Obviously,' said the article, 'the first concern of the proletariat in an imperialist country fighting the Soviet Union is to procure the defeat and overthrow of its own government, turning the imperialist war into a civil war.' But the duties of the proletariat in other imperialist countries 'must be the defence of the Soviet Union, whose defeat would be a terrible blow not only to the proletariat of all countries, but for humanity in general. Every act of the proletarian struggle has to be subordinated to the supreme aim of procuring the victory of the USSR'.[19] The article did not mention anything about the role that the Indian communists were required to play. The question of India was taken up in the September issue of *Labour Monthly*. R. Palme Dutt, in plain terms, told the Indian communists that their support to the war effort of Great Britain should be unconditional and must not rest on the achievement of Independence. 'The interest of the people of India and Ireland and of all colonial peoples of the world, is bound up with the victory of the peoples against fascism; that interest is absolute and unconditional, and does not depend on any measures their rulers may promise or concede.'[20] Simultaneously, another article with the same advice to Indian communists appeared in *Bolshevik*, the organ of the Communist Party of the Soviet Union. In the article titled *The Role of the British Empire in the Current War*, I. Lemin advised Indian communists to support the war effort of Great Britain as long as it fought side by side with the Soviet Union.[21] Both Dutt and Lemin subordinated the question of India's independence, according the first priority to the victory of the Soviet Union. This was an unreal expectation. The people of India, while expressing their sympathy for the Soviet Union, wanted to first become independent, with or without the Soviet Union's victory.

The communists in India were in a dilemma. For quite some time, they could not decide whether to support the war effort of imperialist Britain or oppose it; whether to fight for the independence of their own country to free themselves from colonial rule or fight for the victory of the Soviet Union – the fatherland of the proletariat. However, the communists who were arrested in 1940-1941 and interned in the Deoli detention camp, finally decided to support the war effort of imperialist Britain, camouflaging the imperialist war as the 'people's war'.[22] These old guards sitting in jail perceived a new situation when the news of the alliance among the Soviet Union, the United States of America and Great Britain reached them. They might have been influenced by the articles published in *Labour Monthly* or *Bolshevik* to come to this decision. But Masani thought otherwise. According to him, the 'Deoli Thesis', as it was called, emerged from a letter from Harry Pollitt addressed to the Communist Party of India. The letter, delivered to the Deoli detenues by Reginald Maxwell, is said to have 'ordered for a clear switchover'.[23]

The 'Deoli Thesis' was not immediately accepted by the communists working outside the prison. Led by P.C. Joshi, they stuck to their old policy. In a resolution in July 1941, the polit-buro of the underground Communist Party of India said in unequivocal terms 'that the only way in which the Indian people can help in the just war which the Soviet Union is waging, is by fighting all the more vigorously for their own emancipation from the imperialist yoke. Our attitude towards the British Government and the imperialist war remains what it was. We must continue, nay, intensify our struggle against both. There can be no change in our policy until a people's government…come to power. We can render really effective aid to the Soviet Union only as a free people'.[24] Following this policy, communists outside the prison launched a direct attack on the 'Deoli Thesis' and castigated those communists who formulated it. In October, the underground Communist Party of India said in a statement: 'They are false internationalists and the deceivers of people who say that we can side with the Soviet Union or win the war for the people by aiding the British Government's war effort.'[25] With this expression, the underground communists set to intensify the liberation struggle. They asked the *Kisan Sabha* to take to more militant action[26] and encouraged the students for a nationwide struggle for freedom.[27] The discrepancy cropped up because the two fragments of the party were completely isolated from each other, which resulted in the emergence of two separate, rather, antithetical, policies.

Within a month of the issue of this statement, the underground Communist Party of India had second thoughts about its adamantly anti-imperialist policy. In November, at a meeting of the standing committee of the *Kisan Sabha* held at Nagpur, the communist member of the committee proposed the 'people's war' thesis and managed to pass a resolution stating that the war would become a 'people's war' only after India had achieved independence.[28] Soon thereafter, the underground Communist Party of India did a somersault, abandoned its anti-imperialist stance and embraced the 'people's war' policy. To justify the new stand, the politburo of the underground party said in a resolution, 'We are a practical party and in a new situation it is our task not only to evolve a new form of struggle for it, but also to advance new slogans appropriate to the new stage, suiting the new form of our national movement. The key slogan of our party, which guides all our practical political activity, is: MAKE THE INDIAN PEOPLE PLAY A PEOPLE'S

ROLE IN THE PEOPLE'S WAR.'[29] Thus, six months after the Nazi attack on the Soviet Union, communists in India lined up with international communists.

Once decided, the communists in India laboured strenuously to popularise the 'people's war' thesis. To begin with, P.C. Joshi issued a statement[30] in February 1942 assuring people that the Soviet Union would dominate the allied camp. Popular pressure and Soviet influence would force imperialist Britain to grant independence to India. But this would come only after fascism was destroyed and victory achieved. Therefore, the slogan of the time was to be 'national unity for national defence and national government'.

The slogan 'people's war' turned out to be anti-national as it compromised national interest vis-à-vis British imperialism. It was a misconceived strategy, and violated people's sentiment at the most crucial hour of India's struggle for freedom. The communists realized their folly only too late, when the 'people's war' thesis became a part of history, impossible to erase. However, after speaking at length on the 'people's war' strategy, Joshi turned to its tactical implementation. Instead of looking for unity within the Congress as a national organization, Joshi, on behalf of the communists in India, put the National Congress on a par with the Muslim League. He made it clear that national unity meant Congress-League unity. He defined the Muslim League as 'the premier political organisation of the second largest community in India', the sole spokesperson for the Muslims, and relegated the Congress as the spokesperson for only the Hindus. He refused to call the Muslim League a reactionary communal organization and urged the Congress to concede to the demands of the Muslim League, 'including the demand for a separate sovereign state for Muslims'.[31] This attitude was against national interest. It encouraged the Muslim League to concentrate on the demand for Pakistan, without any tangible gain to the communists.

After hurting the Congress and causing irreparable damage to the nation, the Communist Party of India issued an 'open letter' in the form of a 'healing touch' to the Congress working committee. Praising the National Congress as 'the foremost organization of our freedom struggle', as well as its leadership, the 'open letter' said with a sense of pride: 'We communists are 15 years old, born in the womb of the same broad national movement and we have endeavoured our very best to strengthen it. All of us proudly carry our Congress membership card, as a treasured possession of our national heritage, as a living inspiration to fight the battle of India's freedom, shoulder to shoulder, with our fellow patriots.'[32]

The encouragement to the Muslim League, and the simultaneous flattery and denigration of the National Congress was, in fact, a part of communist tactics. They wanted to eat the cake and have it too. The dubious tactical line adopted by Joshi was first disapproved, but subsequently approved by the Communist Party of Great Britain. About two months after Joshi's policy statement, D.N. Pritt of the Communist Party of Great Britain published an article contradicting Joshi in *Labour Monthly*. Pritt emphatically said 'that the Congress is entitled to be accepted as the representative of the whole Indian people' so long as the terms for settlement to which it agrees 'contain provisions for safeguarding minorities'.[33] He condemned the British government for the creation of the Muslim League and made it clear that the league had no right to speak for the Muslims in India. Ben Bradley, a one-time communist emissary in India, condemned the idea of treating the Congress and the Muslim League on a par, and gave a blank cheque to the National Congress to make a settlement 'on behalf of the Indian people'.[34]

The stand taken by the Communist Party of Great Britain was soon altered. Writing in *Labour Monthly*, R.P. Dutt, contrary to his earlier stand that only the Congress was authorized to negotiate on behalf of the Indian people, called upon the British Government to negotiate 'with all political sections and leaders in India'. He advised the Congress to make 'far-reaching concessions' to the other political group, i.e., the Muslim League. He argued that 'for the present we need not concern ourselves with the representative or unrepresentative character' of groups.[35] This was a temporary accommodation. Soon after the 'people's war' was over and the fascists were subdued, Dutt confessed without regret that it was for 'tactical reasons' that the Communist Party of Great Britain adopted a 'sympathetic approach to the supporters of Pakistan in order to win them for the united all-India national front'.[36] Dutt was perhaps momentarily influenced by V.K. Krishna Menon, the official London representative of the Congress. Menon, in a series of three articles in *Labour Monthly*, pointed out that 'the Soviet Union's entry into the war had transformed the character of the war for the colonial people. The victory of the Soviet Union would guarantee the achievement of freedom to the colonial people as it had always helped them in their struggle for freedom and supported the autonomy of nationalities'.[37]

Meanwhile, the war situation was fast deteriorating to the disadvantage of the allied powers. Japan declared war in December 1941 and by March 1942, after completing the first round, knocked at the doors of India. This perturbed both America and China. To enlist support from India and as a matter of expediency, they discovered legitimacy in India's demand for independence and pressed Churchill for a settlement with Indian leaders. Much against his will, Churchill relented under the pressure, and sent Stafford Cripps with a proposal to negotiate the terms. The Cripps proposal was rejected by all, excepting the communists, as it did not come up to expectations of the Indian leaders. Though the Communist Party of India was not party to the discussion, the politburo of the party approved it and appealed to the Congress and the Muslim League for its acceptance.[38]

Acceptance of the Cripps proposal was a part of the 'people's war' strategy of the communists and, as expected, it paid rich dividends. Cripps came to India in March 1942 and, in April, Maxwell said in the Legislative Assembly, 'If there be any person whose attitude is such that he wishes earnestly to help the war effort, I have no desire whatsoever to keep him in jail.'[39] Following this declaration, on 24 July 1942, the Government of India lifted the ban on the Communist Party of India and allowed it to act freely to popularize the 'people's war' thesis.

It was widely believed that P.C. Joshi had met Maxwell, and perhaps also Cripps, and in the course of the discussion, he had offered to place the services of his party at the disposal of the home department of the Government of India in return for getting a legal status for the Communist Party of India. It was only after this assurance that the ban was lifted. Soli Batlivala, a member of the central committee of the Communist Party of India, narrated some secret correspondence between P.C. Joshi and Maxwell. Batlivala claimed to have seen a confidential file of correspondence between Joshi and Maxwell, but the most serious charge that Batlivala made against Joshi was that, in a letter to Maxwell, Joshi had offered unconditional help to the Government of India and the army headquarters to fight the 1942 underground workers and the *Azad Hind Fauj* of Subhas. These men, as Batlivala said, were termed by Joshi as 'traitors' and 'fifth columnists'.[40]

After obtaining legal status, the Communist Party of India became an ally of the British Indian government. Its support to the imperialist war, euphemistically termed as the 'people's war', satisfied Britain. The communists exploited the hobnobbing to the best of their capacity. To propagate the 'people's war' thesis, they initially brought out an English weekly, *People's War*, followed by a string of provincial newspapers. Significantly, around this time, the British Indian government suddenly became panicky because of an apprehended invasion of India by the combined army of *Azad Hind Fauj* and Japan. Out of sheer desperation and to fight the probably invading army, the British Indian government took a calculated risk and recruited a band of young men, mostly from the communist cadres, to train them as guerrillas. The formation of the 'Red Army' came closer to reality. The communists were elated. However, with the improvement of the war situation, the threat of invasion receded and the British Indian government scrapped the guerrilla training plan, much to the dismay of the communists.[41] Had the war situation not improved and the guerrilla training programme continued, India's freedom struggle would have seen a new phenomenon. Gandhi's khadi-clad non-violent brigade would have been replaced by the 'Red Army', under the command of the communists.

But this loss was partially made up as the political situation in the country took a new turn. With the failure of the Cripps mission, the Congress gave up its lukewarm policy and decided to undertake a mass civil disobedience movement to confront the imperialist government. On 14 July 1942, the working committee of the Congress passed a resolution with the demand that the British must quit India. To consider the resolution, the all-India congress committee met in Bombay on 7 August and, after a threadbare discussion on 8 August 1942, endorsed the resolution with near-unanimity. Only a few communists, viz., K.M. Ashraf, Sajjad Zahir and G.S. Sardesai, members of the all-India congress committee, opposed the resolution, and instead suggested an amendment that embodied the 'people's war' thesis.[42] The communists termed the 'Quit India' resolution 'an abortion' and said with a flush of sarcasm that from the 'nut of inactivity', the Congress 'now seeks to lead the nation into the politics of blind desperation and disaster'.[43]

In spite of the scathing criticism, the 'Quit India' movement was welcomed by the people. It swept India with national sentiment and included the ranks of the communists. Joshi admitted that there was 'vacillation' in the ranks and the 'boys were bogged'.[44] However, as soon as the 'Quit India' resolution was passed, the Congress was declared illegal and its leaders were imprisoned, leaving the field open for the communists to exploit. The communists made good use of the opportunity and spread their influence all around. Through the *kisan* movement, they converted quite a few *kisan* leaders, notably Swami Sahajanarida and Indulal Yagnik, to the main elements of their policy, and brought under control a number of provincial units of the all-India Kisan Sabha. N.G. Ranga, the accepted leader of the *kisans*, had to be satisfied with only six provincial units.[45] Similarly, among the students' front, the communists succeeded in motivating a large number of students to accept the 'people's war' thesis.[46]

The organizing ability of the communists was further reflected in the formation of a number of societies as auxiliaries to the main party. The Indian People's Theatre Association, the Progressive Writers' Association, the Friends of the Soviet Union, the Children's Association and the Women's Association are some examples. These organizations served as effective instruments of action and propaganda, and brought potential recruits closer to marxist ideology. Such activities also gave a new impetus to the communist movement and helped build the party. One index was the increase in the number of members. The party claimed that its membership grew from 4,500 in 1942 to 15,000 in 1943 and 30,000 in 1945.[47] The rapid growth in membership was achieved through diversification of activities. The party also relaxed the standard of admission with the aim of creating a mass party. At a meeting of the central committee, it was decided to 'remove all unnecessary barriers, and throw open party membership to all honest elements who have proved their worth'.[48] Along with the increase in membership, the communists took the initiative to organize a stable system of cadres. By 1943, the Communist Party of India claimed 2,637 *wholetimers*, i.e., full-time salaried functionaries.[49]

In spite of success on all fronts, the communists had to suffer some setback in the trade union movement – the main arena of their political activities. Though the party's influence in the all-India Trade Union Congress increased, it failed to warm up the organization to the 'people's war' thesis. At a session of the all-India Trade Union Congress in 1942, the communists, though they dominated several local unions, countered stiff opposition to their new aims. Nehru, who inaugurated the session, condemned the communists, declaring that India must fight for its own freedom before taking up the cause of any other country. V.R. Kalappa, the president of the all-India Trade Union Congress, asserted that: 'All talk of an anti-fascist front will lead us nowhere' and criticized the communists for their promise of freedom to India after the war. Even N.M. Joshi, the moderate trade union leader, raised his voice against the 'people's war' thesis. In the face of combined opposition, the communists failed to carry through the 'people's war' resolution. They secured simple majority, but failed to get three-quarter majority support required under the rules of the all-India Trade Union Congress for all important decisions.[50] The issue was taken up again at the next annual session in 1943. Feelings ran high. In the midst of the proceedings, communist and anti-communist slogans were raised and the session finally ended in fisticuffs. Once again, the communists failed to push through the 'people's war' resolution or dislodge non-communists from important positions.[51]

However, with the legalization of the party and increased influence in the arena of politics, the Communist Party of India convened its first conference as a legal party in Bombay in 1943. The conference was attended by nearly 300 delegates from all parts of India. In its week-long deliberations, the party approved the 'people's war' thesis as the correct policy and adopted two programmes – the national unity campaign and the productivity campaign – in support of the war effort of imperialist Britain. P.C. Joshi was re-elected as the general secretary of the party.[52]

While the communists in India were meeting at an open conference, the Soviet Union decided to dissolve the Comintern. The Comintern came into existence with the twin purposes of propagating marxism and liberating the oppressed people of the colonies from imperialist oppression. It worked well under Lenin, but when Stalin came to power, it became an appendix to the Communist Party of the Soviet Union. It ceased to be an open forum of communists. It continued to function more as an international refugee camp for marxist revolutionaries than an organization for the growth of the communist movement. When the Soviet Union formed an alliance with imperialist Britain, the greatest colonial power of the time, the Comintern became redundant. The oppressed people of the colonies were asked to shelve their struggle for independence and support the imperialist war effort to defeat fascism for the sake of universal liberty. In fact, the Comintern ceased to be a centre of struggle for the national liberation of the oppressed people of the colonial world.

Besides, when the Comintern came into being, communist parties outside the Soviet Union were weak, both in terms of ideology and organization. They lacked experienced leaders in their ranks, and their membership was quite limited. Such communist parties could deal with the problems of leadership of the revolutionary movement in their respective countries and work out the strategy and tactics of the class struggle only by the joint efforts of all the parties in the collective centralized body – the Comintern. During the heydeys of the Comintern, communist parties developed ideologically and organizationally, accumulated experience in leadership and produced experienced cadres and leaders trained in the strategy and tactics of marxism-leninism. With the passage of time, the activities of the parties became more and more diverse, embracing a variety of fields, but keeping in view concrete national conditions and traditions. This required a greater degree of independence and initiative than before, demanding the abandonment of leadership from a single centre. Taking into account all these circumstances, the presidium of the executive committee of the Comintern decided to dissolve the Third Communist International or the Comintern in the spring of 1943. On 13 May 1943, the presidium discussed the proposal of dissolution and the draft resolution on this question. Dimitrov, the chairman of the presidium, called upon the members to think whether this measure would be timely and politically expedient. Thorez, while seconding the motion of dissolution, commented that the 'old form of international association of the workers has outlived itself …. the movement for dissolution had been well chosen'.[53]

After a thorough analysis of the political situation and the state of affairs of the communist movement, the executive committee of the Comintern submitted a proposal for its dissolution to the communist parties of all countries on 15 May 1943. The proposal was supported by all the communist parties, except the Communist Party of China.[54] On the basis of the majority decision, the executive committee of the Comintern announced on 8 June 1943 that the Communist International would be dissolved from 10 June.[55] The dissolution of the Comintern, however, did not affect the growth of the communist movement. 'On the eve of the war the world had 4,200,000 communists, at the end of the war this figure had risen to 20,000,000.'[56]

As stated earlier, the open conference of the communists held in 1943 approved the national unity campaign and the national productivity campaign as part of the 'people's war' policy. At the heart of the national unity campaign was an appeal for Congress-Muslim League collaboration, or to be more precise, for the recognition of the Muslim League's right to speak for Muslims. This was a profoundly anti-Congress policy. But the communists were happy to brand the Congress a Hindu organization and raise the status of the Muslim League as the sole spokesperson for the Muslims. This uncalled-for advocacy for the Muslim League was amply manifested by Sajjad Zahir, a member of the central committee of the Communist Party of India. Zahir emphatically said that the league would put the Muslim masses on the path to progress and democracy and lead them to their salvation. He felt happy to see the advent and advance of the Muslim League, and said with elation: 'It is a good and fine thing, a happy augury, for Indian Muslims and for India as a whole that the Muslim League continues to grow and gather around it millions of our liberty-loving people.'[57] This soft stance towards the Muslim League was part of the nationality policy. In July 1942, the party issued a statement and stated in unambiguous terms that the basis of the nationality policy should be 'the principle of self-determination including the right of separation for all nationalities that inhabit our subcontinent'.[58] It was further elaborated in September 1942, in a resolution based on a report submitted to the central committee of the Communist Party of India by G. Adhikari. The resolution outlined that 'every section of the Indian people which has a contiguous territory as its homeland, common historical tradition, common language, culture, psychological make-up, and common economic life would be recognised as a distinct nationality with the right to exist as an autonomous state within the free Indian union or federation and will have the right to secede from it if it may so desire.... Thus free

India of tomorrow would be a federation or union of autonomous states of the various nationalities such as, Pathans, Western Punjabis (dominantly Muslims), Sikhs, Sindhis, Hindustanis, Rajasthanis, Gujaratis, Bengalis, Assamese, Biharis, Oriyas, Andhras, Tamils, Karnataks, Maharashtrians, Keralas, etc' (sic).[59]

The resolution appears to suggest that the communists wanted the Balkanization of India. But no one except the Muslims paid any attention to it. They found in this resolution the hope to fulfil their dream of a separate homeland. Though the word 'Pakistan' was not explicitly used in the resolution, it was implicit in it and gave direct encouragement to the Muslims of the Punjab, Sind, Baluchistan and North-Western India to form a separate state and secede. Within a year, the Communist Party of India started supporting Pakistan openly. After criticizing the Congress for its failure to see the anti-imperialist, liberationist role of the Muslim League, Zahir said, 'the demand for self-determination of Pakistan is a just, progressive and national demand, and is the positive expression of the very freedom and democracy for which congressmen have striven and undergone so much suffering all these years.'[60] P.C. Joshi, while supporting Zahir, asked the Congress 'to work out a new platform for the Indian national movement which satisfies the Muslim League and leads to Congress-League front'.[61]

The reason for this blatant pro-Muslim policy of the communists is hard to fathom. Perhaps it was the result of a mechanical application of Lenin's nationality policy. After the socialist revolution, Lenin, as a policy, accepted the right to self-determination as a democratic solution for the conquered and oppressed nationalities of the tsarist empire. The Tsar's policy was forcible occupation and 'Russification' of different nationalities of heterogeneous character. There was no ethnic unity in the empire. It was an amalgam of conflicting nationalities loosely fastened together and wrought into a vast political organism by the awe of imperial authority and the pressure exerted by an omnipotent bureaucracy. In India, on the other hand, the different communities that the communists termed as nationalities had come together neither through forcible occupation nor through 'Indianization'. They had come together through the process of evolution and lived harmoniously. They were a homogeneous group of people, following religions of their choice. The communists in India failed to understand this basic character of the Indian nationality and erroneously applied Lenin's nationality policy. Soli Batlivala, a one-time member of the central committee of the Communist Party of India, said that the communists believed that support to the Muslim League 'will give them a foothold in the Muslim masses, as support of the Congress from 1936 onwards gave them a foothold among the nationalist masses of the country'.[62] However, the Muslim League took advantage of the nationality policy of the communists and, under its shadow, consolidated the Pakistan programme.

Like the national unity campaign, the productivity campaign was aimed at making the 'people's war' programme a success by maximizing India's productive capacity, both in industrial and agricultural sectors, and helping Britain conduct the war successfully. This was sought to be achieved through a harmonious relationship between different productive forces: workers and industrialists, peasants and landlords. In a resolution in 1942, the Communist Party of India gave the blueprint of its wartime economic policy by proclaiming full production as the goal. The party shifted from its policy of proletarian revolution to peaceful cooperation and declared that it would take to agitation only when 'compelled to do so'.[63] In his report to the first open conference of the party, B.T. Ranadive declared that 'strikes should be firmly prevented' and suggested that all economic disputes should be settled through tripartite boards composed of employers, employees and government agencies.[64]

In matters of agricultural production, the party took the same view as in its industrial policy. The demand for land reforms was given up and peasants were advised to cooperate with landlords for full production, while urging reasonable prices to peasants and profits to traders.[65]

The productivity campaign was given the utmost possible emphasis. P.C. Joshi declared that as far as the productivity campaign was concerned, 'everything else is empty phrase'.[66]

Further, the communists formed 'people's food committees' to extend mass contact in rural areas, embracing all sections of the population, except the hoarders and the blackmarketeers. S.G. Sardesai, a member of the central committee of the Communist Party of India, claimed that the mass contact programme paid rich dividends. It strengthened the 'party numerically and politically'.[67] This claim seems doubtful, however. The gains in the trade union movement and the peasant movement were mostly attributed to the lack of opposition. And politically, the party sank in the eyes of the people. The 'people's war' thesis was, in fact, anti-people. The communists failed to attain their goal of national unity or build an anti-fascist front. By abstaining from strikes and land reform agitation in the name of the productivity campaign, the party may have helped the imperialist war effort, but not itself. The Congress represented the sentiment of the people and continued to oppose the imperialist war against heavy odds.

Though the communists were still members of the Congress and continued to hold some important offices, the Congress suspected that they were secretly collaborating with the government, receiving financial aid, undermining its activities and had come to a secret agreement with the Muslim League. The suspicion grew out of a letter supposed to have been written by Joshi to Maxwell. The communists denounced the letter as forgery.[68] But Soli Batlivala claimed that he had seen similar correspondence between Joshi and Maxwell.[69] This letter and various other factors contributed towards widening the difference between the Congress and the Communist Party of India, so much so that a number of provincial congress committees passed resolutions barring communists from holding offices.

The communists, being conscious of their political shortcomings, were frightened at the very idea of expulsion from the Congress. Joshi made an abortive attempt to restore relations to save the situation.

In a bid to placate the Congress, he proclaimed: 'It is the Congress that planted the banner of Indian freedom; it is from the Congress leaders that we got our early lessons in patriotism and it is today congressmen who want to deny us the privilege of fighting shoulder to shoulder with them for the cause they taught us to accept as our main aim in life. To us the Congress is our parent organisation, its leaders our political fathers, its followers our brothers-in-arms.'[70]

The encomiums failed to impress the Congress; thus, in his last bid for reconciliation, Joshi directly appealed to Gandhi to judge for himself the party's patriotism and good faith.[71] Joshi opened the correspondence with a brief note humbly addressing Gandhi as 'the most loved leader of the greatest patriotic organisation of our people'. The correspondence continued for a period of one year, but came to nothing. Gandhi admired the communists as able, selfless and hardworking, and even went to the extent of saying that he would not like to lose such a force because of any preconceived notions, but flatly rejected the 'people's war' thesis. According to Gandhi, it was 'highly misleading' and devoid of any sense of 'reality'. The correspondence finally got down to non-political issues, such as non-violence, *khadi*, non-vegetarianism and morality. Eventually, Gandhi declined to make any firm statement on the status of the Communist Party of India. He believed that the congressmen ought to be guided by their own knowledge and not by his judgement.

The failure to restore relations with the Congress cost the communists dearly. Soon after the 'people's war' was won and Congress leaders released from jail, the Congress appointed a high-power sub-committee comprising Nehru, Patel and Pant to investigate the communists' attitude towards the Congress. The sub-committee recommended the expulsion of the communists from the party. The Communist Party of India did not challenge the decision and instead asked its members to resign from the Congress, excluding those who were members of the all-India working committee. The direction was obeyed and the *entente* between the Congress and the Communist Party of India came to an end. The communists were formally expelled from the Congress in December 1945.[72]

Support to Britain's war effort in the name of 'people's war' and pursuance of the nationality policy severely damaged the prestige of the communists. After their expulsion from the Congress, people expressed their anger through violent attacks on them, particularly in Bombay, and to a lesser extent in Calcutta. Exasperated, and in a bid to stem the tide, Joshi instructed his party comrades to defend themselves by all possible means and warned that 'any comrade who comes back after receiving a beating without giving hard blows in return will be classed as a coward and expelled from the party.'[73]

Notes

1 *Harijan*, Poona, 9 September 1939. It is said that Gandhi wanted Churchill to give up arms and fight the Nazis with the weapon of non-violence and spiritual force. Linlithgo, the then Viceroy of India, to whom Gandhi expressed his views was taken aback by such insolent advice. (Ashutosh Lahiri, *Gandhi in Indian Politics*, Calcutta, 1976, p.64)

2 *The Statesman,* Calcutta, 10 September, 1939.

3 After the outbreak of the war Harry Pollitt, general secretary of the Communist Party of Great Britain, issued a pamphlet entitled *How to Win the War*, asking the communists to support the war effort against fascist Germany. The pamphlet was immediately withdrawn and Pollitt was removed from the office of the general secretary.

4 P.C. Joshi, *Communist Reply to Congress Working Committee Charges*, Bombay, 1945, pp.35-9.

5 *World News and Views*, London, 16 March 1940. Emphasis original.

6 Sitaram Goel, *Netaji and C.P.I.*, Calcutta, 1946, pp.9-14.

7 *Legislative Assembly Debate*; Official Report, Vol. I, No. 2, Delhi, 1941, pp.122-8. Quoted from the *Proletarian Path* by Reginald Maxwell in his speech in the Central Assembly on 12 February 1941.

8 *The Tribune*, Lahore, 21 March 1940.

9 R. Palme Dutt, *India Today* (second Indian edition), Calcutta, 1970, p.431.

10 *The Hindu*, Madras, 15 March 1940.

11 Legislative Assembly Debate, p. 121. (Speech of Reginald Maxwell).

12 G. Kochariants, 'The War and the National Liberation Movement of the Indian People', *Bolshevik*, July 1940.

13 *Communists*, October 1940.

14 ibid.

15 N.N. Mitra Ed., op. cit., Vol. II, 1940, p.415.

16 V.I. Lenin, *Collected Works*, Vol. 27, p.361.

17 N.V. Rajkumar, *The Background of India's Foreign Policy*, New Delhi, 1952, p.85.

18 Bernard Isaacs, op. cit., p.480.

19 *Labour Monthly*, August, 1941, pp.361-2.

20 R. Palme Dutt, 'Notes of the Month', *Labour Monthly*, September 1941, p.381.

21 *Bolshevik*, September 1941, pp.23-37.

22 The 'people's war' thesis was first invented by Roy long before the Deoli prisoners thought of it. Roy characterized the war as anti-facist and demanded India's unconditional participation in support of Great Britain. He visualized that the victory of the fascists would mean the end

of independence and the beginning of slavery. Thus, to achieve political independence the war effort of Britain must be supported to defeat the fascists.

23 M.R. Masani, op. cit., p 80. The allegation seemed to be based on hearsay. Masani has not put forward any positive evidence to substantiate the charge. N.G. Ranga says that it was one of the many stories current at that time (Kisans and Communists, Bombay n.d., p.13).

24 *Soviet German War*: Statement of the politburo, July 1941. Quoted: Acharya Narendra Dev, *Socialism and the National Revolution*, Bombay, 1946, pp.152-3.

25 Acharya Narendra Dev, op. cit., p.153.

26 N.G. Ranga, *Kisans and Communists*, Bombay n.d., p.11.

27 *The Hindu*, Madras, 1 December 1941.

28 N.G. Ranga, op. cit., p.16.

29 P.C. Joshi, *Communist Reply to Congress Working Committee Charges*, Bombay, 1945, p.45. Emphasis original.

30 G.M. Adhikari Ed., *From Peace Front to People's War*, Bombay, 1942, pp.347-77.

31 ibid, p. 347.

32 N.K. Krishnan Ed., *Forgery Versus Facts—Communist Party Exposes Fifth Column*, Bombay, 1943, p.23.

33 D.N. Pritt, *Labour Monthly*, April 1942, p.107.

34 Ben Bradley, 'India Threatened', *Labour Monthly*, May 1942, p.146.

35 R.P. Dutt, 'Notes of the Month', *Labour Monthly*, September 1942, p.266.

36 R.P. Dutt, 'India and Pakistan', *Labour Monthly*, March 1946, pp.88-9.

37 The three articles written by Menon were: 'Freedom Battle' (August 1941, pp.364-7), 'India in the War' (January 1942, pp.26-8), 'India calls for Action' (June 1942, pp.185-8).

38 *Party Letters*, 6 April 1942.

39 *Indian Information*, 1 April 1942, p.332.

40 M.R. Masani, op. cit., pp.82-4. Masani has simply recorded the testimony of Batlivala, but has not produced any other evidence in support of the allegations. At a later date Batlivala repeated the charges in a letter in the weekly *Bombay Chronicle* of 17 March 1946.

41 Rajbans Kishan, 'Fragments from a Guerrilla's Diary', *People's War*, 2 August 1942. One source said that 300 volunteers recruited from all over India were given 12 days' guerrilla training by a British officer. Another source said that in the hills of Poona, units composed of fifteen volunteers each were instructed in guerrilla tactics by American and Chinese officers. (Gene D. Overstreet and Marshall Windmiller, op. cit., p.206).

It is said that side by side with the guerrilla training programme, the communists, instructed by P.C. Joshi, made an attempt to tamper with the Indian armed forces. A few communists, notably Mohan Kumar Mangalam, Parvati Krishnan, Kalpana Dutta, Nikhil Chakravarty, Santimoy Roy, Mohammed Abdul Haq, Santimoy Ghosh, etc., established contact with the armed forces and got favourable response, but nothing came out of it. (Santimoy Roy, *Response of Armed Forces: Freedom Struggle in India*, Calcutta, 1984, pp. 40-42).

42 N.N. Mitra Ed., op. cit., Vol. II, 1942, pp.245-6.

43 *People's War*, 19 July 1942

44 N.K. Krishnan, *National Unity for the Defence of the Motherland*, Bombay, 1943, pp.5-6.

45 N.G. Ranga, op. cit., p.22.

46 *The Student* (An organ of the all-India Students' Federation), February 1942. At a conference of the all-India Student Federation (communist faction) in Patna almost all the 300 delegates who attended the conference approved the 'people's war' thesis.

47 The figures for 1942 are given in N.K. Krishnan Ed., *Forgery Versus Facts: Communist Party Exposes the Fifth Column*, Bombay, 1943, p.4; and figures for 1943 and 1945 are given in P.C. Joshi, *Communist Reply to Congress Working Committee Charges*, p.142.

48 Gene D. Overstreet and Marshall Windmiller, op. cit., p.210.

49 N.N. Mitra Ed., op. cit., Vol. I, 1943, pp.366-9.

50 ibid.

51 ibid., pp.357-8.

52 ibid., pp.304-9.

53 Bernard Isaacs, op. cit., pp.513-4.

54 ibid., p.514.

55 ibid.

56 ibid.

57 Sajjad Zahir, *A Case for Congress League Unity*, Bombay, 1944, p.20.

58 N.K. Krishnan Ed., *Forgery Versus Facts: Communist Party Exposes the Fifth Column*, p.19.

59 N.K. Krishnan Ed., *National Unity for the Defence of the Motherland*, pp.24-5.

60 Sajjad Zahir, op. cit., p i.

61 P.C. Joshi, *They Must Meet Again*, Bombay, 1944, p.30.

62 Soli Batlivala, *Facts Versus Forgery*, Bombay, 1946, p.19.

63 N.K. Krishnan Ed., National Unity for the Defence of the Motherland pp.27-35.

64 B.T. Ranadive, *Working Class and National Defence, Bombay*, n.d., p.34.

65 N.K. Krishnan Ed., *National Unity for the Defence of the Motherland*, pp.63-9.

66 N.N. Mitra Ed., op. cit., Vol. I. 1943, p.305.

67 S.G. Sardesai, *People's Way to Food*, Bombay, n.d., p.34.

68 N.K. Krishnan Ed., *Forgery Versus Facts: Communist Party Exposes the Fifth Column*, pp.3-16.

69 Soli Batlivala, op. cit. pp.7-10.

70 P.C. Joshi, *Congress and Communists*, Bombay, 1944, p.2.

71 *Correspondence Between Gandhi and P. C. Joshi*, People's Publishing House, Bombay, 1945, pp.1-42.

72 N.N. Mitra Ed., op. cit., Vol. II, 1945, pp.112-22.

73 *Peoples Age*, 27 January and 3 March 1946.

6

Indian Marxists on the Eve of Independence

The intervening two years between the end of the Second World War and the achievement of independence were replete with revolutionary potentialities, but the communists in India failed to take advantage of the situation. Isolated from the main currents of Indian politics, and without any guidance and support from abroad, the communists were in a quandary. The Comintern had been liquidated and the Communist Party of Great Britain, as well as the Communist Party of Soviet Union, was cautious about extending any advice. It was busy nursing its wounds. The proletarian revolution was now a thing of the past. The communists in Europe were advised to help their respective governments in their efforts of reconstruction, instead of making any attempt to seize power. As for India, the only advice to the communists was to revert to the pre-war anti-imperialist strategy and collaborate with the national bourgeoisie, instead of looking forward to a proletarian revolution. The Soviet Union prepared itself to consider the United Nation's proposal of trusteeship for the colonies, though it was not quite sure of its outcome and, in fact, was rather apprehensive that the imperialists might try to exploit the arrangement to their own advantage.[1]

The post-war situation in India, as Nehru said, was one of 'frenzied excitement' and 'abiding anger and bitterness' against the British. In June 1945, the British government's policy statement repeated the same old Cripps proposal, which had been rejected by all, except the communists. The unity between the Congress and the Muslim League could not be forged as Gandhi and Jinnah failed to resolve their differences. Adding fuel to fire, the government announced the court-martial of captured officers of Bose's Indian National Army,. The trial drew popular sympathy and raised anti-British feeling to a new high. To mitigate the ill feeling, the Labour government, which had in the mean time come to power by replacing the war-time Tory government of Churchill, announced its intention to grant self-government to India and proclaimed election, both to the central and provincial legislatures, as a step towards establishing a constitution-making body.

The promise of independence failed to satisfy people. In January 1946, the Royal Indian Air Force in Bombay went on strike; in February, the ratings of the Royal Indian Navy rose in revolt, followed by a strike of the Army Signal Corps in Jabalpur. Curiously enough, the Soviet Union paid little attention to these developments and instead dabbled in polemical analysis of the Indian political situation. Soviet commentator A. Dyakov, in his analysis of India's post-war political situation, said, 'A political party like the National Congress embracing comparatively limited circle, is in a position to formulate in its programme a number of propositions which have the support of considerably broader sections of the population.'[2] Simultaneously, he considered the Muslim League as the most influential Muslim organization and accused the Congress of turning down the Muslim demand for secession. As far as the Communist Party of India was concerned, his attitude was one of indifference. Under the circumstances, at least for the time being, communists in India had no option but to shelve the proletarian revolution and take to constitutional communism with a fresh strategy and tactics.

To gain lost ground and maintain the revolutionary zeal of the party, the communists undertook an intensive campaign to prove that they were the rightful heirs of the revolutionary tradition of India. They published a number of short sketches of select underground revolutionaries in the form of pamphlets eulogising their activities. They claimed that a large number of underground revolutionaries had joined the Communist Party of India to fulfil their revolutionary aspirations after being disillusioned by Gandhi's non-cooperation movement. This is a conjecture. In fact, the young revolutionaries gave up terrorist activities when they realized that terrorism would not work. The failure of Gandhi's non-cooperation movement had little to do with it. After giving up terrorism, quite a few of them took to *sanyas*, while the rest joined the Congress, the Hindu Mahasabha or the Communist Party of India. Perhaps the few who joined the Communist Party of India found in it a path to more scientific and successful struggle, in consonance with their revolutionary zeal.

The attempt to identify with the revolutionary heritage did not imply that the communists contemplated reverting to violence, at least in the near future. In fact, they remained passive in all *revolutionary situations*, except the peasant uprising in Telengana[3] in the state of Hyderabad and in Punnapara Vayalar in the state of Travancore. When the ratings of the Royal Indian Navy rose in revolt, the Communist Party of India only lent the red banner and allowed it to fly beside the tricolour of the Congress and the green banner of the Muslim League. The party did not do anything concrete to help the revolutionaries, except by calling the textile workers of Bombay for a general strike. Only a few communists, in their individual capacity, responded positively; the party as a whole failed to rise up to the situation. A few months after the revolt, the central leadership of the party said before the official enquiry committee that the party had no role to play in the revolt and that a few communists took part strictly 'on their own'.[4] It appears that the communists were 'confused and bewildered' and were hankering, not for revolution, but for respectability, by taking part in the ensuing election as an independent political party.

By accepting bourgeois democracy, the marxists in India deferred, rather sealed, the path to proletarian revolution. This was an un-marxist approach. The marxist doctrine clearly indicates that as long as capitalism continues to exist, there can be no real democracy, however widely the franchise may extend. It is meaningless to talk of political rights when people are subjected to gross economic inequality and class exploitation.

As proclaimed by the government, the election for the central and provincial legislatures was held in the winter of 1945-1946. The Communist Party of India, following the footsteps of bourgeois democratic parties, issued a manifesto prepared under the guidance of P.C. Joshi to apprise people of its programme. In it, Joshi clearly stated that the strategy of the party would be 'united struggle for all freedom-loving Indians' against the British who had enslaved India. It criticized big landlords and businessmen, but assured the bourgeoisie that the party would look after their interest and seek from them 'whole-hearted cooperation' to build an 'alliance with the working class in the towns and the peasantry in the villages'. In the sphere of economic activities, the manifesto proposed 'free and equal cooperation between the representatives of the state, the management and labour'. As regards the agrarian policy, the party restricted the slogan to the abolition of *zamindari* and fixing 100 acres as the minimum land holding.[5]

Following the manifesto, the Communist Party issued a number of pamphlets in support of the election campaign. In one of the pamphlets, *Jobs for All,* B.T. Ranadive made an appeal to workers, peasants, middlemen and employers to rally for planned national development.[6] Similarly, in another pamphlet, *Food for All,* G. Adhikari assured rich, middle and poor peasants that they would prosper under the programme of the Communist Party of India.[7]

A section of the manifesto was devoted to the programme for India's constitutional development. After making the usual demand for independence, the manifesto laid emphasis on the implementation of the nationality policy, as defined by the party in 1942. It wanted power to be transferred, not to one, but to seventeen nationalities and asked for the formation of an equal number of constituent assemblies with full and real sovereignty, as well as an 'unfettered right to negotiate, formulate and decide their mutual relations within an independent India on the basis of complete equality'. The communists envisaged the future set-up of India as a confederation of 'voluntary unions of sovereign national states'. The India of tomorrow would be based on democratic principles and would be mutually helpful. The more advanced states would help the less advanced ones through a common federal centre.

Aware of its limited capacity and general hostility towards the party, the communists decided to contest a small number of seats in certain regions in which they had influence with a view to exploiting regional particularism (a term to explain complex social phenomenon in terms of a single causative factor). In an appeal to the Telugu-speaking people of Madras, communists offered to rescue their Telugu brothers from the 'Nizam's *gulami* to build up an independent VISHAL ANDHRA of all the Andhra people'. They claimed support on the ground that only the Communist Party of India had inscribed Vishal Andhra on its banner and was fighting for it.[8]

The communist propaganda failed to produce the desired result. Out of a total 1,585 seats, the communists contested 108 seats and won only 7, whereas the Congress won 930 seats and the Muslim League won 427 seats.[9]

The ratings of the Royal Indian Navy rose in revolt on 18 February and on the following day, British prime minister Clement Attlee announced the decision to despatch a cabinet mission to negotiate a settlement before the transfer of power. The cabinet mission arrived in India in March 1946. R. Palme Dutt accompanied the cabinet mission as a special correspondent of the London *Daily Worker*. Dutt's presence benefitted the communists in India. For quite some time, practically since the liquidation of the Comintern, communists in India were starved of advice from abroad, to which they had become accustomed. Dutt published the account of his visit to India in his journal *Labour Monthly* under the caption 'Travel Notes'. Apparently, he approved the party strategy of 'united struggle for all freedom-loving Indians', but suggested tactical adjustment. He deplored the split between the Congress and the communists and advised the

Communist Party of India to re-establish the old alliance. 'It is to be hoped,' said Dutt, 'that this breach may be overcome at the earliest possible moment, in view of the paramount importance of national unity in the coming period.'[10] To initiate the process, Dutt flattered the Congress by saying that 'it has a long tradition as the main uniting body of all sections of Indian progressive nationalism' and enjoyed the support of 'the overwhelming majority of the Indian-people'.[11] With firm belief in the Congress-communist reconciliation, Dutt met Gandhi, Nehru, Patel and Patil, and seemed to have received favourable response. Gandhi was not averse to the idea and Patel 'expressed full friendliness to the desirability of reconciliation with the communists and letting the past difficulties be buried'.[12]

To give effect to the reconciliation, Dutt asked the communists to modify their tactics and placate the Congress by retracting their open support to the Muslim demand for Pakistan. 'The unity of India is desirable from a progressive point of view,' said Dutt, 'and partition would be a reactionary step.'[13] He advised the communists to distinguish between the Muslim demand for Pakistan and the propagation of the idea of self-determination for the seventeen nationalities, as propounded by the party. In fact, Dutt mainly concentrated on two points. In the first place, the communists must advocate unity and oppose the Muslim demand for Pakistan, and, secondly, they should give up the idea of seventeen constituent assemblies for the seventeen nationalities, as desired by them on the basis of linguistic entities. He proposed a single constituent assembly, directly elected by the people, with sovereign power to frame a constitution for India. But before embarking on framing the constitution, the British must entrust power to a provisional government of India, formed on the basis of parity of representatives between the Congress and the Muslim League. If this fails to materialize, the provisional government should be constituted only by Congress representatives.

The sober advice of Dutt had its desired effect. In a memorandum to the cabinet mission, the Communist Party of India changed its stand. While extending the right to self-determination and sovereignty for nationalities, it urged for a single constituent assembly for India directly elected by the people. It omitted the word Pakistan and declared in unequivocal terms that the Communist Party of India 'is firmly convinced that the best interest of the Indian masses will be served by their remaining together in one common union'.[14] It further asserted that on the basis of parity 'of representatives between the Congress and the Muslim League, the British should constitute a provisional government and hand over power to Indians.'[15] Dutt felt happy. He welcomed the memorandum as 'a clear, practical, constructive and concise document'. It 'kills stone-dead' the 'myth' of communist support to the Muslim League for its demand for Pakistan.[16]

When Dutt advocated an all-India union and a single constituent assembly, both he and the Communist Party of India knew that, over the years, the idea of Pakistan had taken a definite shape. It was difficult to ignore the Muslim demand for Pakistan and impossible to come to a compromise on this issue. Thus, the memorandum of the Communist Party of India to the cabinet mission was 'more a matter of appearance than of reality'. Yet, Dutt appreciated it, because he found in this memorandum a means to wipe out the anti-national image of Indian communists. Keeping in view the Indian political situation, Dutt wanted the communists to put up a neutral appearance, urging unity in conformity with the Congress demand, but not altogether rejecting the demand for Pakistan. Under the circumstances, Dutt urged the communists to 'await the outcome of the political contest between the Congress and the Muslim League'. He had an inkling that the partition of India was inevitable, as was apparent when he said in unambiguous terms that the demand for more than one constituent assembly should be accepted if it comes both from the Congress and the Muslim League.[17]

The cabinet mission failed to come to a settlement. The Congress and the Muslim League could not come together. The cabinet mission, therefore, published its own plan, which was rejected by both the Congress and the Muslim League. The situation became explosive when, in August 1946, the Muslim

League sponsored a 'direct action day' as a first step towards the achievement of Pakistan. It started with the 'great Calcutta killing' and subsequently engulfed the country in the worst communal violence of its kind.

As the cabinet mission failed, Dutt began his exercise all over again. He characterized the cabinet mission plan as a manoeuvre, but desisted from extending any advice to the Communist Party of India on further course of action. Dutt's view was endorsed by both A. Dyakov and P.C. Joshi, who considered the cabinet mission plan an imperialist manoeuvre designed to strengthen the British position in India.[18] However, after analysing the Indian situation once again, Dutt turned his attention towards the Indian states. In his enthusiasm, he made a trip to Kashmir and was enamoured by Sheikh Abdullah's mass action campaign against princely autocracy. He hailed Abdullah as the 'most courageous and outstanding representative of the states people'.[19] In the struggle of Abdullah, he found a model of revolutionary action and wanted the communists in India to look up to Kashmir valley as 'the political storm centre of the Indian fight for freedom'.[20]

On his way back to London, Dutt stopped in Bombay to attend a meeting of the central committee of the Communist Party of India.[21] Inspired by Dutt, the central committee adopted a resolution titled *For the Final Assault: Task of the Indian People in the Present Phase of Revolution*. The resolution, also known as the 'August resolution', was a mixture of moderate and extremist views. The more radical section of the party led by G. Adhikari, B.T. Ranadive and A.K. Ghosh found in Dutt's views support for militant posture. The resolution called upon the party to come forward and take the leadership of a 'bold and militant' working class action, a powerful peasant movement and a broad-based struggle on the pattern of Kashmir in all the princely states. But simultaneously, the same resolution urged the formation of a joint front of three parties – the Congress, the Muslim League and the Communist Party of India. The National Congress, it said, represented the main strand of the independence movement of the country; the Muslim League had behind it the bulk of the anti-imperialist freedom-loving Muslim masses; and the Communist Party of India led the bulk of the organized workers and peasants.[22]

Following the 'August resolution', the party issued a political statement referring to the Kashmir valley as the 'hub of today's freedom battle' and criticized the Congress leadership for its attempt to restrain Sheikh Abdullah, which the party described as a 'terrible tragedy'. Kashmir, it said, cannot wait since it was 'at war'.[23]

The 'August resolution' was an unholy compromise between the radicals and the moderates. For a time, each tried to score brownie points over the other and created a near-split situation in the party. In September 1946, when the interim government headed by Nehru assumed office, Adhikari, a leader of the radical faction, issued a statement criticizing the nationalist leadership as an appeaser of vested interest and asked the comrades to build 'revolutionary unity among Indian people for the final fight for independence and democracy'.[24] In contrast, Somnath Lahiri, a leader of the moderates and the sole representative of the Communist Party of India in the constituent assembly, called upon Indian people to support the interim government. He expressed the hope that the interim government would convert itself into a provisional government of independent India.[25]

Adhikari's radical posture was a purely temporary affair. He soon came under Joshi's influence in believing that the Congress was amenable to influence and that the constituent assembly was an 'instrument for asserting and expressing the will of the Indian people'.[26] Joshi seized upon the weakness of the radicals to work back to the old line, and thus averted a split in the party. Nevertheless, the radicals occasionally flared into militant action, contrary to the accepted moderate line of Joshi.[27]

The failure of the cabinet mission and the subsequent deterioration of the political situation in India worried the Labour government of England. Attlee stated that unless a firm date was announced for the transfer of power, there would never be any solution. Accordingly, on 20 February 1947, Attlee announced that power would be transferred 'to responsible Indian hands by a date not later than June 1948'. The announcement set at rest all speculations about the intention of the Labour government to free India from British control. This was hailed by all, except the communists. The Communist Party of India saw in this announcement a British manoeuvre to hoodwink Indian bourgeoisie to perpetuate its control over the subcontinent through dubious means. By encouraging a few important semi-feudal princely states to remain independent, and then convert them into a 'princistan', the British expected to maintain their commercial interests and military bases in the subcontinent. The Communist Party of India responded with a sense of urgency to frustrate this British design. The party admonished the Congress for its soft policy towards the Indian princes, but expressed the hope that this would be reversed to a hard-line policy.[28] It singled out Nehru and praised him for his confidence in democracy and secularism. It appeared that, at least for the time being, the communists decided to play a constructive role in Indian politics as a gentle critic of the Congress. The reason for this change may be that at this point of time, the communists in India were starved of advice from comrades abroad. The Communist Party of Great Britain was silent and the Soviet Union preferred to postpone judgement till the time India gained independence.

A month after the February announcement, Louis Mountbatten arrived in India in March to replace Wavell, and renewed negotiations with Indian leaders. After an initial setback, Mountbatten succeeded. The delicious carrot that he dangled before the power-hungry bourgeois Congress leaders was too tantalizing to be refused. Prompted by Gandhi, the leaders, particularly Nehru and Patel, agreed to the Muslim demand for Pakistan and threw India into turmoil. At this crucial hour, Hindus failed to put up effective resistance against this nefarious decision, and took it as *fait accompli.* Under the leadership of Gandhi, Hindus in general had become imbecile because of their acceptance of the philosophy of non-violence as the gospel truth and of Gandhi as a *mahatma.* Once the partition of the country was agreed upon, other issues were solved in a few days. V.P. Menon was entrusted with the task of drafting the

Indian Independence Bill in consultation with the Indian leaders. The bill was introduced in the House of Commons on 4 July and it received Royal Assent on 18 July. Power was transferred on 15 August 1947, ten months ahead of the announced date.

The acceptance of India's partition was a scathing blunder. Gandhi realized his folly before long and advised the dissolution of the Congress to get out of the mire. His pretext was that 'the Congress in its present shape and form had out lived its use' and that its 'voluntary liquidation would brace up and purify the political climate' of the country. The leaders of the Congress refused to go by his advice. They were elated to see that their dream had come true and were not prepared to let power go out of their hands. Caught in his own web, Gandhi felt disgusted and perhaps a bit disillusioned too. At the fag end of his life, he realized the truth that the need for him was over. Wisely enough, for all practical purposes, he took leave from active politics and surrendered to *ramdhun* for solace.

Although Gandhi expressed his desire to live longer than usual, God willed otherwise. On 30 January 1948, on his way to a prayer meeting, he was shot dead by Nathuram Vinayak Godse. Godse, like many others, was opposed to the partition of the country and held Gandhi responsible for the catastrophe that followed the creation of Pakistan. Godse cannot be blamed for his action as neither gratitude in politics, nor compassion in revolution go by the rule of ethics. And that is why great personalities in history usually meet their end by unusual means. With the death of Gandhi, the era of sacrifice for the struggle for freedom ended, and a new era of the struggle for power began.

The assassination of Gandhi shocked the nation, but the marxists, ignoring the national calamity, were busy assessing its impact on the Mountbatten plan. The initial reaction of Moscow was one of cautious criticism. A. Dyakov, the Moscow spokesperson on India, denounced the plan as a manoeuvre of the British to continue imperialist control over the subcontinent, and expressed doubts over the motives of bourgeois leaders for accepting the plan. 'We still do not know,' said Dyakov, 'what their motives were, but from the comments in the Indian press it can only be judged that certain political circles thought it better to consent without delay, at least a partial satisfaction of the demand for independence rather than leave the whole question hanging in the air indefinitely.'[29] In June 1947, the Soviet Academy of Science called a special session to discuss the Indian question. Experts on India blamed Mountbatten and the Indian bourgeois leaders. According to them, the partition of India was 'the result of a deal of the Indian bourgeoisie and landlords with British imperialism'. By accepting the Mountbatten plan, the Nehru government, representing the big and middle bourgeoisie, had gone over to the camp of the reactionaries and the imperialists, and had committed an act of treachery. The experts further blamed the Congress and the Muslim League for their reactionary policies, which only strengthened the position of British imperialists and allowed them to manoeuvre their way through.[30] Balabushevich, the main spokesperson at the session, appreciated the difficulties of the communists in India. He concluded his speech with the note that 'the Communist Party of India are conducting a resolute struggle against reactionary bloc of imperialists, bourgeoisie and landlords for complete independence, for liquidation of all remnants of feudalism, for people's democracy.'[31]

When Soviet experts were busy scanning the political situation in India, the central committee of the Communist Party of India met in Bombay and took an entirely different view of the Mountbatten plan and the Nehru government. The party declared the Mountbatten plan as an 'important concession' that would provide 'new opportunities for national advance', and pledged support to the Nehru government. In a policy statement, the party declared that 'it will fully cooperate with the national leadership in the proud task of building the Indian Republic on democratic foundations, thus paving the way to Indian unity.'[32] The views of the Communist Party of India were endorsed by R. Palme Dutt, in spite of his being critical of the Mountbatten plan and agreeing partly with the Soviet expert's opinion. His main concern seems to be Congress-communist unity and support to Nehru for the progress of India, rather than listing the evils of the Mountbatten plan. 'Now more than ever,' said Dutt, 'the situation reveals the urgent need, increasingly recognised on both sides, to endeavour to overcome the past phase of sharp division between the Congress and the Communist Party of India in order to march forward together upon a common programme of democratic advance, for the achievement of full independence.... for the fulfilment of economic and social demands, land reforms, measures of nationalisation and planned industrial development, for which the workers and peasants and masses of the Indian people are looking.'[33]

Dutt iterated this view in an interview with the socialist leader Madhu Limaye. In November 1947, when Limaye met Dutt and expressed his desire to leave the Congress, Dutt advised him to remain with the party and 'agitate for the re-admittance of the communists into the national organisation'. According to Limaye, Dutt believed that at that point of time the Congress was 'divided into two camps, the progressive camp led by Pandit Nehru, Sheikh Abdullah and others, and the reactionary bloc led by Sardar Vallabhbhai Patel. It was the supreme duty of all of us to support Nehru'.[34]

Dutt's support encouraged the Communist Party of India to declare that it would 'join the day of national rejoicing', i.e., the independence day, and vowed to take part in the national movement for full independence, shoulder to shoulder with the Congress.[35] To prove its sincerity, the party suspended the tebhaga movement in Bengal. Bhowani Sen, the foremost communist leader of Bengal, appealed to peasants 'not to launch direct action this year as they did last year'. The new government 'must be given an opportunity to fulfil its promises through legal channels'.[36] During the months of October and November 1947, the party paper, People's Age, flattered Nehru beyond proportions, calling him the 'voice of the people' who 'kept the democratic traditions of the national movement alive ... who alone set her on the road to secularism and prosperity'.[37] The sycophancy continued right up to the end of 1947. In vain the communists expected that, with their support, Nehru would root out the right reactionaries from the Congress and bring in progressive elements.

Notes

1 E. Zhukov, 'The Colonial Question and the Present State', *Marxist Miscellany*, Bombay, 1945, pp.118-9.

2 A. Dyakov, 'India After the War', *New Times*, 1 March 1946.

3 The armed struggle of the people of Telengana (Nalgonda and Warangal district) began in September, 1946. Initially it was a peasant movement for land reforms but soon it took the form of a mass struggle against the feudal autocratic regime of the Nizam and the Razakars, a band of armed rabble protected by the Nizam. The struggle attained its greatest intensity and strength between August 1947 and September 1948. During this period the movement spread over an area of 16,000 square miles affecting 3,000 villages. In the liberated area, bonded labour was abolished, agricultural wage raised, unjustly seized land was returned to the previous holders, and land ceiling which was fixed at 100 acres dry and 10 acres wet was distributed among the landless. The situation changed after September 1948 when the Indian army took over the state. The communist guerrillas whose number at that time was estimated around 2,000 personnel supported by 10,000 village volunteers found it impossible to face the Indian army, though they had collected a large quantity of light arms from the disbanded Razakars. Besides, the slogan of overthrowing the Nehru government did not appeal much to the people as it did against the Nizam. With the loss of popular support the communist guerrillas changed their form of struggle from revolution to isolated action in murdering important individuals. By 1950-51 the movement dissipated.

4 *Towards a People's Navy*, People's Publishing House, Bombay, n.d., p.18.

5 P.C. Joshi, *For the Final Bid for Power: Freedom Programme of Indian Communists*, Bombay, n.d., pp.101-2.

6 B.T. Ranadive, *Jobs for All*, Bombay, 1945, p.30.

7 G. Adhikari; *Food for All*, Bombay, n.d., p.26.

8 *People's Age*, 17 March 1946, p.3, Emphasis original.

9 For a brief account of the election, see: N.N. Mitra. Ed., op. cit., Vol. I, 1946, pp.229-32.

10 R. Palme Dutt, 'India and Pakistan', *Labour Monthly*, March 1946, p.92.

11 ibid., pp.91-2.

12 R. Palme Dutt, 'Travel Notes No. 2', *Labour Monthly*, June 1946, pp.185-8.

13 R. Palme Dutt, *Freedom for India*, London, 1946, p.15.

14 ibid., pp.92-3.

15 The memorandum is dated 15 April 1946. For the text of the memorandum, see: N.N. Mitra, Ed., op. cit. ,Vol. 1, 1946, pp.220-2.

16 R. Palme Dutt, 'Travel Notes No. 2', *Labour Monthly*, June 1946, pp.189-90.

17 R. Palme Dutt, 'India and Pakistan', *Labour Monthly*, March 1946, pp.92-3

18 *New Times*, 1 June 1946, p.20 and also R. Palme Dutt, *India Today*, p.592.

19 R. Palme Dutt, 'Travel Notes No. 3', *Labour Monthly*, July 1946, p.219.

20 ibid., No. 5, October 1946, pp.321-4.

21 ibid.

22 *For the Final Assault: Task of the Indian People in the Present Phase of Indian Revolution*, People's Publishing House, Bombay, 1946, p. 18.

23 Romesh Chandra, *Salute to Kashmir*, Bombay, 1946, pp. 22-3.

24 G. Adhikari, *Resurgent India at the Crossroads: 1946 in Review*, Bombay, 1947, p.24.

25 *Declaration of Independence*, People's Publishing House, Bombay, 1946, pp.5-10.

26 ibid., pp.2-4.

27 The Madras unit of the Communist Party of India took a radical posture and opposed the Congress government in the state to such an extent that the State Government was compelled to declare the party illegal and put under arrest around 700 workers and trade union leaders (*People's Age*, February and September 1947, pp.8 and 12.)

28 *Down with Autocracy: Task Before the State People's Movement*, People's Publishing House, Bombay n.d., pp.3-6.

29 A. Dyakov, 'The New British Plan for India': *New Times*, 13 June 1947.

30 J.H. Kautsky, *Moscow and the Communist Party of India*, New York, 1956, p.24.

31 People's democracy, a new term, was coined by the marxists after the Second World War to explain the theoretical position of the Eastern European countries which had embraced communism through Soviet occupation. In its transitional stage it is neither a bourgeois nor a proletarian government. It utilises the parliamentary bourgeois democracy in the interest of the proletariat and directs its policy against imperialism and feudalism.

32 *People's Age*, 29 June 1947, pp.6-7.

33 R. Palme Dutt, 'The Mountbatten Plan for India', *Labour Monthly*, July 1947, pp.210-19.

34 Madhu Limaye, op. cit., p.57.

35 *People's Age*, 31 August 1947, p.9.

36 ibid., 30 November 1947, p.10. In September 1946, the communists, in response to a call given by the Bengal provincial *Kisan Sabha*, tried to implement through a mass struggle the recommendations of the floud commission which, among other things, said that share-croppers would be entitled to two-thirds of the crop produced, instead of half or even less at times. This movement was known as *tebhaga* because of the division of the crop in three parts. The movement was practically confined to north Bengal, though some pockets of east and south Bengal also felt its impact. The movement took a violent turn in February 1947 when in a clash with the police some twenty people died. Thereafter the movement slowly died down mainly due to the change in the political situation in the country.

37 ibid., 12 October 1947, p.5 and 9, November 1947, p.3.

7

Indian Marxists after Independence

No sooner did India achieve independence than the official policy of the Communist Party of India towards the Nehru government was challenged by the radical wing of the party. The attack was opened by Ranadive with a note of caution that the Nehru government was 'developing authoritarian attributes'.[1] He opposed the policy of 'loyal opposition' adopted by the party and called Joshi a 'petty bourgeois reformist', a popular accusation in marxist terminology. Ranadive's radicalism was largely moulded by Edvard Kardelj of the Communist Party of Yugoslavia. Kardelj, in an article that was later published in the form of a pamphlet, branded the colonial bourgeoisie as reactionary and an agent of foreign imperialism. He asserted that the liberation of colonial people could be achieved only through a violent revolution – a clash 'between the imperialist reactionary forces and the domestic anti-imperialist forces'.[2] Kardelj's formulation was supported by Andrei Zhdanov of the Communist Party of the Soviet Union. But Zhdanov, unlike Kardelj, in a speech delivered at the first meeting of the Cominform, criticized the role of imperialism *vis-à-vis* the colonies. Zhdanov warned that the imperialists were 'seeking to keep India and China under the sway of imperialism and in continued political and economic bondage'. He urged the comrades to intensify the anti-imperialist campaign in the colonies through every channel to stop the imperialists' expansion moves. The main danger for the working class, said Zhdanov, 'lies in underestimating its own strength and overestimating the strength of the forces of the imperialist camp'.[3]

The radicals threw an open challenge to Joshi in December 1947. In a resolution of the central committee of the party, they reversed the existing party line; denounced the policy adopted by Joshi as 'opportunism'; asked for 'unity among workers and peasants and progressive intellectuals'; and called for an uncompromising struggle against the Nehru government.[4] In the resolution that was put to vote, the radicals secured majority support. That was the end of Joshi. Ranadive became the *de facto* leader of the party, relegating Joshi to an insignificant position. To formalize his control over the party, barely two and a half months after the central committee meeting, Ranadive called an all-India party congress.

The all-India party congress was held in Calcutta from 28 February to 6 March 1948. It was attended by 632 delegates and included representatives from the communist parties of Australia, Yugoslavia, Burma and Ceylon. But there was no representative, either from the Communist Party of Great Britain or from the Soviet Union. Ranadive, in his report on the draft of political resolution, set the tone of the congress. The resolution made it clear that Indian independence was a mockery and Britain continued to dominate India. 'Though the bourgeois leadership parade the story that independence has been won, the fact is that the freedom struggle has been betrayed and the national leadership has struck a treacherous deal behind the back of the starving people, betraying every slogan of the democratic revolution.' The resolution condemned the Indian socialists for preaching 'the illusion that socialism may be achieved by constitutional means'. The only change that had taken place in post-war India was that the Indian bourgeoisie had become 'collaborationist and therefore reactionary'. The party, therefore, gave a call for the mobilization of the working class, the peasantry and the petty bourgeoisie to complete the task of the people's democratic revolution for the establishment of socialism.[5] The main emphasis of the political resolution was on armed struggle on the model of Telengana. Ranadive concluded his speech with a note that 'Telengana today means communism and communists mean Telengana.' Ranadive was supported by Bhowani Sen, his principal lieutenant. Sen went a step further and gave an open call for revolution throughout the subcontinent to achieve freedom and democracy. 'The heroic people of Telengana, the great example of fight against autocracy,' said Sen, 'not only show what will happen inside the state, but also what will be the real future of India and Pakistan.'[6]

After the discussion on the main resolution, Joshi took to the floor to perform the ritual of self-criticism – a common marxist practice of penance. Joshi confessed before the house that he had 'confused and corrupted' the party, acted as a 'betrayer', that he was a 'coward', a 'petty bourgeois vacillator' and an 'embodiment of right reformism'. And, finally, he expressed his helplessness – that he had committed all these crimes inadvertently, by an 'accident of History'.[7] But the self-criticism did not help. A new central committee was formed and B.T. Ranadive became the general secretary. Joshi was first suspended and thereafter expelled from the party.

The political thesis adopted at the party congress received a mixed reaction from the communists. R. Palme Dutt endorsed the thesis. In an article in the *Labour Monthly,* he condemned the Indian bourgeoisie and advised the working class to step 'forward to take over the leadership of the battle'. The Indian freedom struggle, said Dutt, had entered 'a new phase'.[8] But A. Dyakov, the spokesperson of the Soviet Union, while accepting certain elements of the thesis, did not approve it in its entirety. He portrayed the Indian situation as being far from revolutionary.[9] The Soviet view was accepted by the Cominform. It accused the Indian bourgeoisie and cautioned Indian communists against adopting violent tactics. Rather, it 'stressed the need for a democratic front to combat the American and British imperialism and the Indian bourgeoisie'.[10]

Thus, the radical posture adopted by Ranadive turned out to be a mistake. He was guided by emotion and the promise of revolution, but there was no preparation for it. In vain he expected that the Telengana movement would serve as a model for his revolutionary plan. Until September 1948, the peasants of Telengana gave a good account of their prowess, fighting the scantily armed army of the Nizam and the Razakar rabbles.[11] But from September 1948 onwards, as the State of Hyderabad became a part of the Indian Union, the peasants of Telengana found it difficult, rather impossible, to face the Indian army. Besides, the integration of Hyderabad with the Indian Union changed the political situation. The people fighting the Nizam's autocracy were reluctant in taking up arms against the Nehru government. The movement that had started with great expectations abated after September 1948, and by 1950-51, ceased to exist. Only a few radicals who believed more in adventure than revolution continued to stick to their guns. Apart from Telengana, the areas that came under the influence of marxist revolution were Calcutta; Andhra, and Malabar in Madras; Ahmadnagar in Bombay; Amritsar; and some places in eastern Uttar Pradesh, Manipur and the Indo-Burma border.

Nehru nursed no illusion about the revolutionary potential of the communists in India. He knew that on the pretext of revolution, the communists could, at best, disrupt law and order, but did not have the ability to initiate a revolution. Therefore, he was not in favour of any drastic action against the communists and preferred to go slow. Instead of declaring the party illegal at the national level, Nehru instructed the state governments to deal with the problem at the local level, without giving much publicity to it. The government's action disappointed the communists. They expected stern action and oppression on the part of the government so that this could be exploited to boost the revolutionary zeal of the comrades.

West Bengal was the first state to ban the party on 26 March 1948. Kiran Sankar Roy, the state home minister, took the pretext that the communists were preparing for an armed revolution and that the police had located arms caches and secret documents belonging to the communists.[12] The example of West Bengal was followed by other concerned states. Party offices of important centres of communist activity were searched; important party comrades all over India were arrested; and party newspapers in West Bengal, Kerala, and Andhra were suppressed. In fact, no sooner did Ranadive set the revolution in motion, than the Nehru government crippled the Communist Party of India. Curiously, the government did not contemplate immediate action against the leaders. Ranadive, Adhikari and Ajoy Ghosh, the leaders of the revolution, enjoyed liberty as usual and they were allowed to continue their activities, i.e., provide incitement for revolt and carry on the publication of pamphlets and the party newspaper, *People's Age*. However, the government soon changed its plan and put under arrest Ajoy Ghosh, S.V. Ghate, S.G. Sardesai, Romesh Chandra and a few others, and issued warrants of arrest against Ranadive and Adhikari. The party paper, *People's Age,* was also restrained by an order of the Bombay government.

During the period of the so-called revolution, the pamphlets issued by the party made it abundantly clear that the communists were actually preparing for a guerrilla war all over the country. In one of the pamphlets, *Course for the Cadres of the Shock Brigade*, the party asked the comrades to collect arms and raid police stations and houses of *zamindars* and *jotedars*; sabotage communication systems by snapping telephone and telegraph-lines; and ambush police parties. These activities, the pamphlet said, would 'help the mass movement developing all over the country and raise it to the higher level when the people in general will take up arms'.[13] Apart from pamphlets, the communists issued a number of circulars, often asking the people and the army to raise the banner of revolt against the Nehru government and attack congressmen. In a circular, the communists asked Indian army personnel to 'fraternise with the revolutionary labourers in the factories and the students in the streets' and 'fire upon the congress fascists'. In another circular, the communists threatened to 'set fire to the whole of Bengal' and asked the people to 'attack the congress brutes in all directions'.[14]

The call for revolution against the Nehru government failed to attract the people, much less the Indian army, but incited the young comrades to take to petty bourgeois adventurism. Bank robberies; train robberies; attacks at public meetings with bombs and acid bulbs; destruction of public property; and murders of police officials, rival workers and other enemies were some of the actions the communists resorted to in the name of revolution.[15]

Ranadive's plan of revolution for the establishment of a socialist state was based on wrong assumptions. He envisaged that the Indian economy had reached a high level of capitalist development and was ripe for a socialist revolution. He presumed that bourgeois democratic revolution, the first stage of a socialist revolution, had been completed with the exit of imperialism and the bourgeoisie coming to power. He, therefore, harped on the anti-bourgeois strategy, hoping to convert the bourgeois democratic revolution into a socialist revolution. In this formulation, he was supported by Yugoslavia, which was the principal adviser of Indian communists for a brief period. The Yugoslav theorist called for drastic action against the national bourgeoisie in the colonies, as it was a reactionary force and an agent of imperialism. Dissent against Ranadive's leadership was not slow to come. The opposition came primarily from trade union leaders of Bombay and the leaders of the Communist Party of Andhra. Trade union leaders disagreed only in terms of the tactics, but Andhra leaders challenged the basic strategy. Ranadive succeeded in diffusing the trade union's opposition, but failed to stand up to the Andhra leaders.

The Communist Party of Andhra was primarily a peasant party. It was dominated by the *kammas*, a class of rich peasants, who owned 80 per cent of the fertile delta land.[16] The leaders of the party were from the landed gentry, mostly *reddy* or *kamma* landlords. Because of the peasant base of the party, Andhra communist leaders found in Maoism a justification for peasant revolution without jeopardizing their interest in land. Mao's liberal attitude towards wealthy peasants suited Andhra communist leaders. Thus, no sooner was the second congress of the party over and Ranadive gave a call for revolution, than Andhra leaders challenged the basic formulation of Ranadive in the so-called 'Andhra letter' of June 1948.[17] In unequivocal terms, Andhra leaders said that the peasant-based guerrilla war on the Chinese model should be the guiding factor for revolution in India.

The Andhra thesis was supported by both the Soviet Union and the Cominform. In June 1949, at a meeting of Soviet academicians, Zhukov approved the Chinese model for India and praised the Telengana movement as the 'first attempt at creating people's democracy in India'. He called the Telengana movement 'the harbinger of agrarian revolution' and 'the most important content' of the liberation movement. He compared the Telengana peasant uprising with that of China to urge Indian communists to follow the Chinese path.[18] The Cominform also approved the Chinese model for a revolution in India. In an article published in its weekly official journal, *For a Lasting Peace: For a People's Democracy*, the Cominform asked Indian communists to draw from 'the experience of the national liberation movement in China and other countries'.[19]

Disowned by the community of international communists, Ranadive issued a statement of self-accusation. He admitted that he had committed 'certain errors in dogmatic and sectarian directions' and pledged to abide by the 'Andhra thesis'. Ranadive's statement was published in the *Communist Review*, the official theoretical journal of the Communist Party of Great Britain.[20] Dutt arranged the publication of the statement, but himself remained silent on the issue.

In May 1950, at a meeting of the central committee of the party, Andhra leaders engineered a coup. Ranadive was thrown out of power and C. Rajeshwar Rao was elected as the general secretary of the party. In haste, Rao accused Ranadive of 'left-sectarianism' in a statement and sent greetings to the Communist Party of China on its twenty-ninth anniversary.[21] Enamoured by the idea of revolution, Rao failed to understand the real situation. He committed the same error as Ranadive and ended up in a mess. His revolutionary strategy failed to enthuse the imagination of the people. The Chinese model fizzled out and, with it, the revolution. The leaders picked up the cudgels once again. The opposition to Rao came from P.C. Joshi and the trade union leaders of Bombay.

Joshi reappeared on the scene after about two years. Though expelled from the party, he maintained contact with his former associates; published pamphlets; and brought out a monthly paper, *India Today,* to prove the hollowness of the radicals' revolutionary strategy. He firmly believed that the situation in India was not ripe for revolution. The best strategy for the party would, therefore, be loyal opposition to the Nehru government. In a pamphlet titled *Views Under the Red Banner*, Joshi wrote, 'I think my comrade holding the present situation to be a revolutionary situation is not only unable to use the evidence of his own eyes and ears but is guilty of repudiating Lenin's own definition of the same. Of all our sectarian mistakes this has been the most disastrous, for it has led to the adoption of tactics suited to an insurrectionary or semi-insurrectionary situation. The result has been that the masses have not responded to our calls and our comrades have landed themselves into the terrorist mire.... The party has ceased to function as an organisation. Every single organisation of the party has been done to death in cold blood ... provincial committees are being reshuffled in an unprincipled manner by a fiat from above ... comrades are expelled without charges being communicated to them .... If some comrades or some units take a determined stand ... they are purged.'

To substantiate the charges, Joshi gave a number of instances indicating the failure of the revolution. These included the following: 'We gave a call for an all-India railwaymen's strike on 9 March 1949, and it was a complete fiasco, it remained a call on paper, unanswered by any section of railwaymen .... In June our comrades in Bengal jails (including our trade union leaders) went on hunger-strike and were fired upon. We gave a call for general strike. Another flop. Not one factory responded.'

Joshi's observation was supplemented by Dange. In April 1950, Dange prepared a critical note on the party policy during the course of the revolution, for circulation among party members.[22] This was followed by another note prepared by Ajoy Ghosh, Dange and Ghate.[23] Both these notes, among other things, exposed the consequences of adventurism. Dange noted that two years of revolution had reduced party membership from 1,00,000 to 20,000, stagnated the trade union movement, practically wiped out peasant organizations, and paralysed the party itself, bringing it closer to disintegration.

At this critical hour, another piece of advice came from London to rescue the party from the cesspool of adventurism. After almost three years of silence, the political committee of the Communist Party of Great Britain sent a confidential letter to the central committee of the Communist Party of India. It asked for a complete reversal of the existing party policy and advised purging the trotskyites and titoites. It prescribed a solution for the party leadership problem through 'full and unfettered discussion' among the rank and file, and election of a new leadership 'enjoying confidence of the members'. At the end, the letter advised party leaders to avail of all opportunities for legal activity and to prepare for the coming general election. The advice to withdraw from the battle front and take to constitutional means was not welcomed by Rao. He made an attempt to suppress the letter but failed. Once the content of the letter was known to the comrades, Rao had no alternative but to convene a meeting of the central committee to take stock of the situation. The central committee was expanded to make the discussion broad based, and a new politburo was formed to represent diverse views. In a resolution, the party decided to revert to united front tactics with other leftist parties and made friends with progressive elements to contest the general election. The resolution further decided to readmit Joshi to the party and hold a party conference.

The political committee letter was followed by a piece of advice from R. Palme Dutt. Dutt urged communists to shun violence and take to united front tactics on a simple democratic programme. He appreciated Nehru's attitude towards the problems of Korea and his support to China in the matter of her entry into the United Nations.

He called this a beginning of Nehru's peace policy and found in him a 'potential friend of peace'.[24]

Before the all-India party conference in April 1951, the new politburo met to draft a programme and a statement of policy.[25] The documents were circulated among the members of the central committee for an open discussion. The central committee met in May and tentatively approved both the draft programme and the statement of policy. It was at this meeting of the central committee that C. Rajeshwar Rao tendered his resignation, and Ajoy Ghosh was first appointed as secretary and then, a few months later, elevated to the post of general secretary of the party.

The all-India party conference was held in Calcutta from 11 to 15 October 1951. The draft programme and the statement of policy were adopted with minor amendments. Joshi was readmitted to the party, and B.T. Ranadive and G.M. Adhikari were put under suspension for two years and one year, respectively.

Though the inner-party dispute on the question of violence versus non-violence continued, the new programme adopted by the party, by and large, leaned towards peace. It adhered to the goal of socialism, but gave up hopes of its establishment in the current stage of development. It compromised with marxist economic policies by pledging to protect private industries and calling for a mixed economy, but remained firm in its attitude towards the Nehru government. The Nehru government was still considered a 'lackey of imperialism', essentially carrying out the 'foreign policy of British imperialism'. In fact, at the end, the communists came round to the democratic process and gave up their premature revolutionary posture. By trial and error, they learnt the simple truth that a people's government could be displaced only with the support of the people. A few armed men, however, dedicated they might be, were not enough to overthrow a people's government unless they were supported by the people. The call for revolution to overthrow the bourgeois Nehru government remained confined to party comrades and did not evoke any response from the people.

The first general election of independent India was held in 1951-52. The electorate numbered 176 million, the largest in the world. The Communist Party of India, in alliance with other leftist parties, came forward to take part in the election and issued in August 1951 an election manifesto largely drawn from the 'draft programme' and the 'statement of policy' approved by the party at the Calcutta conference. The main focus of the manifesto was the failure of the Nehru government and agrarian reforms. 'Five years of Congress rule,' four of them after the attainment of 'freedom' said the manifesto, 'have brought our country and our people to the verge of disaster ... what lies at the root of these miseries? Congress leaders claim that they have ended foreign rule, they have stopped the looting of our people by the British imperialists .... Each one of these arguments is false, each one of these assertions is a lie. The leaders of the Congress have not won freedom for the country. They have betrayed our freedom struggle. They have allowed the foreigners and the reactionary Indian vested interests to plunder and loot our people just as they did in the past. They have themselves joined the loot.'

About the agrarian reforms, the communists promised to 'cancel peasants' debts and transfer all lands and implements of landlords and princes, without payment to the landlords, without any price to the tillers of the soil, taking care to provide for the poorer sections of landlords and without harming the interests of the rich peasants.'[27]

The manifesto was published in full in the official journal of the Cominform in its 31 August 1952 issue. Harry Pollitt and R. Palme Dutt of the Communist Party of Great Britain appreciated the manifesto. In their opinion, it showed the correct path for the people of India to follow. Whether it was on the basis of the manifesto or otherwise, the communists did remarkably well in the election. In the parliament, the communist bloc with 23 seats came second only to the ruling Congress; and in the state assemblies, with 170 seats, it emerged as the main opposition in a number of states. Keeping in view the limited capacity of the party, the performance was encouraging. As the second largest party of the country, it drew the attention of the people, but thereafter, it refused to grow except in a few pockets, namely Kerala and West Bengal.

In Kerala, the marxists progressed well. Taking advantage of the internal bickering, misrule and corruption of the Congress-led government, they revived the *Aikya Kerala* movement and brought the people under their banner.[28] They made their presence felt in the second general election in 1957. In a house of 126 seats, the marxists commanded 60 seats and, together with 5 independents who had won with the support of the marxists, came together and formed the government headed by E.M.S. Nambooderipad. Rajendra Prasad, the president of India, welcomed the establishment of a marxist government in Kerala. In a public meeting in Trivandrum, he declared that 'the experiment which is being made … [is] going to serve as a great lesson not only to other states but to the country as a whole as an example of co-existence, of living and working together in spite of differences for the good of all.'[29] To allay the fear of a red revolution, the marxists on the other hand, promised to work within the framework of the federal constitution as there was no insurmountable difficulty in having a marxist-led government in the state and a Congress government at the centre. In an article titled *Challenge in Kerala,* M.N. Govindan Nair, the secretary of the Communist Party of Kerala, said in unequivocal terms that the marxist government would make all efforts to apply the theory of 'peaceful transition' to communism.[30]

The people of Kerala welcomed the change of government. They hoped the marxists would provide clean, corruption-free administration, but were disillusioned. Instead of taking proper administrative measures to oust corruption, the marxists set Kerala on the road to communism. Special liaison bodies were formed at various levels to link the party with the ministries and other government departments to ensure that the party commands were transmitted and executed. Officers refusing to execute the commands were removed or transferred to remote areas or dismissed. At the lowest level of administration in villages and small towns, the party established 'cell courts' composed of party cadres, which functioned as agencies of class rule in rural areas. They adjudged cases involving party comrades and advised *panchayats* on how justice should be carried out to safeguard the interest of the party.

The first casualty of this gross interference in the administration of the state was law and order. The Kerala State Police Administration Report for 1957 showed that from the installation of the marxist regime on 5 April 1957 to the end of the year, the efficiency of the police department dropped drastically because of political interference. Criminal cases involving 236 marxists were withdrawn from the courts upon government request; cognizable crimes increased by 120 per cent; rioting and general assault, which was mostly of political nature, increased by 81 per cent; the crime detection efficiency of the police reduced by 67 per cent; and criminal proceedings against hundreds of people – needless to say, mostly from the Communist Party or its supporters – were suspended.[31]

In spite of the all-round deterioration in law and order, the marxists continued to enjoy power under Nambooderipad, while the opposition looked on helplessly because of its incapacity to come together and put up effective resistance. Then came the Devicolam constituency by-election in May 1958. By that time, the majority of votes that the communists controlled in the state had dwindled. Victory in Devicolam by-election became a necessity for the party to prove its popularity. The marxists inflated the electoral roll with the names of party comrades from neighbouring constituencies to ensure victory, and in a bid to win the electorate, distributed large sums of money from the state coffer on the eve of the election.[32]

The marxists won the election by a comfortable majority. Nambooderipad declared that the victory symbolized a fresh mandate of the people of Kerala to his party. In a speech at Coimbatore on 3 July 1958, he warned that any unruly behaviour on part of the opposition to disrupt the onward march of the marxists might lead to a 'civil war', as in China.[33] The uncalled for 'civil war' threat startled the people of Kerala and helped the opposition come together, irrespective of their political differences.

In this vitiated atmosphere, a minor clash of students with the government fell like a spark on a haystack. The trouble started when a ticket examiner belonging to the state-owned ferry boat in Ernakulam insulted a student. The student, in turn, assaulted the ticket collector. The encounter resulted in a violent clash in which the police took the side of the transport workers. The government erroneously suspected that the trouble had been brewed by the opposition parties and panicked. Instead of settling the issue through negotiation, it took to high-handed methods.

This use of force was unnecessary. The student agitation would have subsided in course of time, and it was actually cooling down, when the government raised boat fare from 6 paise to 12 paise. This further fanned the agitation. The unrest flared and engulfed practically the whole of Kerala, now with the active support of the combined opposition parties. At this juncture, M.N. Govindan Nair needlessly gave a call to all those interested in the progress of Kerala to organize local *citizen committees* to prevent the opposition from launching unnecessary agitation with the object of pulling down the government in the state.[34]

The upswing affected the party. Radicals who believed that the experiment of peaceful transition to communism had failed in Kerala, wanted the marxists to stay in power at all costs and defend the government, if necessary, by a revolution. The moderates, who constituted the majority, on the other hand, asked for a soft policy. In their view, militant action would invite federal intervention, to the detriment of marxist rule in Kerala. To resolve the issue, the marxists appealed to the fatherland to find out a solution. A three-member delegation comprising Dange, Gopalan, and Ghosh was sent to Moscow for consultation and advice. What transpired in Moscow is anybody's guess. But from the facts it appears that the delegation was asked to adopt a soft policy.[35]

At home, to counter the agitation, the central executive committee of the Communist Party of India sat in a meeting in New Delhi in August 1958 to assess the situation and suggest an effective plan to counter the opposition's move, but failed because of the lack of consensus. It was therefore decided to place the matter once again before the executive committee at its meeting to be held in Trivandrum. At Trivandrum, the executive committee passed a resolution on 11 August 1958 and put the blame on the opposition for creating disturbances, but failed to suggest any effective measures to counter the agitation. The matter then came up before the national council of the party, which met in Madras in October 1958. The national council, while rejecting the notion current among the radical wing of the party, suggested a nationwide peaceful campaign in defence of the government by highlighting its achievements.[36]

The remedy suggested by the national council was ineffective. It failed to stem the tide. Thus, in January 1959, Nambooderipad left for Moscow, apparently to attend the twenty-first congress of the Communist Party of the Soviet Union, but actually to solicit advice. What transpired between Nambooderipad and the Kremlin boss is not known. But from subsequent events, it appears that the Kremlin boss advised Nambooderipad to go slow and avoid confrontation with the Nehru government. The Soviet Union did not like to jeopardize its relationship with India for the sake of the marxists in Kerala.[37]

On his return from Moscow, Nambooderipad issued a call for negotiation. But it was too late. Opposition parties refused to come to the negotiating table and, instead, asked for Nambooderipad's resignation. He refused to step down, the parties formed a *liberation struggle committee* to launch the final assault on the marxist regime. Their only demand was the voluntary resignation of Nambooderipad and they declared 12 June 1959 as 'deliverance day'.

The uncompromising attitude of opposition parties put the marxists in disarray. In July 1959, the national council and the state committee of the Communist Party of Kerala jointly sat in a meeting to decide the plan of action. They ruled out the voluntary resignation of Nambooderipad and, instead, favoured the dismissal of the government by federal intervention. They were under the impression that the union government's action would be undemocratic and would infuriate the people. And they would exploit the situation to stir up a campaign all over India. Thus, to suppress the agitation, as a last resort, they took to repressive methods.[38] After six weeks of chaos, on 31 July 1959, the Union Government dismissed the marxist regime in Kerala and imposed presidential rule.

The mid-term poll following the dismissal of the marxist government was held in Kerala in February 1960. The marxists secured 29 seats, as against 94 seats by opposition parties and 3 seats by other left parties in a house of 126 seats. The debacle of the marxist government in Kerala can be attributed to only one reason – the marxists ignored the ground reality.

The failure of the marxists in Kerala created a sense of despondency among the comrades. The high hopes of a peaceful transition to communism were betrayed and an incorrect assessment of the political situation retarded growth. That apart, at this juncture in 1962, China thrust a war on India, putting the marxists in a dilemma. The pro-Peking faction of the marxists refused to condemn China – socialists could do no wrong. They were elated and expected China to overrun India, helping them bask in the glow of socialism. The halo of socialism was uppermost on their minds; thus, they preferred to live under the tutelage of China as opposed to the bourgeois Nehru government, but there were no takers for this idea. In fact, in the process, they denigrated themselves in the eyes of the populace. However, the real setback to the party came in 1964 when it was split vertically on a flimsy issue of doubtful veracity that, as far back as 1924, Dange had betrayed the party by offering his services to the Government of India.[39] The breakaway faction of the party came to be known as the Communist Party of India (Marxists). And still later, in 1984, the party was split further when Dange with his group dissociated from the parent body and formed the United Communist Party of India – a non-entity in the arena of politics.

The tragedy of marxists in India has been that they have not been able to work in unison. In every crisis, the comrades squabble among themselves, leading to a split or a new party to uphold the purity of marxism. The reason partly lies in marxian ethics, in which fidelity has a low profile. Suspicion and character assassination are common among comrades; and this is done to keep marxism free from dirt and dust.

After the split, the parent body of the marxists, the Communist Party of India, ceased to be a political force for all practical purposes and, in times to come, was reduced to the position of an appendix to its breakaway faction. On the other hand, the breakaway faction, i.e., the Communist Party of India (Marxists), enhanced its position and none-too-soon became a political force to reckon with in West Bengal. The opportunity for the marxists came in 1966 when Ajoy Mukherjee, the president of the West Bengal Congress, dissociated from the parent body and formed the Bangla Congress – a new outfit in the political arena of West Bengal. Mukherjee exited the Congress to give to the people of West Bengal a clean and corruption-free administration. To fulfil the promise, he envisaged a united front with opposition parties, viz., the two factions of the marxists. The marxists welcomed the move and began the process in right earnest.

However, Mukherjee's plan for a united front was shaken when, at the very outset, dissension arose between the two communist parties about the form of cooperation – whether to have a full-fledged united front based on a common programme or a mere adjustment of seats to fight the electoral battle. The Communist Party of India wanted a full-fledged electoral alliance, whereas the Communist Party of India (Marxists) sought adjustment of seats.

Having failed to come to an agreement, rival communist parties formed their own electoral alliances. The Communist Party of India (Marxists), along with the Revolutionary Socialist Party, the Socialist Unity Centre, the Forward Block (Marxists), the Workers Party of India, the Revolutionary Communist Party of India, and the Sanjukta Socialist Party, formed the united left front. On the other hand, the Communist Party of India, along with the Bangla Congress, the Forward Block and the Bolshevik Party of India, formed the people's united left front.

The fourth general election of West Bengal was held in February 1967. In a house of 280 seats, the Congress secured 127 seats; the united left front, 66 seats; the people's united left front, 62 seats; while independents and other non-alliance parties bagged 25 seats. As there was no clear mandate to form the government, the usual process of horse-trading, a part of our democracy, came into operation. The Congress failed to manipulate, but the opposition succeeded and formed a coalition government headed by Ajoy Mukherjee, with Jyoti Basu as his deputy. The defeat of the Congress was not the consequence of any appreciable shift in popular votes towards the marxists or the left in general, but primarily due to defection to Bangla Congress.[40]

The Communist Party of India (Marxists) suffered a temporary setback following its collaboration with the Bangla Congress and the Communist Party of India.[41] The pro-Peking faction of the party disagreed with the party policy. It argued that by collaborating with the Bangla Congress and the Communist Party of India, the party had adopted a neo-revisionist line and discarded the revolutionary ideology of the marxists. Thus, to satiate the revolutionary zeal, the dissidents organized the tribal people of the Naxalbari area for an armed uprising.[42] And in May 1969 they formed a party of their own, the Communist Party of India (Marxists-Leninists).

For the Bangla Congress, the alliance with the marxists proved suicidal. Being unaware of the marxist strategy, Mukherjee strayed into a death trap. Soon after the formation of the coalition government, there occurred a split in the Bangla Congress and Ajoy Mukherjee, the chief minister, became a virtual prisoner of the marxists. In his enthusiasm, and helped by the marxists, Mukherjee had humbled the Congress in West Bengal and cleared the road for the marxists to come to power.

The coalition government of Ajoy Mukherjee survived only for nine months. Shortly after the government was formed, differences arose between the coalition partners on various issues. But the final blow came when P.C. Ghosh, whom Ajoy Mukherjee had managed to include in his ranks, formed a group – the progressive democratic front – and defected along with seventeen other members. Dharma Vira, the governor of West Bengal, asked the chief minister to convene a special session of the assembly to prove his majority. But Mukherjee, instead of facing the assembly, and to the discomfort of the marxists, tendered his resignation. Thereupon, P.C. Ghosh, with the tacit support of the Congress, formed the government and installed himself as the chief minister, with P.C. Chandra as his deputy. The P.C. Ghosh ministry lasted barely three months. Ghosh proved a failure. During his tenure, chaos reigned supreme both within and outside the assembly. The governor recommended President's Rule, which was imposed on the state on 20 February 1968.

The President's Rule was in force for about a year and, then, in February 1969, West Bengal went for a mid-term poll. The united front headed by the Communist Party of India (Marxists) secured 218 seats, whereas the Congress, 55 seats, in a house of 280 seats. The Communist Party of India (Marxists) alone secured 80 seats, becoming the single largest party in the state assembly. Once again, Ajoy Mukherjee became the chief minister, with Jyoti Basu as his deputy. But no sooner than Ajoy Mukherjee had taken the oath of office that dissension arose among the united front partners. It all started with the domineering attitude adopted by the Communist Party of India (Marxists). Instead of working in a cohesive manner to fulfil the aspirations of the people of West Bengal, the Communist Party of India (Marxists) developed a parochial outlook. It wanted to dominate the united front because of its numerical superiority, ignoring the fact that the united front was a coalition of fourteen parties, of which the Communist Party of India (Marxists) was only a fellow traveller. The attitude of the Communist Party of India (Marxists) was resented by other partners of the united front and led to inter-party rivalry.

The first casualty of this rivalry was the industrial sector. The activities of Indian trade union movements were limited to securing petty economic gains. Thus, when the united front minister for labour, Krisna Pada Ghosh, advised employers to 'pay more to get more' he sent the wrong message to workers. Worker unions of different political outfits raised their demand for more pay, without taking into consideration the industry's capacity to pay. When they were refused, they took to *gherao,* a tactic invented by the workers to force the management to succumb to their demands.[43] It spurred furious competition among the united front partners for acts of indulgence in violence and coercion. The *gherao* crippled not only industrial units, but also gradually spread to other sectors, leading to chaos and lawlessness.[44] Yet, the government could not declare *gherao* as illegal. The left, particularly the Communist Party of India (Marxists), opposed it. The situation further deteriorated when the government, under pressure from the Communist Party of India (Marxists), took the unwise step of withdrawing around 1,000 court cases involving those who were held on charges of murder and other heinous crimes.[45]

The Communist Party of India (Marxists) sought to establish its sway over the united front in a distorted manner. Jyoti Basu, the minister of home affairs, in charge of the police and the general administration, set to use his authority to further his party's interests at the expense of other partners of the united front, corrupting in the process both the police and the administration. Anti-social elements, in connivance with the police, continued to indulge in whatever they liked. All moral and ethical standards were run down, and robberies and extortion became the order of the day.

At last, Ajoy Mukherjee made a move when confronted by Jyoti Basu on the question of power and position. The dissension came to such a pass that they ceased to be on talking terms and started communicating through letters. After several rounds of allegations and counter-allegations, Ajoy Mukherjee described his own government as 'barbarous and uncivilized' and sat in a *dharna* or sit-in strike to protest against lawlessness in the state. And when he was unable to rectify the situation, he tendered his resignation on 16 March.

Jyoti Basu yearned for the job of the chief minister and wanted to get rid of Ajoy Mukherjee. He was confident of forming a government without the Bangla Congress, but some of the united front partners stood against him to shatter his dream. The Communist Party of India, the Forward Block, and the Socialist Unity Centre of India threatened to quit the front if it was led by Jyoti Basu. Thus, when Ajoy Mukherjee tendered his resignation, President's Rule was imposed on West Bengal once again.

A day after Mukherjee's resignation, on 17 March, the Communist Party of India (Marxists) called for a general strike in protest against the imposition of President's Rule. The strike call was opposed by some major partners of the united front. What followed were intense clashes between the supporters and opponents of the strike. As many as thirty-five persons lost their life, followed by a trail of murder and bestiality of the worst kind. In most cases, the Communist Party of India (Marxists) was the aggressor; it tried to force the workers and others to join the strike.[46]

The naxalites and lumpen elements took advantage of the situation. Mao's slogans were pasted everywhere, breaking the law became a duty, crackers and bombs were exploded at every public meeting, and the naxalites went on a frenzied killing spree to eliminate class enemies.[47] In fact, civil life in West Bengal became paralyzed, with no remedy in sight.

Mid-term polls were held in March 1971 in the midst of chaos. The united front led by the Communist Party of India (Marxists) secured 125 seats, as against 154 seats by the coalition comprising the Congress, the Bangla Congress, the Communist Party of India and some other parties opposed to the united front. Though the Bangla Congress secured only five seats, Ajoy Mukherjee was elected as the leader of the coalition and formed the government. The government lasted for a few days. No sooner than the assembly met that Jyoti Basu moved a no-confidence motion against the Mukherjee government and voted it out. That was the end of Ajoy Mukherjee. Chaos ensued and, once again, President's Rule was imposed on West Bengal.

The general election of the West Bengal assembly was held in March 1972. The main contenders were the progressive democratic alliance led by the Congress and the united front led by the Communist Party of India (Marxists). The progressive democratic alliance secured absolute majority. S.S. Roy humbled the marxists and made it clear that muscle power and organized manipulations play a crucial role in the electoral battle. Where power is the aim, ethics hardly matter. The Congress alone secured 216 seats, as against 14 seats by the Communist Party of India (Marxists). Jyoti Basu lost the election; S.S. Roy was chosen as the leader of the alliance and formed the government.

Although the Roy government enjoyed a full term, it achieved very little. It succeeded in suppressing the naxal insurgency, but failed to give the people a just and corruption-free administration. Law and order deteriorated, while the hoodlums and lumpen elements, confident of impunity, roamed freely, to the discomfort of the populace. The marxists took full advantage of the situation. Besides exposing the misrule and corruption of the Roy government, they took all care to educate their cadres about electoral manipulations to beat the Congress at its own game.

Roy's victory over the marxists was both short lived and pyrrhic. It cost the Congress dearly. As scheduled, the general election of West Bengal was held in 1977. The united front, led by the Communist Party of India (Marxists), secured absolute majority following the same methods as Roy in the previous general election. The Communist Party of India (Marxists) alone secured 178 seats as against 20 seats by the Congress. Jyoti Basu's dream was fulfilled. He was elected as the leader of the united front and formed the government.

Soon after, the marxists took up the land-reform programme, which they had initiated as a partner of Ajoy Mukherjee's coalition government to offer relief to the rural poor neglected by the successive governments. It was estimated that in West Bengal, 4 per cent families possessed 60 per cent of the land. Thus, they put in place *operation barga,* a pioneering land-reform programme, and distributed 1.04 million acres of land to 2.54 million land-starved sharecroppers. Today, according to government estimate, 40 per cent families possess 80 per cent of the land. The land reform programme has helped the marxists to penetrate into the rural areas of West Bengal.

But in cities and the hinterland, the marxists have failed. Mills and factories have been closed down; investment in the industrial sector has dried up and unemployment among the urban poor has reached alarming proportions. People are sore about it, yet marxists continue to be in power. Since 1977, the united front has won seven assembly elections consecutively – a miracle in democracy.

The success of the marxists in West Bengal can be attributed to three reasons. Firstly, there is no opposition worth the name. The little there is, is hopelessly divided even at the hour of their peril. Secondly, over the years, the marxists have merged the party and the government into one by politicizing the administration and the police force in the state, and then reducing them to the status of a party wing. The real authority, for all practical purposes, is vested with the coordination committees or the liaison groups formed at all the levels.[48] Thirdly, and lastly, the electoral process is skilfully manipulated by dubious means and methods. From the fudging of electoral rolls to the casting of votes, in fact the entire electoral process, is taken care of by the coordination committees, with the tacit support of the election commission, the administration and the police, making the election a mockery of democracy.[49]

The marxists refuse to accept the undeniable fact. The late Anil Biswas, secretary of the Communist Party of India (Marxists), West Bengal, when asked about the rigging and the terror tactics adopted by the marxists in the state, scornfully said that it 'is nothing but a slander campaign launched by a frustrated opposition... Has the Election Commission ever said that we rig the election?'[50] True, the truth is submerged in mystery. The marxists cannot be accused of malpractices – 'Everything is fair in love and war.' After more than eighty years of strenuous efforts, the presence of marxism is negligible except in West Bengal, Kerala and Tripura, a tiny state of little importance – indeed, a dismal failure.

More than three decades of uninterrupted rule in West Bengal made the marxists complacent on one hand while on the other, confident of victory, they became arrogant. The leaders ignored their shortcomings and the cadres tacitly supported by the leaders went on doing as they pleased. There was no accountability. 'Power corrupts and absolute power corrupts absolutely.'

The trouble for the marxists cropped up with the acquisition of farm land for industry. The marxists expected a smooth sailing but a section of the people stood in the way. Supported by Ms Mamata Banerjee, they took to the field and confronted the marxists. Instead of taking corrective measures, the marxists ignored the opposition. They took for granted that the opposition would never unite or even if they unite, it would not make much of a difference. The party was well organized and the cadres were trained to face any adversity. This proved to be an illusion. In their bid for power, the opposition found in Ms Banerjee an astute politician with a clean image – a rare quality of a political leader. For the first time since 1977, under the leadership of Ms Banerjee, the major opposition parties shelved their differences, came to an electoral adjustment and threw a challenge. The marxists were taken aback and caught on the wrong foot. Their promise of good governance failed to enthuse the people. They were in a quandary.

Hoping to better their condition, the common people tired of marxist misrule, looked forward for a change. The change did come in 2011, with the assembly election in West Bengal. In a house of 294 seats, the left front headed by the Communist Party of India (Marxist) managed to get 62 seats as against the combined opposition which secured 227 seats, and others 5 seats only. Power slipped out of the hands of the marxists. Ms. Banerjee's dream was fulfilled. She was elected leader of the house and became the first woman chief minister of West Bengal.

The defeat of the left front can be attributed primarily to anti incumbency and the unity of the opposition, besides strict vigilance and heavy deployment of paramilitary forces. The measures taken scared the marxist cadres from taking to their usual tactics – 'intimidation of non-marxist voters', 'booth jamming', 'booth capturing' and rampant false voting, the underlying election strategy of the marxists.

At the centre, despite their failure to make a mark in Indian politics, the marxists, to their surprise, got an opportunity in 1996 to lead the government. The parliamentary election of 1996 gave a split verdict. No political party could secure a clear mandate to form the government. The Bharatiya Janta Party or the BJP became the single largest party in the parliament, followed by the Indian National Congress. The BJP succeeded in forming a coalition of 24 parties and formed the government at the centre. But no sooner was the government formed than the opposition moved a motion of no-confidence and voted out the government by a slender margin of one vote. The BJP government lasted for only thirteen days.

As the government was pulled down, the opposition came together and formed a rag-tag coalition. Supported by the Congress from outside, the coalition staked its claim to form the government. After a wrangle, the coalition partners sat down to choose a prime minister. In the process, the name of Jyoti Basu was suggested. Basu was willing, rather keen, to accept the responsibility of the august office, but a section of the party leadership stood in his way. The contention was that in the party's programme, there was no provision of joining the government at the centre. Basu's name was dropped.

Disgusted and disheartened, Basu castigated the decision as a 'historic blunder'. The statement sent ripples among the comrades and kicked up a fierce debate. To settle the issue, the central committee of the Communist Part of India (Marxists) called a special party congress and revised the earlier stand. It was agreed upon that, henceforth, given the opportunity, the party would take active part in the centre. The opportunity had come after eight years, but the marxists failed to turn the occasion to their advantage.

In the parliamentary election of 2004, the ruling national democratic alliance or the NDA, headed by the BJP, gave a dismal performance. In a house of 543, it secured only 138 seats, and its alliance partners fared no better. Power slipped out of the hands of the NDA. The opposition performed a little better. The Indian National Congress, having secured 145 seats, emerged as the single largest party in the parliament. The Congress brought together a number of smaller parties under its umbrella and formed the 'united progressive alliance' or the UPA. It still fell short of the required number of seats to constitute a majority to form the government.

At this juncture, the left front, with 61 members in the parliament, came forward to extend support to the UPA coalition from the outside to give it a working majority. The UPA, headed by the Congress nominee Dr Manmohan Singh, formed the government. The tactical move on the part of the marxists enhanced their prestige in the political arena of India. As an ally of the ruling coalition, they got an opportunity to share power at the centre, while keeping the arch enemy, BJP, out of power.

People expected the marxists to play a constructive role to help run the coalition government smoothly, with policy initiatives that could be undertaken jointly. Instead, the marxists preferred to play the role of an opposition party, obstructing every move of the Congress-led government. Taking advantage of the weak coalition, the marxists put spanners in all issues that came up for discussion and decision.

The Congress sought the support of the marxists out of sheer necessity. It was a marriage of convenience, devoid of trust and love. The logical outcome was judicial separation. And the inevitable finally happened on the issue of the Indo-US civilian nuclear deal.

After the break up of the Soviet Union in 1991, the only super power left in the field was the United States of America. The break-up tilted the balance of power in international politics. A realignment of political relations between nations became a necessity. For the first time since independence, India, a non-aligned country with traditional leanings towards the left, turned right. In 1992, the then Narasimha Rao government recognized Israel, hitherto unrecognized by Russia, and reached an agreement on defence relations. The United States of America felt happy and welcomed the move. The process initiated by the Narasimha Rao government continued and, under the NDA, developed into a strategic and economic partnership with the US. The Indo-US civilian nuclear deal was a part of this strategic alliance.

The proposed civilian nuclear deal, with certain riders, promised uninterrupted supply of fuel for India's nuclear reactors, while tacitly accepting India as a *de facto* nuclear power state. The nuclear scientists of India whole-heartedly approved the deal and advised the government to go ahead with it. However, some members of the forty-member nuclear supply group or the NSG objected, as India refused to sign the non-proliferation treaty or the NPT. After prolonged negotiations, they finally came round, gave their clearance and lined up with the US.

The marxists vehemently opposed the deal. Their age-old rabid anti-Americanism played spoilsport. They considered the deal a sell-out to the US and withdrew their support in a bid to pull down the government before the deal could be enacted into law. It was an impulsive and tactless decision. To the surprise of all, the Manmohan Singh government survived the onslaught. The marxists were taken aback. But alas! At this hour of need, no advice came from abroad to rescue them. The situation had changed.

Withdrawal of support from the UPA proved costly for the marxists. The ill-conceived strategy sent a wrong message to the people. They got the impression that the marxists lacked foresight and were incapable of modifying their strategy and tactics in tune with time. This was reflected in the parliamentary election of 2009. In a house of 543 members, the left block managed to get only 24 seats – 37 less than in the previous election.

Notes

1 *People's Age*, 12 October 1947, p.5 and 9, November 1947, p.3.

2 Edvard Kardelj, *Problems of International Development: A Marxist Analysis*, Bombay, 1947, pp.28-32.

3 A Zhdanov, *The International Situation*, Moscow, 1947, pp,40-47. In September, 1947, communist parties of nine countries – Soviet Union, Poland, Czechoslovakia, Bulgaria, Rumania, Hungary, Yugoslavia, Italy and France – held a conference at Sklarska Poreba near Wroclaw in Poland and formed a bureau of information for the communists or Cominform with its permanent headquarters at Belgrade. The idea behind the formation of the Cominform was to encourage the international communists' solidarity by rallying all the democratic and patriotic forces on a common anti-imperialist platform. The formation of the Cominform marked the end of wartime alliances between the Soviet Union and the Western powers, and the beginning of the cold war. However, the lofty ideals of the Cominform could not be achieved as expected, because soon after its formation, differences cropped up between the Soviet Union and Yugoslavia, primarily on the question of authority. The Soviet Union demanded from the communist countries implicit obedience and insisted that they should accept Soviet military and civil advisers for their guidance in the task of building up socialism. Yugoslavia refused to accept the terms and was expelled from the Cominform in June 1948. With the expulsion of Yugoslavia the headquarters of the Cominform were shifted to Bucharest in Rumania. The Cominform had a very short career. It worked only for six years. For all practical purposes, it ceased to function with the death of Stalin in 1953. It was formally dissolved in 1956.

4 *Communist Statement of Policy: For the Struggle for Full Independence and People's Democracy*, People's Publishing House, Bombay, 1947, p.14.

5 *Political Thesis: Adopted at the Second Congress*, Bombay, 1948, containing 95 pages.

6 ibid.

7 Resolution of the central committee of the Communist Party of India on P.C. Joshi's Appeal', Quoted: Gene D. Overstreet and Marshall Windmiller, op. cit:, p.273.

8 R. Palme Dutt, 'Whither India', *Labour Monthly*, June 1948, pp.161-70.

9 A. Dyakov, 'The situation in India'; *New Times*, 2 June 1948 pp.14-7.

10 *For a Lasting Peace, For a People's Democracy* (official journal of the Cominform), April 1948, p.3.

11 From 15 August 1946 to 13 September 1948 the Telengana peasant revolutionaries murdered nearly 2,000 persons, attacked 22 police outposts, captured 20 guns, robbed cash and jewellery worth more than a million rupees, seized and destroyed village records, brunt *chadris* and customs outposts.
Communist Crime in Hyderabad, a. pamphlet issued by the Government of Hyderabad, Quoted: M.R. Masani, op. cit. p.93.
12 M.R. Masani, op. cit., p.91.
13 *Communist Violence in India*, (Ministry of Home Affairs, Government of India), New Delhi, 1949, pp.8-13.
14 ibid., pp.13-34.
15 ibid, pp.59-71.
16 Selig Harrison, 'Caste and the Andhra Communists', *American Political Science Review*, June 1956, pp.380-81.
17 *Communists*, June-July, 1949, p.71.
18 E. Zhukov, 'Problems of National and Colonial Struggle After the Second World War', Quoted: Gene D. Overstreet and Marshall Windmillar, op. cit., pp.293-5.
19 Mighty Advance of the National Liberation Movement in the Colonial and Developing Countries, For a Lasting Peace: *For a People's Democracy*, 27 January 1949.
20 'The Situation in India', *Communist Review*, London, June 1950. pp.175-84.
21 *Communist*, July-August 1950, pp.1-26.
22 P.C. Joshi, *Views Under the Red Banner*, Howrah, 1950. Quoted M.R. Masani, op.cit., pp.100-101 and pp.284-85.
23 S.A. Dange, *Some Notes on the Roots of Our Mistakes After Calcutta*, April 1950.
24 Ajoy Ghosh, S.A. Dange and S.V. Ghate, *A Note on the Present Situation in Our Party*, September 1950.
25 R. Palme Dutt, *The Situation in India*, Bombay n.d., pp.2-6.
26 The draft programme (16 pp.) and the statement of policy (12 pp.) were published by the party from Bombay in 1951.
27 *Election Manifesto of the Communist Party of India*, Calcutta, 1951, Quoted: M.R. Masani, op. cit., pp. 139, 150.
28 *Aikya Keraela* or the united Keraela movement drew its inspiration from an ancient legend when Kerala was a large kingdom under Mahabali. The story goes that under Mahabali all were happy and had lived a prosperous life. The movement though commenced by the Congress failed to give it a united leadership because of internal conflict in the

party. One section of the Congress leadership wanted the four Tamil speaking *taluks* from Travancore to merge with the Madras State, while another section advocated the formation of a large multilingual Kerala. The movement became defunct in 1947 with the merger of Travancore and Cochin into one state. The movement was revived again in 1952 when the marxists took it over and campaigned for the return of those happy days of Mahabali while asking for the unification of all Malayalam speaking areas into a united democratic and prosperous Kerala.

29 *Kerala on the March*, Government of Kerala, Department of Public Relations, Trivandrum, 1957, p.7. Though the president of India felt happy with the establishment of a marxist government in Kerala, U.N. Dhebar, the president of the Congress and other congressmen in general except Nehru did not relish the idea of a marxists-ruled state.

30 M.N. Govindan Nair, 'Challenge in Kerala', *New Age*, Vol. VI, No. 4, April 1957, pp.9-12. Peaceful transition to communism is a post Second World War concept of the marxists. In brief it states that after securing parliamentary majority it would be possible to organize a mass movement and led this into open class struggle to break the power of the opposition parties and then transform the entire government machinery into an instrument of people's rule. The transformation would enable the party to introduce profound political, economic and social changes which, ultimately, would result in the establishment of the dictatorship of the proletariat.

31 *The Kerala Mail*, 15 February, p.9.

32 The electoral rolls in Devicolam constituency were inflated by 17,000 new names. P.K. Chattam, a minister in the marxists government admitted that the government had distributed rupees 1,00,000 in the constituency on the eve of the election. The *Kerala Weekly*, 5 July 1958, pp.2 and 9.

33 Voctor M. Fic, *Kerala: Yenam of India – Rise of the Communist Party: 1937-1968*, Bombay, 1974, p.98

34 *The Deccan Herald*, 22 July 1958; also *The Indian Express*, 22 July 1958.

35 Victor M. Fic., op. cit., p.107.

36 Ajoy Ghosh *On Discussion of the National Council*, the Communist Party of India, New Delhi, 1958.

37 Victor M. Fic, op. cit., p.110.

38 *The Kerala Mail*, 2 August 1959. From 12 June to 31 July 1959, the police opened fire 5 times and killed 17 people, lathi charges were made in 139 places injuring 1605 people, 1,50,000 people were put under arrest of which 40,000 were women. This apart the communist militia

committed 21 political murders. (From the memorandum submitted to the President of Indian Republic on behalf of the Kerala Pradesh Congress Committee, Sri Narayan Press, Quilon 1959)

39 In 1964, in the repository of the National Archives of India, New Delhi, a letter was discovered. The letter dated 28 July 1924 and addressed to the Governor Genaral in Council, was supposed to have been written by Dange soon after the Cawnpore Conspiracy case trial was over. In the said letter, Dange offered his services to the Government of India in return for his release. The discovery of the said letter created a stir in the party circle. Dange denied the authorship of the letter and said emphatically that it was a forgery, but a section of the top echelon of the party leadership refused to give credence to Dange's claim.
For the text of the letter and the subsequent development leading to the split see: Dwijendra Nandi, *Some Documents Relating to Early Communists and Controversies Around Them,* pp.21-27 and 110-12; also Muzaffar Ahmed, *Myself and the Communists Party of India*, pp.383-92

40 The Congress polled 5207930 votes, the Bangla Congress polled 12,86,028 votes and both the communist parties put together polled 31,20,222 votes.
Statistical Report on General Election, 1967 to the Legislative Assembly of the West Bengal, Election Commission of India, New Delhi, p.11.

41 The split registered a serious loss to the party. In 1965, before the split, the party had a membership of 1,19,000 but by 1968 it was reduced to 76, 425 – a loss of nearly 43 per cent.
Political Organizational Report, VIII Congress of the Communists Party of India (Marxists), Cochin December 23-29, Communist Party of India (Marxists), Calcutta 1969, pp.285-86.

42 Led by Charu Mazumdar, Kanu Sanyal, Jangal Santhal and others, the three small towns in the North-East of India, Naxalbari, Khairbari, and Phansidawa, an area comprised of about 250 square miles, rose in revolt. The insurgency started from Naxalbari on 2 March 1967, the day the coalition government took the oath of office. It was essentially an agrarian uprising. The main driving forces behind the uprising were pent-up tribal sentiments in which the peasant seized both, government and private land, looted arms, ammunitions and money, and established people's court to try the class enemies. The movement had the blessing of Peking and spread in several pockets all over India but failed to have any impact on the people. After the first flush of enthusiasm was over, the movement in West Bengal degenerated from revolution to rowdism – killing at will innocent, hapless individuals as

class enemies. The Communist Party of India (Marxist) turned its back on the movement and took all measures to suppress the insurgency as a partner of the coalition government, but failed. Thus rowdism in the name of revolution continued unabated. It was finally suppressed, though not eradicated, when in 1972 S.S. Ray became the chief minister of West Bengal. The Naxals after remaining dormant for quite some time, organized themselves and raised their head once again causing a menace to the country, rather than a mere law and order problem.

43 In literary sense, *gherao* means encirclement. It does not require much of a mobilization. A few determined working people encircle an officer or employer to make him immobile while confining him at one place often refusing food and water till such time he succumbs to their demands totally or partially. The victims of *gherao* were primarily the small and middle industrial establishment.

44 Prafulla Roy Choudhary, *Left Experiment in West Bengal*, New Delhi, 1985, p.99. In the course of a debate in the state assembly, Jyoti Basu admitted that within the first six months of the united front ministry there were 281 *gherao* in the industrial establishments, 34 in educational institutions and 40 in other social sectors.

45 ibid., p.105.

46 ibid., pp.110-11. In one case, a worker was murdered by hammering into his skull large iron nails. In another case, stengun was used to shoot down workers. In yet another gruesome killing in Burdwan town, all brothers in a family were hacked to death in the presence of their mother by a gang of hooligans of the Communist Party of India (Marxists) who were armed with axes, spears, swords, arrows, and other weapons.

47 Surabhi Bannerjee, *Jyoti Basu: The Authorised Biography*, Viking, 1997, p.141.

48 Co-ordination committees or the liaison groups are composed of party functionaries. It acts as a link between the party and the people. The party set its strategy on the basis of feedback received from the co-ordination committees. The members of the co-ordination committees are the real boss, particularly in the rural areas. The police and the administration functions under their thumb.

49 Subversion of electoral process starts with the manipulation of electoral rolls by deleting the names of know anti-marxists voters and inclusion of fictitious names in connivance with the election office. After the electoral rolls are finalized, comes the selection of polling officers, the lynch pin of the election process. They are meticulously selected keeping in view their political leaning. If a non-partisan officer gets in,

the local marxists leaders see to it that he looks the other way. If they fail, the mafias step in to tame the officer. Thereafter the rest of the process is taken care of by the mafias. Localities known for its support or sympathetic to the opposition parties are terrorized. On the day of polling, it starts with booth jamming, an innovation of the marxists to desist anti-marxists or voters sympathetic to the opposition parties from casting their votes. From early morning, the party cadres queue up in front of the polling booths and slow down the process. After waiting for hours in the queue the tired and disgusted voters return without casting their votes. The mafias then take over and cast votes against the absentee voters with the connivance of the polling officer.

50 Interview with *Tehelka*, New Delhi, Saturday, 8 May 2004, p.23.

8

Dilemma of the Indian Marxists

Marxism is a philosophy for the elite, a nightmare for the rich, a hope for the downtrodden and a priceless curio for the petty bourgeois intellectuals. Basically, marxism consists of three elements: a dialectical philosophy taken from the German classical philosopher Hegel, transformed into dialectical materialism, which in turn led to the evolution of historical materialism. A system of political economy is taken from the British school of thought, the dynamic part of which is the labour theory of value and the theory of surplus value. And lastly, it extends a theory of state and revolution in consonance with the revolutionary tradition of France. In fact, marxism is an amalgamation of German philosophy, English economics and French politics. Thus, in true sense, Marx did not make a scientific discovery. Yet, his socialism was scientific in the sense that it sprang from a systematic analysis of social forces that led to a striking discovery. Marx decided before hand what he wanted to discover, and then he did it without fail.

Marxian socialism took much of its shape, rather than content, from the teachings of Hegel. Hegel believed that the determining factor for the progress of society is 'idea', and its gradual realization of which material resources and conditions are but reflections. At every stage, there occurs a conflict in which the superior idea, i.e., the thesis, is challenged by a new idea, its contradiction, i.e., the antithesis. This conflict ends with the fusion of the two, creating a synthesis, a higher idea. This higher idea, in its turn, is challenged by another new idea, its contradiction, which initiates the process towards yet another synthesis, a still higher idea. This contradiction, conflict and synthesis, according to Hegel, is an unending process for the progress of 'idea' and, with it, the society, until it reaches the Absolute, the ultimate reality.

Incidentally, the 'dialectical movement' is an old thought, foreshadowed by Empedocles as early as fifth century B.C. Aristotle embodied it in the 'golden mean', when he said that 'the knowledge of opposites is one'. The supposition remained dormant for centuries until Schelling resurrected the thought. He took the cue from the intellection of Greek philosophers and believed that there was an underlying 'unity of opposites'. The process of evolution is a continuous development of oppositions, and their merging and reconciliation. In the contemplation of Schelling, Fichte found a clue to explicate the thought in the form of a formula – thesis, antithesis and synthesis, the secret of 'all development and all reality'. Hegel seized upon this conception and set it in motion.

Marx took this concept of progress from Hegel but turned it upside down. He contended that for the progress of society, the determining factor is not the 'idea' as Hegel puts it, but the material resources at the disposal of the society. The society, with its knowledge, utilizes the existing material resources at its disposal to the best of its capacity, evolves new methods of production, and designs a new social and economic order to further development. As material resources and knowledge of their use develop, the old economic order becomes untenable, making way for a new one. This necessitates not only redistributing power among social classes, but also changes the social structure and class relationship, and gradually leads to a higher order.

Although Marx adopted Hegel's dialectical method as the basis of his theory of 'dialectical materialism' he was rather emphatic in justifying that his method was different from Hegel's. In the introduction to the first volume of *Capital*, he stated categorically that his 'dialectical method is not only different from Hegelian but is its direct opposite'. And then he qualified his statement that Hegel's 'thinking process is the demiurge of the real world and the real world is only the outward manifestation of "the Idea". With me, on the other hand, the real world is nothing else than the material world reflected by the human mind and translated into terms of thought.'

From dialectical materialism, Marx derived a philosophy of history or a materialist concept of history, as it is popularly known. This concept emanates from two assumptions. The first is that economic causes are fundamental for social changes, while the second is that they operate in accordance with the dialectic principle. Marx, in his *Critique of Political Economy*, raised a fundamental question about the principle that governs all human relations and answered that the base of social relations comprises productive forces or the production of the means to support life and the exchange of the things produced. Man has to live before he starts to think. Marx, in fact, tacitly implied that economic causes are fundamental for all social changes and political liberty or social justice or any other ideological formulations act as an auxiliary force and are subservient to the economic causes. Marx's thesis has had profound influence on writers of social history. Even the staunch critics of Marx accept this formulation rather than any other part of his doctrine.

It may be stated that like dialectical materialism, economic fundamentalism is an old thought. Kautilya, who lived in fourth century B.C., observed in his *Arthashastra* that of the three objectives of human endeavour – *dharma, artha* and *kama*, '*artha* is the most important, for *dharma* and *kama* are both dependent on it'. In fact, Kautilya came, as did Marx, to the same conclusion that in a society economic activities reign supreme, while other activities are subservient to them.

However, Marx's second thesis that history operates in accordance with the dialectical principle is of doubtful veracity. The dialectic speaks of gradual progress towards the Absolute through contradiction, conflict and synthesis. History does not follow the dialectic principle. It is not a tale of continuous progress towards the Absolute, but a record of hope and despair, rise and fall, decay and dissolution.

Similarly, Marx deduced his economic theory from the labour theory of value propounded by the British school of economists. Locke, while defending private property made labour the criterion of value. He ascertained that 'a man is entitled to that to which he had given value of his labour.' Following Locke, Ricardo, with certain reservation, put forward a theory of value, according to which 'the value of a commodity depends on the relative quantity of labour necessary to its production' and held what Lassalle said in his theory of 'Iron Law of Wages', that the value of labour itself or the rate of wages depend upon the cost of the labour's subsistence. Marx seized upon this theory of value and, by an ingenious way, dismissed the orthodox view of production vis-à-vis the labour.

The orthodox theory calls for the cooperation of four agents to produce a commodity of value. The four agents are land (raw material), labour, capital and organization, and each in turn gets a share of the value: land as rent, labour as wages, capital as interest and organization as profits. Marx disagreed with this view of distribution of value. He insisted that if labour is the criterion of value, then he alone is entitled to the value he has created by his labour.

Before Marx, Adam Smith had stated that 'the value which the workers add to their materials resolves itself into two parts of which one pay their wages and the other is the profit of the employer.' Marx called the second of these parts 'surplus value' – a fraud upon the labourers. This is often taken to be his distinct contribution to economic theory, though Marx never claimed to have invented it.

From the theory of surplus value, Marx inferred three golden rules that predict the doom of the capitalist system of economy. Firstly, competition will force capitalists to take to automation to save labour and increase production. Secondly, under competition, the bigger units will either swallow or drive the smaller units out of the market and lead to a swell in the ranks of unemployed workers. Thirdly, and lastly, the misery of unemployed workers will increase in proportion to the development of capitalism. This will help, according to Marx, in the emergence of an 'industrial reserve army' of wage earners. In times to come, when the misery of wage earners will become more and more unendurable, they will be forced to unite for their survival and eventually throw a challenge to the capitalist system to destroy it altogether.

In the realm of the theory of the state and revolution, Marx could not extricate himself from the influence of France's revolutionary tradition. The origin and nature of the state and the limits of its authority is a matter of controversy. But that they exist and/or should exist is accepted universally. Hegel, on whom Marx relied heavily for his philosophic theory, visualized the state as a divine institution in which an individual achieves self-realization only as a member of it. Marx, on the other hand, denied the existing concept of the state and took a diametrically opposite stand. In the *Communist Manifesto*, he defined the state as 'the executive committee of the bourgeoisie'. Engels, in his *Anti-Duhring*, elaborated the concept further. He stated that the state is not a natural institution, and it arises 'when the society is cleft into irreconcilable antagonism which it is powerless to repel'. It is a product of the class struggle and will 'wither away' when a classless society comes into existence. In the introduction to the 1891 edition of Marx's *Civil War in France*, he states once again that the 'state is nothing more than a machine for the oppression of one class by another'. The proletariat will throw it upon the scrap-heap as 'useless-lumber' when they come to power.

A complete exposition of Marx's theory of the state can be found in Engels' *Origin of the Family Private Property and the State* published in 1884, within a year from the death of Marx. Marx perhaps wanted to write a treatise on the subject, but failed to do so. However, he left behind his notes, which Engels used as the basis of his book.

Lenin interpreted the theory further in the first chapter of his *State and Revolution*.

The idea of the liquidation of the state did not originate with Marx. Long before Marx, even before he was born, William Gordon drew the attention of people towards the coercive nature of the state in *Political Rights* (1795). Gordon contended that if the state were abolished, men would live together in accordance with the principles of right reason. Proudhon, an anarchist by faith and a contemporary of Marx, held the same view as Gordon. He propagated the idea of replacement of the state with free, decentralized self-governing committees.

By advocating the abolition of the state, Marx did not imply anarchy. The abolition of the state would mean that the state would lose its political character or, as Engels said in his *Anti-Duhring*, 'the government of persons would be replaced by the administration of things' to watch over real social interest.

Marx's theory of the dialectic of revolution evolved from two factors – class antagonism, and proletariat organic unity. At one point, the landed gentry controlled the state and moulded the society in accordance to their needs to serve their class interests. Then came the industrial capitalist and the mercantile classes who, over the years, gained sufficient strength to throw a challenge to the traditional authority of the landed gentry. From this conflict emerged a new governing class – a fusion of the two classes. The authority of this new class is, in turn, destined to be challenged by the workers, initiating a conflict towards a synthesis.

In Marx's perception, revolution will come in two stages. The first stage will involve a bourgeois democratic revolution, when the bourgeoisie, with the support of the proletariat, will be the master of the state and serve the bourgeois class interests. In the second stage, the proletariat will capture the state through a revolution to usher in socialism in the interest of all.

Paradoxically, in the *Communist Manifesto*, Marx paid a handsome tribute to the capitalist order. In his opinion, barely in one hundred years, it had 'created more massive and more colossal productive forces than have all preceding generation together'. By rapid improvement of all means of production and communication, it had drawn 'all, even the most barbarian into civilization'. By creating great cities, it had 'rescued a considerable part of the population from the idiocy of rural life'. It had established 'universal inter-dependence of Nations' and subjected 'Nature's forces to man'. Yet, in Marx's assessment, the working class, i.e., the proletariat, is destined to overthrow the capitalist class and capitalism as an economic order.

But socialism cannot be achieved by merely ousting the capitalist class from its pre-eminent position; there will be a period of transition between the fall of capitalism and the establishment of socialism. The intervening period will not witness a free society. As an exigency, the proletariat dictator would be obliged to retain the state, the coercive machinery of the predecessor. Therefore, in this period of transition, the victorious proletariat must be the dictator not only to consolidate its power, but also to defend itself against the onslaught of counter-revolution to build up for itself the social habits and forms of organizations necessary for the functioning of a classless society. The proletariat will not merely capture the state and use it for its own ends, but destroy it altogether, along with the class it represents. With the disappearance of classes, the state – an emanation of class relationships – will 'wither away' and be substituted by a new institution that will administer the community's resources in the interest of all. This will end the exploitation of man by man – resulting in the creation of an ideal society or utopia where every one is happy and without conflict forever more, i.e., in hegelian terms, the Absolute.

Marxists agree to this analysis of social progress but differ widely as to the nature of the new institution that will come up in place of the state and the method by which the replacement will be achieved.

Marx's doctrine was clearly outlined as early as 1848, when he and Engels published the *Communist Manifesto*. But its impact was felt much later, though socialism of one sort or another figured in the movements of 1848. The main conflicts of 1848 were based on attempts to establish parliamentary democracy, or to secure national unity and independence, rather than any bid on the part of the working class to overthrow capitalism. The impact of the manifesto was felt with the rise of social democracy after the formation of the First International in 1864, and the rise of communism after the socialist revolution in Russia in 1917.

Apparently, marxism is a simple philosophy, yet complicated and often confusing. It is said that in 1895, when Lenin on his visit to Paris told Paul Lafargue, the son-in-law of Marx, that Russians were studying Marx's writings, the latter replied that 'even after twenty years no one in France understood them'.[1] And this is true for all countries. The majority takes to marxism, swayed by its populist approach, without understanding what actually it speaks about. It is the duty of marxist intellectuals to make marxism intelligible to common men. Marxists in India have failed rather miserably. They kept talking and writing about marxism at a level only few could reach. The common men who took to marxism in India carried with them obscurantist ideas. Thus, from the very outset, the marxists had to fight obscurantism both within and outside the party. They opened the fight with the zeal of a missionary, but from a wrong perspective. They neglected the social environment and psychology of the people. They failed to comprehend that the politics of a country could not be divorced from the social system with which it was linked, both supplementing each other. Marxists in India ignored this basic fact and tried to transplant marxism in its orthodox form, bothering in the least about the social psychology of the people. They were under the impression that social justice and economic equilibrium, the basic tenets of marxism, would sweep the country, and this, followed by a proletarian revolution, would solve their problem. The downtrodden in India looked for social justice and aspired to better their economic condition, but were not prepared to accept the marxian view of proletarian revolution to turn society upside down. Age-old obscurantist ideas and innate faith in the Almighty stood in their way. They were in a quandary about how to make it appropriate to Indian conditions by weeding out what was uninspiring.

In India, the major challenge to the marxists came from Gandhi. Gandhi's love for religion, absolute faith in non-violence and aversion to class struggle were all diametrically opposed to marxism, but aligned with the Indian mind. His politics was universal in character, based on humanism, and never attached to any political ideology. His approach was always mild and flexible, slow but steady. Quite often he flattered the minorities, but never accused the majority. His humanistic approach captivated people from all strata of society, irrespective of caste or religion. He was the true representative of India. Marxists failed to assess this trait of gandhism. They vacillated and shifted their stand vis-à-vis Gandhi from time to time.

Marxism, with its concept of welfare, is a philosophy not akin to the Indian mind. The concept of class struggle and proletarian revolution is antagonistic to the Indian social system. To plant this new philosophy on Indian soil, the marxists needed constructive thinking in consonance with the Indian social system and the psychology of people, besides a personality to match Gandhi. Muzaffar or Dange, Singaravelu or Ghate, Adhikari or Joshi, Ghosh or Ranadive were no match for him. They were sincere and dedicated, but lacked the charisma of Gandhi.

As against Gandhi's universal appeal for independence, the marxists' appeal to the people was lopsided. It was primarily confined to workers and peasants in search of social justice and better economic status. The major political programme of the subservient country should be independence which was not their immediate concern. And the marxists cannot be blamed for this. According to the marxian dictum, the proletariat is the vanguard of revolution. Collaboration of the bourgeoisie is necessary only to achieve a bourgeois democratic revolution, after which, the proletariat will take over to convert the bourgeois democratic revolution into a socialist revolution. Thus, the major emphasis of marxists all over the world is on the appeal to workers and peasants, as was the case in India. This exclusive appeal to workers and peasants made marxism in India synonymous with trade unionism and led to its isolation from the main currents of the freedom struggle.

In India, the freedom struggle was mainly a bourgeois nationalist movement. The role of workers and peasants was minimal and momentary. In this predominantly bourgeois nationalist movement, only a handful of the bourgeoisie took to marxism. Bourgeois intellectuals, in general, play a significant role in propagating marxism. It is through them that the message of marxism reaches the downtrodden. In fact, marxism in any country, in the initial stages, is a bourgeois intellectual movement. The Indian bourgeoisie that took to marxism primarily comprised arm-chair politicians who cherished lofty ideals and supposedly sympathy for the poor, but were simply happy to be members of the privileged class. They failed to turn marxism into an intellectual movement and kept it confined within their coterie. They placed marxism on a philosophical plane just to satisfy their intellectual curiosity and did not accept it as a creed to fight and formulate an action plan for the proletariat.

Apart from the failure to contain Gandhi and manipulate bourgeois intellectuals, marxists in India committed a series of grievous errors one after another. The first was the preaching of the people's war thesis, followed by the opposition to the 'Quit India' movement, and then the nationality theory which helped evolve the Muslim demand for Pakistan.

When the Second World War broke out, the marxists regarded the war as an opportunity to free India from British control by converting the imperialist war into a revolutionary one. They took full advantage of Gandhi's ambivalent attitude towards imperialist Britain and made some headway with the masses. This was in accordance with the people's aspirations to see India free from British control. But no sooner did Germany cross into Soviet territory and Gandhi adopted a jingoistic posture, than the marxists did a volte-face. To the marxists, the imperialist war suddenly became the people's war, and defeat of fascism and the victory of the Soviet Union became the supreme concern, in preference to national independence. The marxists extended their cooperation to imperialist Britain, when all the people of the country were intently anticipating her defeat in the war. The unconvincing plea of the marxists was that fascist victory would enslave the whole world, not sparing even India. This support to Britain's war effort on the pretext of people's war was a big blunder – it was anti-people.

After espousing the people's war thesis, the marxists committed another folly when they opposed the Quit India movement. Although the Quit India movement was thoughtless and sporadic, without any plan or preparation, it was all the same a people's movement to end British rule in India. Opposition to such a movement, however justified, tantamonted to treachery. The marxists, advised by the Communist Party of Great Britain, took this step wilfully to fulfil their obligation to the people's war thesis.[2] They condemned the leaders as fifth columnists and opposed the movement, which led to their separation from the masses. The Congress and the socialists took full advantage of the situation and accused the marxists as traitors and agents of British imperialism. The marxists, in their turn, retaliated by calling the leaders of the movement gangs of criminals in the pay of the fascists. In a resolution adopted by the first congress of the party, it was laid down that 'the groups which make up the fifth column are Forward Block, the party of the traitor Bose; the CSP which betrayed socialism at the beginning of the war, and pursued a policy of opportunism and disruption; and ended in the camp of the trotskyite traitors and finally, the trotskyite groups which are criminal gangs in the pay of fascists. *The Communist Party declares that all these groups must be treated by every honest Indian as the worst enemy of the nation and driven out of political life and exterminated*'.[3]

The marxists committed another serious error by giving a fillip to the Muslim demand for Pakistan at a time when Gandhi was trying to narrow down the differences between the different communities in India through his liberal policies. The ethnic multiplicity of India fostered a variety of particularist* currents with a strong regional bias, but they never considered themselves as separate nations and lived together as Indians bound by a common thread. The marxists, in their enthusiasm, took the initiative to transplant in

India the nationality theory as propounded by Stalin.[4] In imitation of the Soviet Union, they considered India not to be a nation, but a conglomeration of seventeen nationalities. They asserted that in India every section of the people 'which has a contiguous territory as its homeland, common historical tradition, common language, culture, psychological make up and common economic life would be recognised as a distinct nationality with the right to exist as an autonomous state within the free Indian union or federation and will have the right to secede from it if it may so desire'.[5] The Muslims, with an overwhelming majority in the north-western region and in eastern Bengal, found in this theory a support for their demand for a separate homeland, i.e., Pakistan, with the right to secede from the Indian Union.

The nationality theory contradicted the one-nation theory of the Congress. Till the early thirties of the twentieth century, it was accepted by all, including the Muslims, that India was one and indivisible. But from the mid-thirties, the Muslims started thinking in terms of a separate homeland to counter the 'Hindu Congress', though not a separate nation. This separatist tendency got an impetus from the nationality theory, in which the Muslims found both justification for a separate homeland, i.e., Pakistan, and a separate identity as a nation.

Faced with the insistent demand for Pakistan, marxists in India adopted the right-opportunist approach and accepted religion as one of the factors in the national make-up. By supporting the Muslim demand for Pakistan, the marxists compromised their views on religion, in total disregard of marxism-leninism. They tacitly accepted that religion was no more an 'opium of the people', at least as far as Muslims in India were concerned. The Muslims were not impressed by marxism, but simply exploited the marxists' support to their advantage. The marxists realized their mistake, only after it became impossible to rectify.

Of all the errors committed by marxists in India, the most distressing was the exclusive reliance on foreign advice. It cannot be denied that foreign emissaries contributed substantially to the growth of marxism in India. But it is equally true that the advice received from abroad was out of tune with the situation prevalent in India. Whether it was a wrong assessment of Gandhi, the people's war thesis, opposition to the Quit India movement or the nationality theory; at every step, it was foreign advice that worked at the roots. Marxists in India never tried to think for themselves, and always looked for guidance from abroad. In the earlier phase of the movement, or till the time that India got her independence, marxists in India were mere page-boys of the foreign advisers. Leaders of the Comintern and the Communist Party of Great Britain took upon themselves the responsibility to guide marxists in India. They were well versed in the theory of marxism-leninism, but were ignorant of the Indian political scenario. Their advice was based on the experience of their own country, disconnected from India. The marxists in India never questioned their right to advise and worked as agents of foreign governments in the country. Since Moscow was the epicentre of marxism, anything said and done there became sacrosanct for marxists in India. It was only after India achieved her independence that marxists in India gradually reduced their dependence on foreign advice and learnt to think for themselves, but not in consonance with the social system and psychology of Indians. No political party, however dynamic its programme, can grow if it fails to understand the psychology of the people and works in opposition to it.

Notes

1 Pierre Chasles, Vie de Lenine, Paris, 1929 p.39.
Referred: R.N. Carew Hunt, *The Theory and Practice of Marxism*, Pelican, 1969

2 In a letter dated 2 August 1942, addressed to the Communist Party of India, R. Palme Dutt wrote: 'By the time this reaches you, events will have moved very much further and you maybe in the midst of a big issue. The general line is clear; maximum mass mobilisation against fascism; full cooperation in practical action with all who oppose fascism, irrespective of political differences; no action of the present rulers so long as they stand by the alliance to resist fascism, should deflect us from this line, which is in the interests, not merely of the world front of the peoples, but of the Indian people whose future cannot be separated from the world front of the peoples.'
Quoted: M. R. Masani, op. cit., p.278 fn.

3 Madhu Limaye, op. cit. pp.48-9. Emphasis original.

* Exclusive or special devotion to a particular interest

4 The question of nationality from the marxian point of view was first formulated by Stalin as far back as 1912. Since then it had become the touchstone of nationality policy for the marxists all over the world.
For details, see: J.V. Stalin, *Works*, Vol. IV, Moscow 1953, pp.300-81.

5 N.K. Krishnan, *National Unity for the Defence of the Motherland*, Bombay, 1943, pp.24-5.

9

Indian Marxists at the Crossroads

Whether socialism of the kind visualized by Marx will ever be established is anybody's guess. The proletarian revolution, the collapse of capitalism, the dictatorship of the proletariat, the establishment of a classless society and withering away of the state, all of which occupy key positions in the theory of marxism, are in jeopardy. Marxists have failed to come up to the expectations of people. The era ushered in with the blood of the Romanovs promised eternal bliss, but none too soon turned into a nightmare. After more than seven decades of the dictatorship of the proletariat, the Soviet Union, the fatherland of marxists all over the world, has been forced to discard marxism and shift to bourgeois democracy, starting with *perestroika* and *glasnost*. To the surprise of all, the union itself has been disintegrated, raising grave doubts about the feasibility of forming a super state through the conglomeration of a number of nation states with wide ethnic diversity, solely on the basis of economic determination, ignoring the national and cultural aspirations of the people.[1] The dictatorship of the proletariat is no more acceptable to people as it tends to ignore democracy and suppress civil liberty.

The concept of classless society and withering away of the state has turned out to be utopian.

Marx considered, as did Plato, the society to be a mass of clay and wanted to fashion it at will. Nevertheless, till date, only a few can claim to have acquired the astute intellect of Marx in the realm of political economy. Basing himself on the works of classical English economists, Marx accomplished a veritable revolution by throwing a challenge to the capitalist system of economy, though his thesis has often been criticized and he has even been accused of plagiarism. In fact, Keynes described *Das Capital* as 'an obsolete economic textbook... scientifically erroneous...',[2] while certain followers of the German economist Rodbartus have accused Marx of plagiarizing from the work of their master.[3] Yet, *Das Capital* remains the most influential piece of writing produced in modern times. It is more a revolutionary treatise than a mere exposition of the capitalist system of economy. The power of *Das Capital* lies in its central idea. The arguments put forward in support of the thesis may not always be tenable, but that is beside the point and should not deter us from appreciating the genius of Marx.

Lenin ignored the utopia ingrained in marxism and sought to implement the theory of Marx into practice. Long before Lenin, Plato had also tried to give a practical shape to his 'utopia' and ended up with disastrous consequences.[4] Utopia is a fantasy. It is an extraordinary exposition of a brilliant mind, apparently true but impossible to achieve. Enamoured with his own imagination, Plato could not foresee the impracticability of turning his utopia into a reality; the experiment of Lenin, as of Plato, was therefore doomed from the start. Yet, looked at objectively, it would be too early to say that the thesis propounded by Marx has been disproved in toto.

The bolsheviks occupied the seat of power in the wake of chaos. It was an accident of history. The revolution happened in Russia not because of a crisis in the capitalist system of economy, but because of all round disorder deliberately created during the war by the corrupt bureaucracy and the propertied class. The bureaucracy undertook to wreck Russia from within, in order to make separate peace with Germany, while the propertied class sabotaged the economy and war efforts of Russia to initiate a political revolution, which they thought would help them wrest power from the Tsar. 'They wanted Russia to be a constitutional republic like France or the United States: or a constitutional monarchy like England.'[5] The bourgeois intellectuals of Russia, besides being divided among themselves, had no knowledge of a revolutionary upsurge. They considered revolution a 'sickness' and erroneously believed that like all other sicknesses, the revolutionary sickness could be cured by administering 'medicine' perhaps not by the Russians, but by some other foreign powers, viz., Germany.[6] They remained unconcerned of the impending revolution and all round disorder and suffering of the common populace. They continued with their petty conventional life, ignoring the revolution as much as possible. The masses wanted peace, liberty, food and clothing, and looked forward to a revolution to cure the ills plaguing their lives. They lost confidence in the monarchy and loathed the bureaucracy and the propertied class.

Away from this anomalous situation, the army as a whole was loyal to the monarchy. Only a faction of the officers desired the deposition of the 'colonel', as Nicholas II was called in the military circle.[7] The bulk of the officers had a very poor opinion about bolsheviks. On 7 November, the day the bolsheviks fired the first shot, captain Gomberg, a menshevik by faith and secretary of the military section of the party, when asked about the prospect of the socialist revolution, shrugged his shoulder and said, 'Well, the bolsheviks can seize the power but they won't be able to hold it more than three days. They have not the men to run a government. Perhaps it is a good thing to let them try – that will finish them.'[8]

Captain Gomberg's observation had some truth in it. The bolsheviks knew that theirs was a party primarily composed of workers and peasants, and had poorly trained and educated personnel. So, a section of the bolsheviks was in favour of an all socialist government, instead of a purely bolshevik rule. They argued in the same vein as Gomberg, 'We cannot hold on, too much is against us. We haven't got the men, we will be isolated, and the whole thing will fall.'[9] But Lenin, supported by Trotsky dismissed the idea and favoured going ahead with his plan for an all-bolshevik government.

To counter the anarchic state of affairs, the Kerensky government vacillated between ineffective reforms and repressive measures, allowing the situation to deteriorate beyond repair. Kerensky believed that for Russia time was not yet ripe for a socialist revolution. The masses were not educated enough to take over power. Any attempt to do so would inevitably help the reactionaries and a ruthless opportunist might restore the old regime. Russia must pass through the stage of political and economic development and take to bourgeoisie democracy before taking a plunge towards full-fledged socialism. The bolsheviks who believed to the contrary exploited the situation to their advantage and converted the people's rage into a revolution. To begin with, bolsheviks were initially supported by a few thousand sailors of the Baltic Fleet and the Red Guards.[10]

The ease with which bolsheviks achieved the revolution was a miracle. In ten days, the provisional government of the mensheviks succumbed before the bolshevik onslaught. The reason was that no sooner did the revolution begin than the bulk of the army switched its loyalty to the bolsheviks, because of the vacillation and inaction of the Kerensky government.

The success of the bolsheviks dismayed the middle and upper strata of the society. They were taken by surprise and in sheer desperation attempted a counter-revolution to meet the challenge, but failed to come up to the situation.[12] The resistance they put up was partial, while the revolution was total. The lava of the revolution engulfed the whole of Russia, as it had in France in 1789. Nevertheless, disillusioned and disheartened, Russia accepted bolshevism as a fait accompli. No matter what one thinks of bolshevism, it is an undeniable fact that the socialist revolution in Russia was one of the greatest events in human history – a phenomenon of worldwide importance.

The socialist revolution inaugurated an era only apparently, except for the abolition of the capitalist system of economy and the liquidation of the counter-revolutionaries, everything continued as before. The bourgeois state without the bourgeoisie was allowed to continue with its coercive functions as in the old order. Differences and even unjust differences of wealth persisted, and workers continued to be paid 'according to their work and not according to their need'. In fact, the socialist revolution simply turned tsardom upside down, with the promise of equality and social justice to all, irrespective of religion, sex, or nationality.

The socialist revolution destroyed the capitalist system of economy but failed to eradicate the evils of the capitalist order. Corruption, indiscipline, selfishness – in fact everything that rules the capitalist order – continued unabated. People took full advantage of socialism but, in return, gave back very little to the society. Socialism made people conscious of their rights, but failed to make them recognize their duties. It is good to plan a society where no distinction is made between individuals and all are treated as equals. But to extend such a lofty ideal to all would mean dilution of responsibility. When everything belongs to everybody, no body takes care of anything. This is exactly what happened in the Soviet Union. There were many who accepted socialist laws and practices and managed to get from them all that was possible, but in return shared very little with the society.[13]

Yet, under the dictatorship of the proletariat, the Soviet Union emerged as a powerful modern state to reckon with. This was no mean achievement. The Soviet Union was created with Russia as the centre, the most backward among the states of Europe. Peter the Great equated Russians with 'cattle' and Tshaadayeff, the man who headed the reform movement in the reign of Nicholas I, dismissed Russia as a 'superfluous member of the body of humanity'. Tshaadayeff lamented, 'No great truth has ever come from out of our people. We have discovered nothing, and from all the discoveries made by other nations we have borrowed only the outward simulacrum of useful luxury.'[14]

The reason for the success of bolsheviks was Lenin's realization of the ground reality that the transition to socialism would be impossible without experts who are in the main bourgeois. Before coming to power, Lenin's views on administration were naive. He reduced administration to the level of 'registering, filling and checking' which can 'easily be performed by every literate person' and declared unequivocally that 'we must break the old, absurd, savage, despicable and disgusting prejudice that only the rich (i.e. educated) can administer the state'.[15]

But no sooner did he come to power than his illusion was over. At the ninth party congress, he declared that 'For the work of organizing the state we need people who have state and business experience, and there is nowhere we turn to such people except the old class … we have to administer with the help of the people belonging to the old class we have overthrown.'[16] This open policy, though a deviation from the tenets of marxism, prompted a large number of bourgeois specialists to collaborate with the state in order to secure a privileged position. This was a temporary set-up. It was expected to continue till such time as a new generation of experts, of whom a majority would be of proletarian or peasant origin, assume power.

This apart, the marxists succeeded in bringing together a set of people who sincerely believed that socialism would liberate people from ignorance, hunger and prejudices. For the first time since the dawn of history, the marxists successfully forged a link between intellectuals, workers and peasants, with a promise to bring them to the centre stage. They awoke the populace from its deep slumber, disciplined it and raised it to the level of an advanced nation. Yet none too soon the people felt disgusted with marxism. The high promise made to the people by the marxists proved to be an illusion. The melding of thought and action did not lead to the liberation of men, but to totalitarianism, while degenerating the working-class power into tyranny. Genuine socialism means uniform development of the social whole. The marxists, instead, treated a part as the whole and the remainder no better than a serf under the Tsar.

That such a situation would arise was long expected. With the first flush of bolshevik success, Trotsky, in the name of the Military Revolutionary Committee, declared: 'We are going to find a power which will have no other aim but to satisfy the needs of the soldiers, workers and peasants.'[17] He excluded the bourgeoisie and elite intellectuals from assuming power in a new social order – an experiment unique in history. The proletariat dictator robbed intellectuals of their liberty and terrorized those who were outside the pale of marxism or disagreed with the dictator. And there was no remedy to this tyranny. Those who tried to raise their voice were ruthlessly suppressed and, all along, it was made to appear that everything was in order. 'Propaganda of success – real or imagined, gained upper hand. Eulogizing and servility were encouraged, the need and opinion of working people, of the public at large, were ignored. In social sciences, scholastic theorization was encouraged and developed, but creative thinking was driven out from social sciences and superfluous and voluntarist assessments and judgements were declared indispensable truth.'[18] The change came with the collapse of the economy, as it affected all aspects of Soviet society. The economic debacle followed by *perestroika* and *glasnost* opened the floodgates of liberalism and led to the collapse of marxism in the Soviet Union and, along with it, the East European countries.[19]

As to the achievement or failure of marxism, there are two sets of opinions diametrically opposite each other. This is because, like the alexandrite,[20] it is difficult to determine the true colour of marxism. It all depends on how one looks at it. Marxists look only at the brighter side of the doctrine, while non-marxists only see the darker side of it; what they overlook in this process is that there are other shades in between.

As a viable political ideology, marxism in its orthodox form is on its way out from the arena of politics. Lenin's experiment has failed, to the great relief of the capitalist order. Yet marxism will not perish altogether; at least some of its elements are here to stay. For years to come *Das Capital* will be studied and analyzed by intellectuals all over the world and the ideas of socialism will continue to hang like a Damocles sword on the capitalist order.

The debacle of marxism in the Soviet Union has put marxists in India in a state of disarray. They can no longer hope to get financial assistance or advice from the fatherland.[21] Besides, at this hour of peril, they have been called upon to face a new challenge – *Hindutva* or the Hindu consciousness movement, which in modern times began with Swami Vivekananda and is now reaching maturity. The movement with its vast potential and immense social implications has dismayed marxists. It has created a crisis in the arena of Indian politics by augmenting Hindu consciousness, which had long been absent because of centuries of political servitude. Any political movement that aims to capture the masses must endeavour to identify a *symbol* that can seize the imagination of the people and inspire them to action. The votaries of the Hindu consciousness movement have found a symbol in *Hindutva*. It has seized the imagination of a large section of the Hindu populace and, sure enough, it will inspire them to action, though much will depend on how the leaders discharge their responsibilities.[22]

The marxists in India, instead of taking up the gauntlet in right earnest to counter the movement, are in a quandary. They are neither adequately equipped, nor sufficiently organized to challenge the movement on their own. They ignore the positive side of the movement. With a handful of self-appointed guardians of secularism, they try to whip up a fear psychosis among a section of the populace by dubbing the movement as communal. They refuse to learn from history. History has shown time and again that in a political crisis people lean towards the ideology that power-hungry politicians seek to suppress the most. The constitution of a joint front of marxists to counter the spread of Hindu consciousness is a misconceived strategy. Instead, the socioeconomic political changes that the marxists intend to introduce in India can be brought about by preventing exploitation of the poor and organising the peasants and workers in productive activities. The majority population of India comprises Hindus; thus, any movement detrimental to Hindu interest is bound to be counter-productive in the long run. Marxists in India are yet to understand this fact and act accordingly. This apart, the collapse of marxism in the Soviet Union and the East European countries has raised grave doubts about the feasibility of marxism as a viable alternative to India's existing politico-economic system. Marxists in India need to develop a realistic approach for a positive view of things. They should stand on their own by bringing together the different splinter groups and shun the joint front strategy of pre-independence days. Endless compromises with diverse political groups may get short-term advantages, but ultimately lead to oblivion.

The marxist aspiration for class struggle leading to a socialist revolution in India has turned out to be a pipe dream. The dictum of Marx has failed, at least for the time being, to the detriment of marxists all over the world. Marx, through a scientific analysis of the capitalist system of economy, came to the conclusion that class struggle is 'as objective a fact as the law of gravitation': socialism is inevitable, if pursued, it will come sooner, if not, it will come a little late. The form of socialism may change, but its basic character will remain the same. The capitalist system of economy is bound to collapse because of its internal contradictions. The super structure of laws and institutions, which has come up to safeguard it, has long since become fetters on productive forces. Capitalism cannot be reformed. The majority of marxists have shifted from this position after the dissolution of the Soviet Union. Marxists all over the world have taken to bourgeois democracy and adopted the much condemned capitalist mode of production. They have become pragmatic and no longer aspire to achieve a proletariat revolution as a first step towards socialism. Only a small segment of marxists are still harping on the prophecy of Marx and blissfully basking in the halo of socialism with the hope that at the end Marx's prophecy will come true. In India, marxism is limping, though more than eight decades have passed since the ideology set its foot on the country's soil. Confined to a few pockets, it is struggling for survival through means and methods often in total disregard of the tenets of marxism.

The survival and expansion of a political party largely depends on four factors – a leader with foresight, an ideology in consonance with the spirit of the time and akin to the socio-political perception of the people, a programme that meets the needs of the people, a regular process of recruitment to infuse new blood into the party. The Communist Party of India has an ideology but the other basic factors are lacking, so the future of the party is bleak. In times to come it will cease to be a political force, yet survive as a non-entity in the arena of politics. It will be admired by the intellectuals while being despised by the common populace.

Notes

1 The Soviet Union was an amalgam of fifteen nation states. It was created over a period of time both by forcible annexation and voluntary accession. The entire edifice was built up with Russia as the centre – the largest amongst the states of the Soviet Union having 76 per cent of the territory and more than 50 per cent of the population. The states which comprised the Soviet Union were Armenia, Azerbaijan, Byelorussia, Estonia, Georgia, Kazahkistan, Kirghisa, Latvia, Lithunia, Moldova, Russia, Tajikistan, Turkmenistan, Ukraine, and Uzbekistan.

2 J.M. Keynes, *Essays in Perceptions*, New York 1932, p.300.

3 E.H. Car, *Karl Marx – A Study in Fanaticism*, New York 1934, pp.270-71.

4 In the year 387 B.C., Dionysius, the ruler of Syracuse, invited Plato to turn his kingdom into an 'utopia', Plato accepted the invitation hoping to give a practical shape to his thought. But no sooner did Plato set to put his thought into action, Dionysius realized that if he agreed to the concept of 'utopia' as Plato had visualized, he should either be a philosopher or cease to be a king. So he bulked. The upshot was a bitter quarrel. The story has it that the king sold the philosopher into slavery only to be rescued by his friend and pupil Anniceries who came forward and paid the ransom money.

5 John Reed, *Ten Days that Shook the World*, (Reprint), New York 1938, p. VIII. In 1915, when the war was on in some sections of the Russian trenches there was only one rifle for every four or five men because of short supply. The manufactures crippled the production to the ground. The coal mines near Kharakov were set on fire and flooded. The engineer of the textile mills at Moscow put the machines out of order, the factories closed the gate, the railways broke down and food disappeared from the market. The speculators took full advantage of the situation and piled up fortunes to meet their fantasies.

6 ibid., p.7. A few days before the revolution began, Stephen Georgevitch a cadet by political faith and commonly known as 'Russian Rockefeller' said that 'revolution is a sickness' and made a prophecy that sooner or later foreign powers would intervene to cure Russia of her 'sickness' as soon as they realize 'the danger of bolshevism in their own country'.

7 E.J. Dillon, *The Eclipse of Russia*, London 1918, p.385.

8 John Reed, op. cit., p.76.

9 ibid., pp.123-24.

10 The Red Guards were a band of armed factory workers untrained and undisciplined but full of revolutionary zeal. They were first organized in 1905 and then again sprang up in March 1917. All efforts to disarm them

by Kerensky government proved futile. With the first sign of revolution they came out on the streets of Petrograd in support of the bolsheviks.

11 To check the bolsheviks, at the last stage of the revolution, a few counter revolutionary groups sprang up. The two most notables of them were the White Guards and the Death Battalion. The White Guards were drawn mostly from the students of the university and the unemployed youths. And the Death Battalion was composed of young people form amongst the sons and daughters of the propertied class with the active support of Kerensky.

12 Mikhail Gorbachev, *Perestroika*, London 1988, p.3.

13 E.J. Dillon, op. cit., pp.11-12.
For subtle observation and pungent criticism of the Russian society Tshaadayeff was shut up in a mad house.

14 V.I. Lenin, *Collected Works*, Vol. II, p.258

15 ibid. p.556

16 John Reed, op. cit., p.86

17 Mikhail Gorbachev, op. cit., p.21.

18 Taking lessons from the collapse of marxism in the Soviet Union and in the East European countries, socialist countries such as China, Cuba, Vietnam, and North Korea are drifting towards market economy while keeping the administration in the hands of the communist party.

19 The Alexandrite is a gem, more expensive than the diamond. It was first discovered in the Urals in 1833 and named after the Tsarevitch who was to become Alexander II. The peculiarity of the gem is that it is green in daytime but at night under artificial light it turns fiery red and gleam like the star Actures.

20 To propagate marxism, financial assistance to fraternal organization was started by Lenin. At the initial stage, the fund used to be disbursed through the Department of Foreign Relations, a wing of the central committee of the Communist Party of the Soviet Union and thereafter through the K.G.B. It is difficult to assess the total amount disbursed form the Soviet coffer and the share of the Communist Party of India. But since 1987, the amount disbursed was to the tune of $20 million. According to a document dated 25 February 1987, the share of the Communist Party of India came to be $5 lacs.
Rosia, a Soviet weekly, and also *Washington* Post on the basis of a report published in Ogonyok. Quoted: *The Times of India*, New Delhi, Saturday 12 October 1991: and Sunday 22 March 1993.

21 The demolition of the Babri Masjid and the demand for the restoration of the Krishna Janmabhoomi and the Yaganvapi Mosque speaks only of

Hindu consciousness or *Hindutva.* A large section of the Hindu populace considered the Babri Masjid a monument of disgrace and looked forward for its demolition as an act of self-respect. They firmly believed that the said mosque was constructed by demolishing a temple dedicated to Sri Ram, an incarnation of Sri Vishnu, with the sole purpose of humiliating the Hindus by a band of zealot, professing Islam, who swooped down on India from across the border.

A Note on Internationals

The idea of forming an international association of workmen did not surface all of a sudden. It has a long history behind it. Like many great things, the beginning was modest, when in 1843 a few German exiles in Paris formed a small society of ten to twenty artisans under the name The League of the Just. Its leader was Wilhelm Weitling, a disciple of Louis Blanqui, the head of a small revolutionary group in France. Blanqui drew his inspiration largely from the Jacobins of the French Revolution and, particularly, from Babeuf, the founder of the only socialist movement of the period. Babeuf was not a communist, but had proclaimed that 'nature has granted to every man the equal right to enjoy all the goods.' However, after the failure of Blanqui's coup, some of the members of The League of the Just shifted to London and founded the German Workers' Educational Society. In 1845, when Marx visited London, Engels introduced him to this group. Marx was impressed. On his return to Brussels, he founded a German Workers' Association on the model of the German Workers' Educational Society. Engels, in turn, organized a Paris committee of Marx's German Workers' Association.

In 1847, the German Workers' Association organized a congress in London in which the Brussels, London, and Paris committees took part and founded the Communist League. Marx did not attend the congress but the responsibility to draft a constitution for the league was entrusted to him. The result was the Communist Manifesto – the classic formulation of the marxist creed. The manifesto was printed in German in 1848. London became the headquarters of the league.

As the league came into existence, there arose a difference of opinion among the executive members of the league over the timing of revolutionary action. Karl Schapper insisted on immediate revolutionary action but Marx opposed it. The matter was ultimately put to vote. Marx won a narrow victory, but realized that the rank and file were against him. He carried a resolution and transferred the headquarters of the league from London to Cologne, where he had a group of adherents. That was the end of the league. It ceased to be an effective organization.

The First International – 1864-1876

With the *de facto* dissolution of the Communist League, Marx did not, however, snap his contact with the proletarian movement. He continued to be active in the German Workers' Educational Society till such time the First International was founded. The process to form the First International began unnoticed in 1862. In the summer of that year, a group of French workers visited London to see the international exhibition. They were entertained by a group of British workers. Next year, British workers organized a meeting in support of Polish revolutionaries to which French workers sent a delegation. This was followed by another meeting in September 1864, which was attended by French, German, Italian, Swiss, and Polish workers, mainly to consider a proposal from British workers for cooperation against the practice of importing cheap foreign labour. It was at this meeting that an International Federation of Working Men or the First International was founded to destroy the existing economic system. Though Marx had no role in organizing the meeting, he was elected as one of the thirty-two members of the general council, and at once assumed the leadership. The drafting of the constitution was first entrusted to a disciple of Mazzini, but Marx, because of his experience of working-class movement, came to the fore and drafted the constitution in the form of an inaugural address delivered at the second congress, which met at Geneva in 1865. In the address, Marx introduced as much of his doctrine as he could convince his colleagues to accept. The address was concluded with the tailpiece of the *Communist Manifesto*, 'Workers of all Lands, Unite.'

The First International was a centralized body, based primarily on individual membership and organized local groups integrated in national federations, though some trade unions and associations were collectively affiliated to it. The supreme body of the international was the general council. The international met every year either in Switzerland or Belgium to formulate principles and policies to organize collections for the support of strikes in various countries; and, in general, to advocate its goals.

The international held its annual conferences regularly from 1866 to 1869. Marx and Engels did not attach much importance to these conferences as they were in control of the general council in London. Although the statutes of the international called for an 'eternal union of brotherly cooperation', the elements of which the international was composed were too heterogeneous to come to an agreement on any important issue. The British, on whom the international depended for financial resources, were primarily interested in the extension of the franchise, strengthening of trade unions and introduction of reforms. Germans were divided into marxians and liassalleans, while the French were bound to Proudhon's anarchist thesis.

Nevertheless, the international did encourage the development of a sense of proletarian unity, which had not existed before. By the end of the sixties, its membership increased to 800,000. And if the strength of other labour groups with which the international had alliances is added, the total strength stands at around 7,000,000.

Marx was very hopeful and saw great possibilities in the international. In September 1867, he wrote to Engels: 'By the time of the next revolution, which may perhaps be nearer than it seems, we (that is you and I) will have this powerful engine in our hands.... We may consider ourselves very well satisfied.'[1]

The revolution came with the Paris Commune in 1871, when the masses inspired by Bakunin and Blanqui took to the barricades and brought the first proletarian government of the world. During its short existence, it abolished the standing army, introduced universal suffrage with the delegates subject to recall, and kept salaries of public offices down to the level of workers' wages. The immediate cause of its fall was that it acted moderately by refusing to seize the Banque de France and march on to the Government of Versailles. The revolution began on 17 March and was finally suppressed on 28 May, by which time at least 20,000 people had lost their lives. The Paris Commune became a legend, the most conspicuous achievement of the revolutionary working class, until the bolsheviks seized power in Russia.

Marx, in his *Civil War in France*, defended the Commune. Both he and Engels conceded that the First International had fulfilled its mission and its reputation had been raised by the Commune. With the collapse of the Paris Commune, however, a split occurred in the international because of a clash between Marx's centralized socialism and Bakunin's anarchism at the Hague Congress in 1872. In order to prevent the bakuninists from assuming the leadership of the international, the general council, prompted by Marx, shifted the headquarters from London to New York, where the international languished until it was formally dissolved at the Philadelphia conference in July 1876.

The breakaway bakuninists' group assumed the leadership of the truncated international. They held annual conferences from 1873 to 1877, when the social democrats abruptly left it because their motion to restore the unity of the international was rejected by the bakuninists. The bakuninists, however, failed to keep the international alive. In 1881, after the London Anarchist Congress, it ceased to represent an organized movement.

The Second International – 1889-1923

After the dissolution of the First International, Marx did not make any attempt to found another. In a letter to a Dutch socialist, Marx wrote: 'It is my conviction that the critical juncture for a new International Workingmen's Association has not yet arrived and for this reason I regard all workers' congresses, particularly socialist congresses, in so far as they are not related to the immediate given conditions in this or that particular nation, as not merely useless but harmful. They will always fade away in stale generalised banalities.'[2] Engels not only held the same view as Marx, but also added: 'I think the next International – after Marx's writings have had some years of influence – will be directly communist and will openly proclaim our principles.'[3] Engels' prophecy did not come true. In less than a decade, the Second International was founded with a mixed bag of marxists and non-marxists.

In 1889, two congresses were arranged in Paris – one by marxists and the other by non-marxists. The two were persuaded to combine and, thus, on 14 July, on the centenary of the fall of Bastille, the Second International was founded at a meeting under the joint chairmanship of Liebknecht and Edouard Vaillant.

There was a marked difference between the First and the Second Internationals. The First International had a genuine revolutionary attitude in spite of disagreement over the methods to be followed. But the Second International was a loosely organized assembly representing many shades of opinion with varying degrees of maturity. It was based on only membership of national parties and trade unions. Any political party or labour group that evinced adherence to its principles was admitted. It formally adopted the basic principles of marxism: class struggle, universal brotherhood of workers and peasants, proletariat action and socialization of the means of production.

The Second International did not meet in conference annually, but met every two or three years up to the First World War. It did not set up a central organization either, until eleven years after its foundation. The International Socialist Bureau, the central organization, was set up in 1900, with headquarters at Brussels.

Though committed to marxian ideology, the international confined itself to improving the economic conditions of workers within the framework of the existing system, rather than making any attempt to destroy the system in accordance with the marxian principle. It believed in peace abroad, legality at home, free trade, universal suffrage and extension of parliamentary institution. In fact, it deviated substantially from the basic principles of marxism. Yet, Engels supported the international with the hope that, none too soon, the marxists would acquire control over it and that 'the real need of the day was not direct revolutionary action, but rallying the masses and winning them to socialism'.[4]

The issue that confronted the international from the beginning of the twentieth century was what attitude should the working class adopt in the event of a war. Ever since the Moroccan crisis of 1905, the international became increasingly concerned with this problem. The issue was discussed at length at the Stuttgart congress in 1907, in Copenhagen in 1911, and again at an extraordinary congress at Basle in 1912. At Stuttgart, the international adopted a resolution calling upon socialists to work on measures such as abolition of standing armies, disarmament and international arbitration.

When the war actually broke out in 1914, the international was split into three groups. A majority of the socialist parties comprising the right wing chose to support the war effort of their respective national governments. The centrists condemned the national chauvinism of the right wing and sought the reunification of the international under the banner of world peace. The left wing led by Lenin rejected the national chauvinism of the right wing and the pacifism of the centrists, and instead asked for a socialist drive to transform the imperialist war into a transitional class war. The hope that the international might prevent the war proved to be an illusion. In almost every country, the appeal to patriotism proved stronger than the appeal to working class solidarity, excepting to the socialists of Serbia and the bolsheviks of Russia. In Germany, the social democrats voted in favour of appropriation, while in France, socialist leaders joined the government in the face of German invasion. This prompted Rosa Luxemburg to say with sarcasm that Karl Kautsky, the theoretician of the Second International and a leader of the right wing socialists, had made an important amendment to the *Communist Manifesto*: 'Working men of all countries unite in peacetime and cut each other's throat in wartime.'[5] After the split, though it was not dissolved, the activities of the international came to a standstill, at least during the early part of the war.

In 1915, however, some opposition to the war began to be expressed by a small section of socialists from France, Germany, Italy and some neutral countries. To give a concrete shape to their ideas, the socialists, particularly those of the left wing and the likeminded, met in a conference at Zimmerwald in Switzerland, where Lenin and his associates were already residing.

The conference at Zimmerwald was attended by thirty-seven delegates from twelve countries. It was a heterogeneous group. Only eight out of the thirty-seven delegates took a consistent revolutionary nationalist stand and formed the Zimmerwald left group, commonly known as the Zimmerwald minority, an ideologically cohesive unit. It was composed of the Russian bolsheviks; the Polish rozlanists; the leftist social democrats; and the left elements in the social democratic parties of Sweden, Norway, Switzerland, and Germany. Later, this group was further reinforced by the left socialists of the Netherlands, Serbia, France, Bulgaria, Austria, and the USA.

The other twenty-nine delegates formed the right wing and came to be known as the Zimmerwald majority. This group was composed of the kautskyites, the pacifists and the consistent internationalists who hovered between revolutionary action and reformist tactics. The chief item of discussion at Zimmerwald was the question of the proletariat's action for peace. The left Zimmerwald wanted to put an end to the imperialist war by calling the masses of workers to a revolutionary struggle against the capitalist governments to win political power and usher in a socialist state. The right Zimmerwald, on the contrary, contended that the time for revolution had not yet come and that it was too early for the proletariat to take the path of revolutionary action against imperialism. It preferred the conference to confine itself to a general appeal for peace, and in no case should it embark upon revolutionary action or create a new organization as opposed to the old international. When the resolution was put to vote, the left Zimmerwald lost. It was rejected by the majority.

As a follow-up to the Zimmerwald conference, the socialists held another conference at Kienthal in Switzerland the following year. The conference was attended by forty-one delegates from eight countries. But the left Zimmerwald was again a minority. It had the support of only ten delegates, though it was supported on a number of issues by another twelve delegates. The main issue of controversy was whether the workers should be asked to restore the old international or establish a new international. The majority voted for the former, but were forced to adopt a resolution condemning the socio-chauvinist policy and the failure of the International Socialist Bureau. However, in the meantime, opposition to the war among the left wing of socialists had grown sufficiently strong, leading to the socialist revolution in Russia and the founding of the Third International.

It only remains to be added that the parties that had withdrawn from the Second International, but were not prepared to affiliate with the Third International, formed the Two-and-a-half or Vienna International. Any attempt to amalgamate all strands into a single international failed, mainly due to the opposition to the Third International. Disillusioned and disheartened, in 1922, the Second and the Two-and-a-half or Vienna International met at Hague and resolved to call a conference at Hamburg to decide further course of action. The conference, as scheduled, was held in May 1923. It was attended by 620 delegates from 30 countries. By a majority decision, both the Second and the Vienna International were dissolved, and in their place, the Labour and Socialist International was formed. The Labour and Socialist International continued to exist until 1945, when it was replaced by the International Socialist Conference. In 1950, at a conference at Copenhagen, the International Socialist

Conference transformed itself into the Socialist International – an organization for discussion and exchange of views.

The Third International – 1919-1943

The Third Communist International or the Comintern was founded in 1919 after the socialist revolution in Russia. Lenin was willing, more than ever, to hasten worldwide revolution to create necessary conditions for the survival of the Soviet regime. The socialist revolution gave a new impetus to the working class for a revolutionary struggle against imperialism, both in developed capitalist countries and in backward countries. This resulted in the founding of communist parties and groups in a number of countries, and created a favourable condition for the formation of an international.

The move to form a Communist International was taken up at a preliminary meeting of the communists at Petrograd in January 1918. The meeting decided to call a conference of the left, which was engaged in revolutionary struggle for immediate peace and was prepared to support the socialist revolution and the Soviet government. The decision was communicated to all left parties and groups. The January 1918 meeting was followed by another meeting in January 1919 that unanimously accepted Lenin's proposal for convening an inaugural congress of the Third International in the near future. The members present, in an appeal, briefly formulated the ideological and political platform of the proposed international and spelt out the aims, tactics and organizational principles of the international communist movement. The appeal was sent to thirty-nine fraternal parties, groups and organizations to discuss the question of founding the international and to take part in the congress.

Following this appeal, delegates began to arrive in Moscow by February 1919. On 1 March, a preliminary meeting of the delegates, chaired by Lenin, was held to discuss the constitution and the agenda of the forthcoming congress. Hugo Ebertein of the Communist Party of Germany resented the immediate founding of the international. His objection was that many delegates from important countries had not arrived. In view of Ebertein's objection, it was resolved to go in for an international communist conference. Accordingly, on 2 March, the International Communist Conference met in Kremlin.

The question of founding the Third International was once again taken up when new delegates arrived on 4 March. The representatives of the communist parties of Austria and Hungary, as well as of the Swedish Left Social Democratic Party and the Balkan Revolutionary Social Democratic Federation, issued a joint statement to the effect that the foundation of the Third International was a necessity and the international communist conference must realize this. The joint statement had the desired effect. The 4 March session of the International Communist Conference was converted into the inaugural congress of the Third Communist International or Comintern. The conference was attended by fifty-two delegates from thirty-five organizations of twenty-one countries of Europe, Asia and America.

The policy and programme of the Comintern was given actual shape at the second congress, though it was discussed and framed at the first congress. The decision to set up an executive committee of the Comintern was taken, but not implemented; it was left to the second congress to decide the choice of the members. However, pending the formation of the executive committee, the first conference constituted a five-man bureau to look after the working of the Comintern's secretariat. Somewhat later, Zinoviev was selected as the chairman of the executive committee, with Angelica Balabanova and J. Berzin as secretaries.

In between the first and the second congresses, the communist movement took a big stride worldwide. Communist parties were formed in Yugoslavia, Denmark, Indonesia, Iran, Turkey, Great Britain, the USA, Mexico, Uruguay, and Astoria. Besides, quite a number of socialist parties and trade unions announced their affiliation with the Comintern. In fact, when the second congress met, the world communist movement had firmly established itself.

The most important deliberation of the Comintern at the second congress was the thesis on the national and colonial question and Lenin's twenty-one conditions for admission to the Comintern. The salient features of the twenty-one conditions were recognition of the dictatorship of the proletariat; complete break with the reformists and the centrists and their expulsion from the party; and submission to the decisions of the Comintern or its executive by the parties affiliated to it. In other words, Lenin, through his twenty-one points, made the Comintern a monolithic organization of the international proletariat.

The administrative structure of the Comintern resembled that of the Communist Party of the Soviet Union. An executive acted when the congress was not in session and a smaller presidium served as the chief executive body. Moscow became the permanent headquarters of the Comintern.

During the life-time of Lenin, the Comintern maintained a somewhat consistent policy. But as Stalin came to power, the Comintern became a tool of Soviet foreign policy. International proletariat solidarity and the revolutionary action of the proletariat ceased to be the primary objective of the Comintern. Under Stalin, the policy of the Comintern was dictated by Soviet national interest. When the Second World War broke out and the Soviet Union formed an alliance with imperialist Britain and the USA against the fascists, Stalin dissolved the Comintern in 1943 to allay fears of communist subversion among his allies.

The Fourth International – 1938-1953

The idea of a fourth international was mooted by Trotsky's followers after the death of Lenin, when Stalin came to power and made Comintern an adjunct to the Communist Party of the Soviet Union. Trotsky opposed the idea at that time because he felt that the Comintern, despite its flaws, was still the vanguard of the working-class movement. However, after his expulsion from the Soviet Union and the rise of nazism in Germany, he felt the need for a fourth international to reorient and oppose the Comintern's policy.

The first conference of the Fourth International was held in September 1938. The immediate task before the international was to undermine the base of the ruling class and mobilise the masses for revolution. To achieve this, the international adopted Trotsky's transitional programme, which called for minimum reform, i.e., higher wages and better working conditions, and maximum programme, i.e., overthrow of capitalism and transition to socialism.

However, the lofty ideas of the international could not be realized as they failed to make an impact on the working-class movement. Its activities remained confined to a small coterie of intellectuals preoccupied with Trotsky. Apart from disseminating information to the extreme left groups, it was dead wood for all practical purposes. The only active unit of the international was a small Socialist Workers' Party of the United States.

In 1940, with the murder of Trotsky, the international lost its mentor. The two Belgian trotskyites Michael Pablo and Ernest Germain who assumed leadership, failed to activate the international. But it continued to survive in a state of coma. In 1949, when Pablo called for its dissolution, a factional fight erupted. In 1953, the international was split into two – the International Committee and the International Secretariat.

The story of the internationals shows that the First International was an experiment towards mobilizing the working class under one banner; the Second International was a poor attempt to fulfil the task left by the First International; the Third International was a calculated move to give proper shape to the marxian concept of proletarian brotherhood, leading to the overthrow of capitalism; and the Fourth International was a mere shadow of the Third International, few cared to be aware of its miserable existence.

Notes

1 R.N. Carew Hunt, op. cit., Pelican, 1969, p.137.

2 ibid., p.146.

3 ibid.

4 J. Lenz, *The Second International, New York*, 1932, p.12.

5 Bernard Isaacs, op. cit, p.27.

Index